DISNEY WORLD
Within Reach

MEETING THE MOUSE WITHOUT BREAKING THE BANK

By

Lauralyn "LJ" Johnson

Disclosure

_____

This book contains affiliate websites. This means that when you type in and make a purchase or sign up at a site I have provided, I make a small commission at no additional cost to you. I am disclosing this in accordance with the Federal Trade Commission's 16 CFR, Part 255: "Guides Concerning the Use of Endorsements and Testimonials in Advertising."

But just so you know, it's my personal policy never to lie to save or make money. I made that commitment a long time ago and it's a big part of who I am. This means that if I recommend something, you can trust that I personally use it and find it to be good. I would never trade your confidence in me for money. Your trust means too much to me.

Thank you for supporting the book!

2017

I dedicate this book to all mothers everywhere:

May you know in your heart that what you are doing

matters more than anything else in the world.

And may you never believe it when they say you

matter less because you are a woman.

2018

I add this the second edition:

May you also know you are not alone. Even at 3am,

when she won't stop crying, we're all here cheering

for you.

Table of Contents:

Chapter One: Introduction and How to Read This Book 1

Part I: Discounted Gift Cards 13

Chapter Two: Eight Websites You Need to Know About 15

Chapter Three: Sam's Club and BJ's 37

Chapter Four: Target 59

Chapter Five: My Grocery Store Can Get Me to Disney? 65

Chapter Six: Buying Disney World at Big Box Stores 93

Chapter Seven: Your Mileage May Vary Options 113

Chapter Eight: What Do We Do Without the DVA??? 119

Part II: Accounts Bonuses 133

Chapter Nine: Checking Accounts to Disney 135

Chapter Ten: $500 Fast 143

Chapter Eleven: Chase Sapphire Preferred 155

Part III: Staying Onsite for Less 171

Chapter Twelve: Disney Resort Basics 173

Chapter Thirteen: Disney Resort Discounts 187

Chapter Fourteen: Disney Resort Hacks 211

Chapter Fifteen: Agency Exclusives 227

Chapter Sixteen: Deluxe for the Price of Moderate?

Or Value?!?! 235

Chapter Seventeen: Renting DVC Points Wisely 255

Chapter Eighteen: Military Discounts 271

Part IV: Lowering the Price of Disney World

Admission 279

Chapter Nineteen: Annual Passes for Everyone 281

Chapter Twenty: Authorized Resellers 295

Chapter Twenty-One: Lesser Known Ticket Savings Tricks 303

Part V: Dining Well on the Cheap— With or Without

the Dining Plan 309

Chapter Twenty-Two: Intro to the Dining Plans 313

Chapter Twenty-Three: "Should I Get the Dining Plan?" 321

Chapter Twenty-Four: Dining Comparisons 333

Chapter Twenty-Five: Hacking the Disney Dining Plan 349

Chapter Twenty-Six: Stretching the Dining Plan 371

Chapter Twenty-Seven: Hacking Disney Dining Without the

Dining Plan 381

Part VI: Travel and Staying Offsite 397

Chapter Twenty-Eight: Flights 399

Chapter Twenty-Nine: Rental Cars 415

Chapter Thirty: Driving, Food, Hotels and Gas 421

Chapter Thirty-One: Staying Offsite 427

Part VII: Saving via Mindset Change **433**

Chapter Thirty-Two: Lower Taxes, Please 435

Chapter Thirty-Three: Tax Savings via Disney 465

Chapter Thirty-Four: Saving on Life and Applying It to Disney.487

Bonus Chapter Thirty-Five: Planning for All the Hidden

Expenses 497

Afterword: Learning to Find These Strategies Yourself 503

Part VII: Appendices **511**

Appendix A: Strategies to Save the Most 513

Appendix B: Strategies to Use if You're Super Busy 523

Appendix C: Strategies to Use if Your Trip is Soon 535

Appendix D: Strategies Without Credit Cards 541

Appendix E: Strategies to Use Time and Time Again 547

Chapter One:
Introduction and How to Read this Book

I go to Disney World a lot. Almost every month. Sometimes twice a month. And I've been doing it for years: more than 200 days spent on vacation at Disney World in the last three years. That means 20% of my life these days is on Disney soil. I get asked a lot of questions about it like:

Q: **"Why do you go so much?"**
A: I just love it. I don't know why, but it's part of the fabric of who I am. I'm happier when I'm there, so I try to be there often.

Q: **"Do you ever want to go anywhere else?"**
A: Does Disneyland count? Just kidding, yes, I do go other places sometimes, but Disney World will always be my favorite. We travel quite a lot, but I'm

never as happy heading anywhere else. God just made me this way.

Q: **"Haven't you done everything by now?"**
A: No, I could live at Disney and never do everything. There's just too much there. But I'm going to continue to try to do it all. Just when I think I'm getting sort of close, they add more stuff for me to do, and I love that!

But by far, the most common question that I hear is **"How do you afford it?"**

And I never really know how to answer this question, because how I afford it is in a million tiny ways. There's no quick answer. So, I jokingly answer sometimes, "I'm independently wealthy." But this isn't true. My income is fairly low in the grand scheme of things- under the median income— in Kentucky, which has a low median income as far as states go. We are under the median even with the money I make from Smart Moms Plan Disney because I re-invest most of the earnings back into the business and only take a small salary. However, that's good news for you. If I can figure out how to afford Disney World almost every single month for the last three years, you can easily use my strategies to bring Disney World within reach.

Not all of these strategies will work for every person. I don't use them all, every time. And in this edition, I even added some that I haven't done yet. I use whatever is best at that moment and trust that there will always be some way for me to save enough and get to Disney.

So, if you read a strategy and think, "That won't work for me" follow these two steps:

1. Think it through again. Why won't it work for you? Is there a way to overcome that? For instance, if you don't qualify for a credit card that I recommend, don't just stop there. Think about how you can correct that so you can use that strategy down the road. More commonly, when I hear people saying that something won't work for them, what they mean is that they aren't willing to try. Don't be that person! Or if you are going to be that person, then realize that the only reason you can't go to Disney World is because of that decision. Tough love, people.

2. If you've truly looked at a strategy with an open mind and open heart and conclude that it won't work for you (for instance, maybe you don't live close enough to use a certain store I use), then just let it go and move on to the things that will work. Do not let yourself get stuck on the things that won't work. There are things that don't work for me. Or they worked once, but won't work again. Or they worked once, but now I've

found something better. That's ok. It's not hurting a thing. Just move on to the next one and give that a try.

So, what do you need to make these strategies work? Not much:

1. Time. If you are trying to go to Disney next week, I can help you a little. If you're going in two months, I can help you a lot more. If you're going in six months or more, or if you haven't even begun planning your trip, this system is going to save you a lot of money!

   If you don't have a ton of time before your trip, don't worry. There's still plenty you can do. And I've even created an appendix just for you (Appendix C).

2. An open mind and a willingness to learn. You might have to do something you're not 100% comfortable with-- and that's ok. I'm certainly never going to tell you to do anything immoral, but there might be things you aren't used to doing that I might ask you to do- like using a coupon. Some people feel like that makes them look or feel poor, but I think it makes you look smart.

   For others, the math might be challenging. My husband is a genius when it comes to anything physical. He can fix anything, and build anything. But numbers make him nauseous. If that's you, please know that you aren't alone. Your gifts are somewhere else and that's not a problem. Find someone close to you who can help you, or follow the examples I'm going to give you closely. You can also email me with specific questions:

LJ@SmartMomsPlanDisney.com

I'm kind of geekily in love with math so I'll be happy to help (just don't ask me to build anything, because that's not where my strengths are!)

3. For some strategies, you need access to certain stores. Kroger, Giant Eagle and Albertsons are regional. Sam's Club and BJ's are membership stores. You can always join though. And if these won't work, move on to another strategy.

4. Decent credit will help. If you can get approved for a couple of credit cards, it could make a world of difference in your Disney budget. If you can't, there are still plenty of strategies you can use so don't despair. There are thirty-four chapters in this book and only two of them are exclusively about credit cards. All the other chapters have ways to work the strategy without a credit card. You can also begin planning to have better credit in the future so you can take advantage of certain deals later.

Repairing your credit is a whole other topic, but I do want to take the time to say: you can do it. And it's not as hard as you think. I've included bonus pages in the Disney World Within Reach Workbook that will walk you down the path to repair your credit and I promise you, it's not as hard as it seems.

If your credit isn't great or you just don't want to open more credits cards, there are lots of strategies you can use, and I even summed them all up in an appendix just for you (Appendix D).

5. Money. If you're thinking, "Wait, how can money be a thing I need to make this work when I'm telling you I need money?", I hear you. However, this book isn't titled, "Go to Disney World for Free." (Side note, it is possible, but takes a lot of creativity and time!) You need money to be able to take advantage of deals. If a deal pops up to pay $75 that will net you $100 toward your trip, you need to be in a position to take advantage of that. But you don't need a lot to start and Disney World will be there in 5 or 10 years if you need that long to save up. At least I hope it will be there.

(Off topic tidbit: once I told someone that I was learning Spanish in my spare time and he said, "That's going to take you forever!" He said it in a tone that sounded like he meant, "You're wasting your time." But I thought to myself, it might take me a long time (15 minutes per day for two years and counting so far), but the time will pass anyway. So, I should do something with it. I might as well take 10 years to learn Spanish because then I'll know Spanish in 10 years. You might as well save $20 a month and plan to go to Disney in 10 years. The time will pass anyway. You might as well make a plan to do something with it. End rant.)

That's it! Time, an open mind, and money are all you really need though access to certain stores and decent credit would also help.

How to Read this Book

I'm going to present these strategies from easiest to hardest. For me "easiest" means "most easily replicated" and "least amount of work." And the ideas will build on each other. The first time we encounter a new idea, I'll explain it as clearly as I can. The next time, I'll just refer back to that explanation so you aren't reading the same ideas over and over. Writing it this way means that you should start at the beginning and read through to the end. If you can't use that particular strategy, feel free to skim over and just see if there's any part of it that you CAN use. I'm also a mother of young children and find myself explaining things thoroughly. So, if you find you have the general idea and want to skip ahead, I often mention where you can do that. I feel that I'm morally obligated to do my best to help you learn this incredibly valuable information so I often tell it several ways to be sure it's understandable to as many people as possible.

The strategies in this book fall into two categories: specific and general. Specific savings will save you the same amount as they'll save me. There's no human involvement or decision making to them. For instance, Target's RedCard is going to give us both the same discount no matter what. Other topics are more general. They are more dependent on timing and on skill level of the person buying, and on the market— supply and demand.

For the general strategies, I'll give you the process and speculate on how much you can save based on various levels of effort. I can't tell you, "This will save you $200," but I can say "this saved me $200 with minimal effort" or "I think you can save $200 this way." It will ultimately be up to you to decide how much savings you want to get from those methods and how hard to work at them.

At the end of each chapter about specific savings strategies, I'll sum up how you can stack the strategies we've discussed to that point, if it's possible, and I'll tell you what percent you'd save if that strategy worked for you. And to help you look at how it could affect your trip, I'll use these two fictitious families and give you the numbers for them:

Fictitious family #1: The **Smiths**. They are a young couple with two kids, ages five and eight. They're staying at a Disney Value Resort— Pop Century. They are staying for four nights, with four day tickets, without Park Hopper. They have the Quick Service Dining Plan which includes two quick service meals and two snacks for each person per night. Their total cost with Disney is $2,500.

Fictitious family #2: The **Robinsons**. They have three kids ages seven, nine and eleven. One of them is a Disney adult (age ten and over.) They are staying at a Disney Deluxe Resort: The Grand Floridian. They are staying for seven nights, and they have seven day tickets with Park Hopper. They are doing the regular Disney Dining Plan which includes one quick service meal, one table service meal and two snacks for each person per night. Their total cost with Disney is $9,500.

We aren't discussing how these two families choose to do Disney (I'm strictly no judgement!) We're just using them to help us with comparing the savings.

The Afterword and the Appendices need a little more explanation. I thought I'd explain here because it might help you to know about them now, especially if you're in a hurry to get started on your savings journey. The Afterword is about learning to find these strategies yourself. The savings arena is ever changing as loopholes close and open and retailers change. The last chapter will help you with that.

The five Appendices at the end of the book are more reference items, less reading material. There aren't new ideas in them, just the ideas we've discussed already, but organized in different ways.

- Appendix A ranks the strategies in order of how much you can save with each. As you are beginning to try new things, you can flip to Appendix A and see which ones will save you the most and start there. Work your way down the list until you find something that works for you.

- Appendix B has the strategies listed according to the amount of time that it will take you to complete the steps needed to take advantage of the savings. We're all busy and we all want to spend our time doing something other than typing gift card numbers into accounts. But we have different situations and some of us have more time than others. There was a time when I was nursing the baby non-stop and I spent at least a half hour a day earning points on M+ (a now defunct app that paid you for looking at advertising.) Now, I would consider that half hour impossible for me to carve out of my day, and I certainly wouldn't do it at the expense of the rest of my life. But then, it felt nice to be "accomplishing something" even while I was tied to the chair nursing for hours every day. Side note: breastfeeding is COMPLETELY accomplishing something. But it didn't feel like it at the time. Appendix B will help you with which strategies you should attempt if you only have a little time to devote to this idea of saving money and want it to go a long way.

- Appendix C is a list of strategies that you can take advantage of even if you don't have a lot of time. Not in terms of your actual time spent, but in terms of how long the whole process will take. For instance, ordering a hard-plastic gift card instead of an egift card will involve waiting for it to come in the mail. This is important if you're going to Disney soon. You lucky duck! I've also included a specific strategy that we've used many times to help last minute Disney-go'ers inside the Disney Within Reach Private Facebook Group (if you aren't a member, you should be, you paid for it with your purchase and it's awesome. Search Disney Within Reach on Facebook.) That strategy I mentioned is right at the beginning of Appendix C.

- Appendix D is all about what you can do if you don't want to use credit cards. I personally loathe debt, but I'm not against using credit cards as tools. If you can use them, they can be a great help. But if they use you, stay away from them. If you find yourself getting into trouble with them, you need to tighten the reins, or give them up altogether. I'm coming from a place of being in horrible debt and clawing my way out of it, which you'll read more about in the upcoming chapters.

I respect you immensely if you are mature enough to realize that you can't handle credit cards and have given them up because of that. Don't let me urge you to do anything you aren't ready for. But if you can use them responsibly, credit cards are a tool like any other. Not inherently bad or good. Like a chainsaw. Some people get hurt by chainsaws, but that doesn't make them bad. Learn to use a chainsaw and it can be very beneficial. Take the time to think about this and decide if you want to use credit cards. And if not, Appendix D is for you.

- Appendix E is about what you can do over and over again to get to Disney every time. This is an addition to the Second Edition. It's a question that was coming up on the regular so I'm answering it. There is SO much that you can do continually, and it will help you quite a bit to have that spelled out for you.

Let's jump in!

Part I:
Discounted Gift Cards

I see comments in the big Facebook group all the time, "Why is everyone so crazy about Disney gift cards? Why would I want them?" And I remember my first foray into discounted gift cards- it was a little nerve wracking, but I was so happy and proud to be saving 5%. 5% is a cute little savings now that I've learned all these different tricks, but we all start somewhere and 5% is a lot better than 0%.

There's a lot of information in the next few chapters and there's a lot of math along with it. Just take it slow, read it as many times as you need to if math isn't your thing. I try to be really clear with the math. There are more than 15 different ways to get Disney gift cards at a discount in the chapters to come. There are really easy predictable ways to get them at 5%, 10%, 15% off, there are harder ways to get them at 20%, 25% even more % off if you do all the steps and everything works out.

Get ready to print some Disney money...and it's not even illegal.

Chapters in this section:

Chapter Two: Eight Websites You Need to Know About

Chapter Three: Sam's Club and BJ's

Chapter Four: Target

Chapter Five: My Grocery Store Can Get Me to Disney?

Chapter Six: Buying Disney World at Big Box Stores

Chapter Seven: Your Mileage May Vary Options

Chapter Eight: What Do We Do Without the DVA???

Chapter Two:
Eight Websites You Need to Know About

This chapter is a "laying the foundation" chapter. I'm a little scared to put this chapter second, because this is a strategy that seems like it doesn't have a huge pay off, but anyone can do it, and it can be the basis to save even more when stacked with other strategies. And using these websites can SURE add up over time. This is a chapter I get emails about. It's a chapter people close this book over. They think, "I'm not doing this piddly little stuff. It's a waste of my time." It should take you less than 45 minutes and make you over $150. So, if you're making more than $200 an hour somewhere else, go do that, and skip this chapter.

Two more thoughts on this:

1. Ok, fine. Maybe you're making boatloads of money elsewhere and this stuff really isn't

worth your time. In that case, skip this chapter with my blessing and don't look back, and also don't let this derail you from doing the other strategies in this system.

2. If you aren't making boatloads of money elsewhere, don't let your ego trip you up here. Yes, these are small amounts of money, but the funny thing about that is that large amounts of money are always made up of small amounts.

Just so you believe me, I rounded up my lifetime savings from a few. These are just my accounts, not any that my husband might have (we'll learn more about that), and these are just the ones that made it easy for me to see how much I've saved.

Check them out:

102,096 SB
Lifetime

Account Overview

❗ Please can you help us?		
Outstanding	Paid	Total
$795.33	$2,158.22	$2,953.55

Welcome,

LJ

Member since 6/23/15

Lifetime Cash Back
$565.68

$2,049.40
Savings to Date

(In case you're wondering a SwagBuck "SB" is worth a penny so 102,096 SBs translates to $1,020.96)

$2,158.22
$565.68
$2,049.40
+$1,020.96
$5,794.26

If you add these four up, it's comes to $5,794.26 that I've already been paid ($6,589.59 if you include the $795.33 that's still outstanding) in the past two and a half years. What would you do with an extra

17

$2,317.70 each year? That's enough to pay for your vacation each year if you were smart with it (and you will be if you use this system.) And remember, this is only four of the eight and doesn't include my husband Mike's earnings. Little things add up to big things, my friend!

I also include this so that you can see I use these strategies. I'm in the trenches with you day in and day out. I'm not some wealthy person pointing and telling and not actually doing. I don't make more money than your family (almost guaranteed, as we are well under the median income) and I'm using the tools I'm giving you on a daily basis. I just earned $3 cash back today in fact. I'm just a few steps ahead of you on this path and can show you the way.

Now that you know this stuff is worth learning, let me tell you about these eight websites. The first three are similar, the next four are similar and the last one is in a category all its own:

Raise, Cardpool, and CardCash: These are gift card resale sites. There are others out there, but these three are my go-to. They are good at what they do, and are reliable in my experience. If anything goes awry, you can count on them to take care of you.

These sites sell gift cards at a discount. If your grandma gives you a Forever 21 gift card, and you're about 29, you can sell it on Raise, Cardpool or CardCash and recover some of the cash. If you have the need to buy a gift card, you can find it on Raise, Cardpool or CardCash at a discount.

Now before you go checking, I'll just tell you they usually don't have Disney cards, and when they do, I don't buy them. I can't usually tell if they'll work for Disney World, or if they are Merchandise Only so I steer clear. But that doesn't mean the websites aren't useful. Just stick with me and I'll show you how. And I'll also tell you the pros and cons of each.

TopCashBack, eBates, Mr. Rebates and CouponCabin: These are cash back sites. Again, there are others, but these are my favorites for their ease of use, good percentages, and reliability. Anytime you are going to buy something online, you can click through one of these sites and you may earn a small percentage of your purchase back in cash. I have earned a lot of money with these four sites over the past two years, but I do a lot of shopping online for my businesses. I think the average household could easily receive a few hundred cash back each year just for their regular online purchases, not including anything Disney World related.

Swagbucks: This is the one that's in a category all by itself because it truly has so so SO much going on. In the last version of this book, I only talked about this website in passing and it was in the Saving on Life and Applying It to Disney Chapter near the end of the book. It just wasn't a big part of my strategy until this year.

Swagbucks gives cash back on purchases so you'd be tempted to put it into the cash back category, but it does so much more that wouldn't do it justice. Swagbucks also sells gift cards, and sometimes they are discounted, so you could put it in the gift card resale category too, but that also doesn't do it justice. In fact, neither of those things are the most valuable feature. The best thing about Swagbucks is that you can earn money doing small tasks online every day. I interviewed several Smart Moms and created a blog post (smartmomsplandisney.com/swagbucks/) that explains best practices to earn the most in the least amount of time. I'm honestly surprised by how much I'm earning each month from Swagbucks.

I won't go into it all here since the blog post does such a good job, but please don't waste too much of your time on the surveys if they aren't working for you. I hear tons of people saying, "the surveys are a waste of time" and I agree (although I do hear some people say they make quite a bit from them so definitely try them before you decide.) I only do the surveys that I have to do to for my Daily To Do List. There is a video on the blog post that will help you quite a bit too.

Where to Begin

If you aren't a member of these sites yet, you should be. And you can earn quite a nice chunk of change toward your trip just by signing up, and having your spouse sign up. My husband is signed up for many things that he's completely unaware of... #justsaying

Ok, here's how to earn a nice little bonus to get your trip fund started. First, full disclosure, if you use my links/urls to sign-up I earn referral bonuses (thank you!) So, click through (or if you're reading a paper copy of this book, type the urls in- I've shortened them for you and they are <u>case-sensitive</u>), sign up and you'll earn the following bonuses on your first transaction.

Raise: http://bit.ly/SMPDRaise $5 off your first order

Cardpool: http://bit.ly/Cardpoolbonus $5 off your first order (They sometimes ask you to also put in a code to get this. It should show you that code when you click through or type in this link.)

CardCash: www.cardcash.com No referral or sign-up bonus, but they are worth having in your back pocket, because they offer some really exceptional deals sometimes. Sign-up for their newsletter if you want to save. If you're in the Facebook group for the Disney World Within Reach System: (https://www.facebook.com/groups/18841493 35165319 or just search Disney Within Reach on

Facebook), I announce Disney applicable deals in there.

Top Cash Back (TCB): http://bit.ly/SMPDTCB No bonus usually, but you still want to sign-up for what we're going to do later.

eBates: http://bit.ly/SMPDeBates Get $10 back after your first transaction.

Mr. Rebates: http://bit.ly/SMPDMrRebates $5

Coupon Cabin: www.couponcabin.com No referral or sign-up bonus, but you can earn up to $23 extra with your first transaction if you plan it correctly (more info to come, but don't sign up until you read about it.)

Swagbucks: http://bit.ly/SMPDSwagbucks $3

Let me break this down a little bit better. Spouse #1 signs up for:

> Raise: $5
> Cardpool: $5
> CardCash: no bonus ☹
> Top Cash Back: no bonus ☹
> eBates: $10
> Mr. Rebates: $5
> Coupon Cabin: $23 (if you follow the instructions to come)
> Swagbucks: $3

Total: $51

Spouse #1 refers spouse #2 to:

> Raise
> Cardpool
> CardCash (No referral, just new
>   account to earn bonuses
>   through CouponCabin)
> Top Cash Back
> eBates
> Mr. Rebates
> CouponCabin (No referral, just new
>   account, so that you can earn
>   bonuses)
> Swagbucks

Spouse #2 earns the same $51 bonus as Spouse #1 did. Now you have a nice $102 for maybe forty-five minutes of typing your emails in. Make sure that you use a different email and credit card for your spouse or they might say that you're the same person and that you aren't eligible. If you have another address that you don't mind using, that would make you extra safe. I use my PO box sometimes, or a work address would be good too— that's not necessary, just being extra safe.

But wait, there's more (please read that in Billy Mays' voice, thank you.) Spouse #1 also earns referral bonuses:

> $5 from Raise,
> $5 from Cardpool,
> $10 from Top Cash Back,
> $25 (This changes regularly, but it's $25 as I write this. If it's lower, wait. It'll go back to $25 at least quarterly) from eBates,
> 20% of all activity from Mr. Rebates (so if you refer your spouse and then use their account for all of your activity, you will earn 20% more)
> $3 from Swagbucks,

If you want to share this info with your mom or dad or siblings, you could make even more in referrals. You can even go hang out and show your family how to do this (or do it for them) and make them a little extra cash and yourself a little extra too. If they are going with you to Disney, they'll be super willing, I'm sure!

So, Spouse #1 makes $48 from referring Spouse #2. Now you've made $150. Spent about 45 minutes in your pajamas while also half watching Grey's Anatomy. Nice. That'll buy your first day's ticket to Disney with enough left over for lunch. It sounds like it's small and doesn't matter, but when you put it all together, it's a lot of money. For me, these strategies have made all the difference in making Disney World affordable. Stay with me.

You do need to make a purchase on all these accounts to get the bonuses, but this will not be hard. Let me tell you how to do it to maximize the savings.

Here are the limits to earn the bonuses:

> **Raise:** $5 off your first purchase, your referral gets the same when they make a purchase within 30 days of signing up. When they order, you get your $5 referral bonus.

> **Cardpool:** You get $5 off your first order; your referral gets the same and you earn another $5 after they place their first order.

> **CardCash** has no bonuses.

> **Top Cash Back:** person referred must earn $10 cash back to qualify you for bonus.

> **eBates:** you must spend $25 through eBates within the first year of signing up to get your bonus. Your referral must do the same to earn his/her bonus and to qualify you for the referral bonus.

Mr. Rebates: you get $5 off after your first transaction no matter how big or small. Same with your referral and you also earn 20% of their cash back earned for as long as they are active with Mr. Rebates.

Swagbucks: You earn an extra $3 after you earn your first $3 (not hard to do). You earn $3 when your referral earns their first $3 and 10% of your referral's earnings for as long as they are active on Swagbucks.

To earn the $23 from **Coupon Cabin**, you need to be strategic. Coupon Cabin will offer amazing bonuses to entice you into signing up. The key is that you can't already be signed up, so don't just mosey over and sign up. Think about what you want to do. Here are a couple of the offers that I've thought were valuable to Disney funding:

This first one gives you 20% cash back on Target up to $15. Just click "get bonus". You would need to spend $75 to earn the full $15. You can buy Disney gift cards from Target (see the Target chapter to maximize that.)

This is the one you need to get the full $23 from signing up for Coupon Cabin. And I would advise you to wait for a decent sale at CardCash. They do sell LOTS of different gift cards that can be used for Disney so you may want to get through the rest of this book and then revisit your plan here. I've seen CardCash hold a sale on certain gift cards that could be used to purchase Disney cards. They were 10.5% off. I also used a 2% cash back credit card. If you did that and coupled it with this new CouponCabin member bonus, you'd spend $100 on $110.50 and get $20 back from CouponCabin, and $2 back from your credit card. You just turned $100 into $132.50 in about 5 minutes. 32.5% return. Dang. Try and ask your banker for a 32.5% return and he'll laugh at you.

To get the other $3 from CouponCabin you have to do a couple little tasks:

Thank you for downloading the CouponCabin Sidekick for Chrome!

Your download will complete shortly.

Next steps:

- It's common to see a warning message appear at the bottom of your screen whenever you try to download an extension. The CouponCabin Sidekick is safe to download, so simply click "Continue" to proceed.
- A dialog box will appear to ask if you want to install the CouponCabin Sidekick. Just click "Install" and the install will begin.
- You may be prompted to restart Chrome.
- Go to Sears.com to see the CouponCabin Sidekick in action.
- **Click the 'Sign In' button to login and get your $2 credit.**

> I have read these Cash Back tips!
> Please credit me $1*

*Valid once per account

Download their Chrome extension and earn $2, read their tips and earn $1. Honestly, their Chrome extension is so helpful, I would probably pay to use it rather than have them pay me! There have been a lot of times where I would have probably forgotten to use a cash back site and their extension alerted me that they have an offer that would save me some cash. And if you hate it, delete it! Keep the $2.

To earn the other bonuses, you would do the following:

- Open one of the cash back sites (eBates, Top Cash Back, Swagbucks or Mr. Rebates) in your browser.

- Find one of the discounted gift card sites (Raise, Cardpool) and click through to it by clicking "Shop now." (There may be better offers available here too, so look.)

- Then look for a gift card that you can use to buy a Disney gift card. Kmart is my go-to. Be aware that right now they are allowing gift card to gift card transactions, but they could change their policy at any moment. Even now, some Kmarts do not allow gift card to gift card transactions I only invest money that I can afford to actually spend at those stores, just in case. Kmart has groceries, so I can buy a Kmart gift card knowing that if I can't turn it into Disney money, I can buy some milk or eggs and use my grocery budget to get my cash back out and back into my Disney fund.

- eBates only pays 1% while TCB pays 2%, the others will vary too so I would look to spend the minimum at the places with lower payouts. So, for eBates look for a $27 Kmart gift card. You should be able to get it for 2%-7% off if you keep watching. That way if you get it for 7% off, you'll still be above the $25 threshold.

- Once you get the gift card, walk into Kmart (it won't work online) and buy a Disney gift card with it.

With that transaction, you'll earn two of the bonuses: the cash back site's and the discounted gift card site's. Refer your spouse and have him/her take the same steps. Rinse and repeat with the other cash back and discounted gift card sites. Cardpool isn't always available through the cash back sites. If it's not, you can wait and it should pop back up or you can just go ahead knowing you're missing out on 1% of your purchase. No big deal.

A note on Top Cash Back: it is the hardest (by hardest, I don't mean in time or skill, but in money invested) to earn the referral bonus. You would need to have your referral order $500 of gift cards through Raise to get the bonus. This isn't hard, but there may be better ways to save. Just be smart and take it slow and if you're confused about whether you should go ahead with any one thing, just ask in the Disney Within Reach Facebook group.

Buying discounted gift cards from Raise is a solid strategy for decreasing the amount of money that it takes to go to Disney World. It's repeatable and it stacks well. It has long been a part of my strategy and you'll read more about how to stack it as we continue. I do want to give you a couple caveats here so you're prepared:

- You can only earn cash back from any site (eBates, Swagbucks or Top Cash Back) on the first $1,000 spent on Raise or Cardpool.

- In my experience, they don't catch that right away and will keep paying for far more, but their terms say it's only good on the first $1,000. I feel like it's closer to $2,500, but I was also moving fairly quickly so maybe they just check monthly or something.

- Your spouse will have the same limits.

- You can save money on Cardpool and Raise indefinitely, but you can only earn the cash back on the first $4,000 ($1,000 each for Raise and Cardpool for you and your spouse.) Again, that number was more like $10,000 for us- $2,500 each for Raise and Cardpool, but they might have better systems in place to stop those payouts now.

- Top Cash Back typically pays better, so after you get the eBates bonuses, run the rest through Top Cash Back.

I've told you above how to maximize CouponCabin, so that just leaves Mr. Rebates and Swagbucks (because remember, CardCash doesn't offer any bonuses.)

Mr. Rebates is easy. You can click through to Raise and buy a card for any amount. I'd keep it small since Mr. Rebates doesn't pay as much as others, so you're really just capitalizing on the $5 right now. Refer your spouse and have "him" (ha, ha, ha!) do the same.

Swagbucks can be a little trickier to maximize. You have to earn $3 (which is 300 Swagbucks) and then you're credited $3 extra. If you are in the Disney Within Reach Facebook group, I often announce moneymakers from Swagbucks. These are things like doing a free trial or investing a small amount of money to earn more than that back. I just did one for a free trial of Hulu. You signed up for Hulu and earned 3,000 Swagbucks, which is $30. I canceled Hulu before I got charged and still pocketed the $30.

Stuff like that happens on the regular on that site and if you're willing to sign-up and tell Siri to remind you when to cancel, you can earn around $50 a month. So, you can go check out the "Discover" tab and see if you can find a quick way to earn your 300. Or you can shop through their portal, watch videos or concentrate on your daily to do list. Definitely check out the blog post on Swagbucks. It's worth your time! smartmomsplandisney.com/swagbucks/

A couple more tips with Swagbucks: if your antsy about junk email, you can open a separate email to use on Swagbucks. I don't do this and don't feel like I get much junk. You can also grab a Google Voice phone number (which is a free number that rings to your phone) to use if you're concerned about giving your phone number out. Finally, if you want to sign up for these "Discover" deals, but worry about turning them off on time, you can pick up a Visa debit card from the grocery store and use it to sign up for things. You can reload it on line and put just enough on it to sign up. Then if you forget and don't cancel in time they won't be able to pull any funds from you. I also don't do this, I just tell Siri to remind me and then I turn it off in time, but if you know yourself, you may want to take precautions.

Another thing that I want to note: sometimes the cash back sites change their bonuses and the stores that they offer. I have everything accurate now at the time of print, but things change. Mostly you'll be able to cope if things shift a little, but if you have a question, please email me (LJ@SmartMomsPlanDisney.com) or ask me in the Facebook group.

We're going to discuss these sites more in the following chapters and you'll come to understand when to use which, so don't stress about that now. For now, we're just earning a quick $150 for our trip and laying a solid foundation for the rest of the tricks we're going to employ.

Let's check in on the Smiths and Robinsons:

The Smiths will save $150 using the eight websites.

Needed for Vacation	$2,500.00
8 Sites Bonus	- 150.00
Total	$2,350.00

Savings of $150 or 6% so far.

The Robinsons will save $150 using the eight websites.

Needed for Vacation	$9,500.00
8 Sites Bonus	- 150.00
Total	$9,350.00

Savings of $150 or 1.6% so far.

Note: this technique is probably just a part of the stacking that we're going to do. But you could use the Raise/Cardpool, eBates/TCB strategy for all the money you need for Disney. This is one of those General Strategies, where I really can't calculate the savings because it would be different for everyone. If you were in a hurry you could probably consistently get 4% off. But if you had time and patience, you could get 5%-7% off so it just depends. That's something to keep in mind if you don't like any of the other strategies. We'll discuss this in detail in a later chapter.

All Summed Up:

You can save around $150 (probably more) by signing up through these cash back sites and earning your referral bonuses for referring your spouse. Except for the Top Cash Back referral bonus, this should take less than a $300 investment.

These sites can be beneficial for saving other ways as well. We will learn more about that as we go on.

No matter which savings method you use, you should take advantage of these sign-up and referral bonuses. Earning $150 on less than $300 is a no brainer, plus you'll get the 1-2% from the cash back sites and save 2%-7% off the face value of the card. You should end up with at least $462 for a $300 investment. Do it!

Chapter Three:
Sam's Club and BJ's

Here's where things get fun. The first time I learned these techniques, I had to stop and just marvel for a while. It's like printing Disney money.

You probably already know that Sam's Club and BJ's are wholesale clubs. Their premise is that they charge a membership fee and then you can save big with wholesale pricing. I can't comment to the whole "saving big" thing because I don't use them that way, but they have saved me a lot of money on Disney World.

The good news for us is that they sell Disney gift cards at "wholesale pricing." The gift cards are about 4% off online.

Let me pause for a second and explain that Disney gift cards are good for (almost) ANYTHING Disney sells. You can use them at the Disney Store. You can use them to buy merchandise at Disney World. You can use them to pay for your Disney hotel, your food, your tickets, your dining plan, tips, special events at Disney, basically anything. The only thing you can't use Disney gift cards for are places that only take cash. There are very few of those now. I can literally only think of one, and that's one of the food trucks on the boardwalk at Disney's Boardwalk Resort.

You can also use Disney gift cards at Disneyland, Aulani (Disney's Hawaiian resort), Disney's Vero Beach Resort, the Disney Cruise Line, and Adventures by Disney. You cannot use them at Disneyland Shanghai or Disneyland Paris or any of the other overseas Disney locations.

I haven't paid Disney with any form of payment other than gift cards in years. But I'm getting ahead of myself. Let's go back to Sam's Club.

Online, Sam's Club offers three gift card options at the time of this writing, though they do occasionally go in and out of stock. The prices have also fluxuated slightly now and again.

- The $150 pack- 3 $50 gift cards for $142.98 (free shipping)- 4.7% off
- $500 plastic card for $484.98 (free shipping)- 3% off
- $500 digital card for $484.98 (no shipping)- 3% off

Here's what you'll see online:

You can also find these in stores (despite the fact that it says, "Online Only,") but the prices may vary slightly (usually by a buck up or down.)

The $150 pack is more work, but it pays off. The numbers work out like this: you pay $142.98, but get $150. A savings of $7.02 That's 4.7% off (7.02/150=4.7%). You could also take $7.02 and divide it by $142.98 and get your ROI (return on investment), but most people are more comfortable talking about "percentage off," so I will stick with that throughout the book. The ROI here is 4.9% in case you're interested. The $500 card is $484.98, a savings of $15.02, which is 3% off (15.02/500= 3.0%)

So, the Smiths would need to buy seventeen $150 packs which would cost them $2,430.66 (142.98*17), but would give them $2,550. A savings of $119.34 before expenses.

The Robinsons would need to buy sixty-four $150 packs which would cost them $9,150.72 (142.98*64), but would give them $9,600.00. A savings of $449.28 before expenses.

What expenses? Well, you need to buy a membership to use Sam's. This should be $45, but you can often get deals for $30 on Groupon with a $10 bonus gift card for signing up. Remember Chapter Two? You can also click through a cash back site when you sign up. eBates gives 1.5% at Sam's, but Top Cash Back gives 7% back on a new membership. (Neither will pay on gift cards though, bummer. But I always try, because occasionally they don't catch it and they do pay.)

So, if you get the Groupon and the $10 offer and click through Top Cash Back, you would end up paying less than $20 for the membership: $30-$10= $20-($30*7%)= $17.90

That $17.90 will eat up most of your savings on your first $450, but it's worth it.

If we stopped here our fictitious example families would look like this:

The Smiths would buy seventeen $150 packs for $2,430.66 (17*$142.98). They would get $2,550 but only pay $2,430.66. That's $119.34 in savings ($2,550-$2,430.66), but they paid $17.90 for their membership. So, they come out $101.44 ahead ($119.34-$17.90). On $2550, that's 4% off ($101.44/$2,550= 3.97%, rounded to 4%).

The Robinsons would buy sixty-four $150 packs for $9,150.72 (64*$142.98). They would get $9600, but only pay $9,150.72 That's $449.28 in savings ($9,600-$9,150.72), but they paid $17.90 for their membership. They come out ahead $431.38 ($449.28-$17.90). On $9600, that's 4.5% ($431.38/$9,600= 4.49% rounded to 4.5%).

Not too bad, but we aren't stopping here.

Take It to the Next Level

The great thing about buying gift cards from Sam's Club is that you can pay however you would like. You don't have to use a certain form of payment to get the discount. This creates the opportunity to stack more savings in from the form of payment.

One of the best ways to do this is to use a credit (or debit) card that gives you cash back. I think most cash back cards are around 1%. That's good, but we can do better.

Before we go further down the rabbit hole on cash back credit cards, I want to spend just a minute making sure that you know you have options to get cash back even if you don't do credit cards.

When I was digging us out of $248,000 in debt not too long ago, I only used my debit card to keep us under control—amazing how well that works. I was not savvy enough to realize that there are actually debit cards that will pay you to use them. So, I have not tested the options below, but they come highly recommended:

- Disney Chase Visa Debit Card (this actually doesn't pay you, but gives you many Disney perks.)

- Discover's Cash Back Checking Account

- KeyBank's Debit Card

- PayPal had a business debit card that pays, you may not qualify now, but my hope for you is that by the time you finish this book, your brain will be figuring out a way to qualify. Just hang tight.

- Local Banks and Credit Unions are also good places to check for cash back debit cards or checking accounts.

Ok, now let's look at credit cards. Below are five different credit card options that will give you more than the average 1% cash back card. Pick the one that works best for you.

- **The Barclaycard CashForward World Mastercard** is actually the only one of these cards that I don't have myself. They keep sending me applications, but so far, I've been ok with what I have. But I do want to let you know that I don't have this one, just as a matter of conscience- this is not firsthand experience.

  This one pays you 1.5% on everything and also gives you another 5% back on your rewards. I almost feel like this is just to confuse us consumers and make it look like we're getting more than we are. But we aren't that gullible- let me do the math for you. You spend $1. You get 1.5 cents back. You also get 5% of the 1.5 cents which ends up being .075 of a cent. So, when you spend $1, you get 1.575 cents back, making this a 1.575% cash back card. Still much better than the popular 1% cards. But we can do better! You also get a $200 bonus if you open this and spend $1,000 in the first month.

- **The PayPal MasterCard** gives two points for every dollar spent with PayPal (and these days, I find I can use PayPal most everywhere), but be smart. This is not 2%, like it sounds. You get two points when you spend, but it takes 6,000 points to get a $50 statement credit. This means that the points are worth eight tenths of a cent (does this make your brain hurt? It's ok, keep going, I will summarize.) So, two points per dollar is worth 1.6 cents or 1.6%. It sounds like that's basically the same as 1% but it adds up. I'm going to show you that later.

Don't forget all the ways you can earn rewards

3x The Points for every $1 spent on gas and restaurant purchases

2x The Points for every $1 spent on PayPal and eBay purchases

1x The Points for every $1 spent on other Mastercard purchases

*See Rewards Program Terms included in your Cardholder Agreement for more details.

- **The CitiBank DoubleCash Rewards** card is one of my favorite cash back cards. It gives you 1% when you spend, and another 1% when you pay it off. 2%, and you don't have to keep track of quarterly categories. I use this for all my normal expenses. My husband uses it for everything so he doesn't have to keep track of anything.

- **Even better: Chase Freedom**. You do have to keep track of categories on this one, but quite often wholesale clubs are one of the bonus categories. And when they are, you get 5% back. Stack that with the 3-4% from Sam's and you're doing all right! Alternatively, Walmart is occasionally a category with Chase Freedom.

You can purchase Walmart gift cards earning the 5% and then take those to Sam's and stack them with the Sam's discount. Options are good! (Always check on Shopkicks with Walmart because there are sometimes options for Kicks (covered in more depth later) when buying from Walmart.

If you don't have one yet, sign up here: http://bit.ly/ChaseFreedomLJ (this is case sensitive if you type it in) and you'll get $150 cash back for signing up and spending $500 on the card; $25 more for adding an authorized user. Earn 5% cash back on quarterly categories (you need to activate!) up to $1,500 a quarter. Earn 1% on everything else. Good solid card to have in your wallet.

- **Even better: Discover** also gives 5% in certain categories, and wholesale clubs are frequently on the list.

What makes this better than Chase Freedom is that they will double your cash back earned for the first year of having the card. Now it's not immediate, you do have to wait until the end of the year for the second 5%, but 10% cash back is a pretty big deal.

You'll earn a bonus $50 (that is also doubled) when you sign up through this link:

http://bit.ly/Discover_Bonus Earn 5% cash
back in categories that change each quarter,
up to the quarterly maximum ($1,500) when
you sign up (be sure to activate your cash back
categories!). Earn 1% cash back on all other
purchases

There's one more strategy you can use at Sam's Club,
but before I explain that, let's check in on the Smiths
and the Robinsons to see how they're doing.

- With this strategy alone, the Smiths would
  buy $2,550 in gift cards from Sam's, but they
  would only pay $2,430.66 because of Sam's
  Club's discount. So, they would have
  cashback of:
  o Generic 1% card (there are many):
    $24.31
  o BarclayCard: $38.28 + $200 sign up
    bonus
  o PayPal: $38.89
  o Citibank: $48.61
  o Chase Freedom in a 5% quarter:
    $121.53 + $150 sign up bonus
  o Discover in a 5% quarter, doubled to
    10%: $243.07 + $100 sign up bonus
    ($50x2)

Obviously, Discover would be their best bet, so let's
assume they choose to do that. Discover has
warehouse stores as the bonus category quite

regularly, but the 5% is only good on $1,500 each quarter, so the Smiths will need to buy $1,500 in one quarter and then wait for another quarter for the other $900. They will receive the $50 (doubled to $100) for signing up too. Let's look at where the Smiths are now. Remember that they received $300 from the eight sites maneuvers from the last chapter. I had them buy $2,250 from Sam's because it came out that way with the $150 packs from Sam's so they are going to end up with $2550 ($50 spending money.)

As we move forward, I'll always put how the Smiths and Robinsons procured their funds off to the side in parenthesis. "($2,250 Sam's Club, $300 Eight Sites)" means that they acquired $300 from the eight sites and $2,250 from Sam's. That's what all the savings will be based on. I will choose the most lucrative way for the Smiths and Robinsons, but know that there are many ways to acquire savings and if you can't do exactly the best way, you can still save a ton. I will also show this only in ways that make sense as far as stacking goes. If the Smiths procure $300 from the eight sites, they won't be able to run that $300 through Sam's because it's in Disney gift cards now, not cash. You can use this to see where you can and cannot stack.

Here's the Smiths savings so far:

Needed for Vacation	$2,550.00	($2,250 Sam's, $300 Eight Sites)
Eight Sites Bonuses	- 150.00	

47

Subtotal	$2,400.00	
Saved via Sam's	- 105.30	($7.02*15)
Subtotal	$2,294.70	
Paid for Membership	+ 17.90	
Subtotal	$2,312.60	
Cash Back, Discover	- 214.47	($2,250-($7.02*15)*10%
Subtotal	$2,098.13	
Discover Sign-Up	- 100.00	($50, doubled)
Total	$1,998.13	

$1,998.13 for $2,550 in Disney gift cards! That's a savings of $551.87! This is 21.6% off. Are you getting excited yet? You should be, because this is just the beginning of the book. So much more to come!

And a note on the Smiths: They could both sign up for the Discover card and double their sign-up bonus, but I suggest that they wait to do that. They should wait until just before a year and then have the first spouse refer the other spouse. Then, the first spouse would earn a referral that would be doubled AND they can do this whole strategy again next year. (And if they do plan to go two years in a row, they should also check out the Annual Pass chapter because it could save them a bundle!)

Let's check in on the Robinsons now:

- At Sam's Club alone, the Robinsons would buy $9,600 in gift cards from Sam's, but they would only pay $9,150.72 because of Sam's discount. So, they would have cashback of:

- Generic 1% card: $91.51
- Barclaycard: $144.12 + $200 sign up bonus
- PayPal: $146.41
- Citibank: $183.01
- Chase Freedom in a 5% quarter: $457.54 + $150 sign up bonus
- Discover in a 5% quarter, doubled to 10%: $915.07 + $100 sign up bonus ($50x2)

They would chose Discover too. But the Robinsons need a lot of Disney gift cards. They need to have time and be a little strategic in making purchases at Sam's because Discover only gives the 5% cash back on $1,500 each quarter.

If both spouses sign up for the Discover Card, they'd be able to buy $3,000 per quarter with the bonus. Right now, as I write this, wholesale clubs are included in this quarter's bonus categories. They were included in last quarter's bonus categories, and they will be included in next quarter's bonus categories. That's all the information Discover has given at this time, but it's enough to make me think that the Robinsons will be able to get all the money they need through this strategy, as long as they are smart and patient and have a while before their payments are due to Disney. (Second edition note: Wholesale Clubs were not included as often in the quarters to come, but still often enough to get most trips budgets handled over a year.)

Both spouses received the $50 (doubled to $100) for signing up too, AND the first spouse refers the second spouse. That also gives the first spouse a $50 referral bonus (doubled in the first year.) Cha-ching.

Here's a complete look at where they are now:

Needed for Vacation	$9,600.00	($9,300 Sam's, $300 Eight Sites)
Eight Sites Bonuses	- 150.00	
Subtotal	$9,450.00	
Saved via Sam's	- 435.24	($7.02*62)
Subtotal	$9,014.76	
Paid for Membership	+ 17.90	
Subtotal	$9,032.66	
Cash Back, Discover	- 886.48	($9,300-($7.02*62)*10%)
Subtotal	$8,146.18	
Discover Sign-Up	- 200.00	($50 for each spouse, doubled)
Subtotal	$7,946.18	
Referral Bonus	- 100.00	(spouse #1 refers #2: $50 doubled)
Total	$7,846.18	

The Robinson's paid $7,846.18 for $9,600 in Disney gift cards. They saved $1,753.82. They saved 18.3% (1,753.82/9,600) Pretty good for taking a few little steps.

I estimate that this whole process would take less than one and a half hours of Mr. or Mrs. Robinson's time. I wish I could always make $1,169.21 per hour, while shopping online in my pajamas... It's nice work if you can get it.

A note: You may not think that someone who is about to drop almost $10K on a vacation would take the time to save this way. Well, if you thought that, you'd be wrong. People with money know how to save money. That's why they have money. If you don't believe me, take a look at the book *The Millionaire Next Door* (http://amzn.to/2nCyKYD). It's a study of how millionaires really spend their money. It changed my life. Ok, back to business.

Now, I mentioned there was one other way to save at Sam's. This is a good option if you don't want to sign up for a credit card, or can't. It does take more time and effort, but you can still save a lot using Raise, CardCash, Coupon Cabin, Top Cash Back (TCB) and eBates.

Now remember, eBates and Raise say they'll only pay cash back on the first $1,000, but in my experience, they'll pay on more like $2,000-$2,500. But to be fair we're only going to use the $1,000. I don't want to over-promise you anything.

The best way to optimize these payouts is to use eBates only for $25. That's how much you need to spend to get the referral and sign up bonuses. Then run the rest through Top Cash Back. Always check this though because things change regularly.

- $25 through eBates: $0.25 cash back (but don't forget you're netting another $45 for you and your spouse)

- Another $25 through eBates to earn your spouse's bonus: $0.25

- $975 through Top Cash Back: $19.50

- Another $975 through Top Cash Back on your spouse's account: $19.50

So, you'll end up with $39.50 from the cash back above.

But what are we buying?

Good question. Not Kmart this time. Not Disney either.

We're buying Walmart gift cards. Why? We want to go to Disney, not Walmart. Well, Sam's Club accepts Walmart gift cards. You could buy Sam's gift cards, but they are never really at favorable percentages.

As I write this, there are no discounted Walmart gift cards on Raise. But if I sit here and hit refresh they'll appear and disappear. Yep, there's one. 2.3% off. You have to be quick. There's another. 2.1% off. You have to decide what discount will make you move, and you have to move when one appears that is discounted enough. Have your card loaded in to pay or someone will snatch it out of your cart as you're typing in the numbers.

You'll miss out on a lot of them. It will take time and patience for you to get them for high percentages off. I do not think you will be able to get them for more than the Discover card will net you. And the Discover card avenue is a heck of a lot easier! But if you watch, you should be able to get them for more than 5% off. If you pay with a credit card that gives you another 2% off and click through Top Cash Back for another 2% off, you'll be in the ball game.

I have seen Walmart cards for as much as 24% off on Raise, but it's sure hard to get them.

I only recommend this if you have plenty of time, nothing better to do with it, and no option of opening the Chase Freedom or Discover accounts. Or, if you need to move fast on a small amount of money and it's not the right quarterly bonus time for Chase or Discover. Say you needed the $200 for your deposit with Disney and were just looking to get it as cheap as you could. You could do all the referral and opening bonuses and end up with that $150 off. Maybe you'd be satisfied with 3%-4% off from Raise and whatever cash back credit card that's already in your wallet.

A note on this: some Sam's Clubs will allow you to combine all your Walmart cards at the service desk.

This can be helpful if you have a bunch of printed paper cards because the plastic ones always seem to be easier.

Since this is general theoretical savings, not specific, I'm not going to show you the Smiths and Robinsons savings with this method. There's just no predictable way to say how much they'd really save this way.

Moving on to BJ's:

It is the exact same set up. Only two things are different:

1. You don't have the option of going through Raise for BJ's gift cards, so if you aren't signing up for a credit card, go with Sam's to stack. You can still go through the eight sites to get the sign-up bonuses, you should just get Kmart gift cards from there and turn those into Disney gift cards. We'll talk more about Kmart soon. When I say you don't have the option, I mean that BJ's gift cards on Raise are few and far between and at a low discount. There are conflicting reports on whether you can buy a gift card with a gift card through BJ's. I have not personally tried buying a gift card with a BJ's gift card.

2. BJ's offers Disney gift cards in several denominations. The $500 option isn't always available, but when it is, it's much more

convenient than buying the $50s, but you are losing some of your savings, so you just have to decide what your time is worth to punch it all in as $50s.

$100 Disney Gift Card
🖥 Online
$95.99
Free Shipping

☐ Compare

$500 Disney Gift Card
🖥 Online
$484.99

☐ Compare

$50 Disney Gift Card
🖥 Online
$48.49
Free Shipping

☐ Compare

$25 Disney Gift Card
🖥 Online
$24.49
Free Shipping

☐ Compare

They offer free shipping so the discount on the cards winds up being as follows:

- $150 for $144.99- 3.3% off (this has fluctuated lately)
- $25 for $24.49- 2% off
- $50 for $48.49- 3% off
- $100 for $95.99- 4% off
- $500 for $484.99- 3% off

I won't rehash the entire conversation above because I value your time, but I will tell you to run the numbers because though the percentages are less with BJ's, you can buy a very inexpensive online-only membership ($10 at the time of this writing) and that lower cost can make up for higher prices if you only need a small amount of Disney money.

One note: I've been hearing that BJ's is being more careful about their online orders. I've had my own orders from BJ's canceled and when I called they said it was a security issue and they would be happy to take my order over the phone. This doesn't make me happy because I lose out on the chance to earn that extra 1%-3% from eBates or Top Cash Back, but I went ahead with it and it was fine. I just want to make you aware of the situation. The cash back sites are paying less and less often on gift cards, but they occasionally do. I view this as an unpredictable bonus.

Here are the numbers for the Smiths and the Robinsons:

The Smiths bought $2,200 in $100s from BJ's and $300 through the Eight sites to capture those bonuses.

Needed for Vacation	$2,500.00 ($2,200 BJ's, $300 Eight Sites)
Saved via BJ's:	- 88.22 (22*$4.01)
Subtotal	$2,411.78
Cash Back, Discover	- 211.18 (($2,200-$88.22)*10%)
Subtotal	$2,200.60
Discover Sign-Up	- 100.00
Subtotal	$2,100.60
Eight Sites Bonus	- 150.00
	$1,950.60

This saved the Smiths $549.40 off $2,500. This is 22%

And now for the Robinsons:

Needed for Vacation	$9,500.00 ($9,200 BJ's, $300 Eight Sites)
Saved via BJ's:	- 368.92 (92*$4.01)
Subtotal	$9,131.08
Cash Back, Discover	- 883.11 (($9,200-$368.92)*10%)
Subtotal	$8,247.97
Discover Sign-Up	- 200.00 ($50 for each spouse, doubled)
Subtotal	$8,047.97
Discover Referral	- 100.00 ($50 for spouse #1, doubled)
Subtotal	$7,947.97
Eight Websites	- 150.00
	$7,797.97

The Robinsons saved $1,702.03 off $9,500. This is 17.9%

All Summed Up:

Sam's Club and BJ's can save you money by allowing you to buy Disney gift cards at a discount. If you throw in a cash back credit card (or discounted gift cards at Sam's Club), you can save even more.

Chapter Four:
Target

But what if you don't have a good cash back card and don't want to open a credit card, but still want to save on your Disney vacation? This short chapter is just one of the many strategies in this book that you can use.

Target is a great option for you because they give 5% off Disney gift cards that are purchased in store or online with a Target RedCard.

Right now, you're thinking, "I thought you said I don't need a credit card for this one." And you're right. You don't need a credit card— Target has a debit version of their RedCard that still gives the 5% discount. This means that all you need is to connect your checking account to a RedCard debit account and you'll score 5% off your Disney gift cards in store.

Simply take your checkbook into Target with you and ask at check out or at the customer service desk to apply for a RedCard debit card. It will take a few minutes. They will use your checkbook to find the routing number and account number for your checking account. This process should take less than fifteen minutes and it really couldn't be easier.

You will receive a receipt that will act as your new "RedCard" until you get your debit card in the mail. With that receipt or your new card, you're totally set to use your RedCard account to save 5% on everything at Target, but especially on Disney gift cards.

The bad news is that since the 5% is contingent on the form of payment, you can't stack like you can with Sam's and BJ's. But this is still a good savings for the effort. It's SO easy and predictable. You can order online from home in your pajamas and save on Disney.

Smiths:

Needed for Vacation	$2,500.00	($2,200 Target, $300 Eight Sites)
Saved via Target:	- 110.00	(22*$5.00)
Subtotal	$2,390.00	
Eight Websites Bonus	- 150.00	
	$2,240.00	

$260 saved. 10.4% Not too bad. Go to any Disney Facebook group and say you're saving 10.4% on

Disney gift cards and see how many people want to be you.

Robinsons:

Needed for Vacation	$9,500.00 ($9,200 Target, $300 Eight Sites)
Saved via Target:	- 460.00 (92*$5.00)
Subtotal	$9,040.00
Eight Websites Bonus	- 150.00
	$8,890.00

$610 saved. 6.4% Not as good as some other methods for sure, but I've never been handed $610 and thought to myself, "Jeez, I wish I didn't have this money."

A few more tips about Target:

You used to be able to use Target gift cards to buy Disney gift cards, but in June of 2018, Target changed their policy and they no longer allow this in-store or online. This is not a huge problem in my mind as their RedCard savings is decent and the Target gift card route only saved marginally more for a much larger hassle.

To be honest, I rarely bought Target gift cards with Disney gift cards for any kind of savings. I was more likely to get Target gift cards just because I wasn't sure what I'd ultimately need (Amazon, Disney, Lowe's, gas or food, etc.) and I could grab Target knowing I could purchase any of them with it. Now, that's not the case. A little less convenient, but really no loss.

You can still save a little money with Target gift cards over the RedCard and I do that when I need to make a larger purchase—say I'm about to buy a camera or phone from them. I would buy Target gift cards at say 6-7% off at Raise/Cardpool (you'll learn all about this in the Big Box chapter) and then stack with my cash back card for another 2% off, ending at 8-9% off. That additional 3-4% can be worth it when you're spending $1,000. That really isn't Disney related except for the fact that any dollar saved is a dollar you can put into your Disney fund. #amIright

Also, check ShopKick when you are buying anything at Target. They sometimes have a 1 ShopKick/$1 spent at Target which isn't a ton of money, but free money is free money. And there are always some things to scan for kicks at Target too, if you have the time and inclination. My kids love it. It's a scavenger hunt that pays.

Lastly, I might be crazy here, but I feel like I've found a way to get Target to send me $5 off coupons. AND they work on Disney gift cards. This is completely me guessing, so if you try this and it works, let me know and the more data I have maybe we can get this down to a science. Here's what I do: go login to Target.com and put some items in my cart and then don't check out. Make sure you're signed up to receive Target's promotional emails. After you leave items in your cart, watch your email. You may receive a $5 off a purchase at Target. In store, it works on Disney gift cards. I do it every few weeks and it seems to work. But maybe I'm just getting targeted and I don't realize.

All Summed Up:

Target Debit RedCard is a great option if you don't have a credit card and can't or don't want to open one.

The credit or debit RedCard (along with the other things we've learned) would save the Smiths: $260 which is 10.4%.

The credit or debit RedCard (along with the other things we've learned) would save the Robinsons: $610 which is 6.4%.

Chapter Five:
My Grocery Store Can Get Me to Disney?

You may be surprised to hear that my grocery store is one of the greatest assets in getting me to Disney. This strategy has actually been the <u>best</u> long-term strategy for me. It's predictable, it continues to work and it doesn't rely on me opening a new credit card every 15 minutes. I mean, you can open a credit card to add to this strategy, but once you do open it, you can use it consistently every year. The Discover deal is better, but only for the first year. And actually, I've found a way to make this an even better deal than Discover, but I'm getting ahead of myself.

The credit card that you may want to open is called the American Express BlueCash Everyday or the American Express BlueCash Preferred (http://bit.ly/BlueCashLJ). Let me explain the difference between the two.

The Preferred has a $95 annual fee. I'm usually anti-credit card fees, but I choose the Preferred card and I pay the fee. It's worth it in this situation. Here's why:

- The Preferred gives 6% cash back at grocery stores (up to $6,000) 6%!
- The Preferred gives 3% back at gas stations and select department stores
- The Preferred and the Everyday give 1% back everywhere else
- The Preferred gives you $250 for signing up (http://bit.ly/BlueCashLJ case-sensitive) and spending $1,000
- The Everyday card gives 3% back at grocery stores (up to $6,000)
- The Everyday gives 2% at gas stations and select department stores
- The Everyday gives you $100 for signing up and spending $1,000

So, some quick math just assuming you spend the $6,000 at grocery stores: the Everyday would give you $180 and you'd have no annual fee. The Preferred will give you $360 and you'll pay $95 for the Annual Fee for a net of $265. For me, I knew I would spend the $6,000 every year so I went with the Preferred.

Always do your own math. How much are you going to spend in a year at the grocery store? If you spend more than $3,166.67 it makes sense to go with the Preferred. This is because the extra 3% that the

BlueCash Preferred gives you on grocery stores will cover the $95 fee if you spend at least $3,166.67. That's only $263.88 a month. Even if you do a small trip like the Smiths, you could probably pay for your trip and then still hit the $6,000 by buying actual groceries with the card. Or Amazon gift cards, or Lowe's gift cards, or restaurant gift cards. Go to your grocery store and take a look at what they offer by way of gift cards. If they don't offer any (unlikely), look for a grocery store that does sell gift cards. But let's back up.

If you're quick on the uptake, you're probably realizing how this helps me get to Disney World. I'm not buying milk with my American Express BlueCash. I'm buying Disney! You can buy Disney gift cards from the grocery store. American Express doesn't know (or care) what you're buying so you earn the 6% back. Then you can take the gift cards and stack the savings. Later, I'll show you my way of stacking.

Smiths:

Needed for Vacation	$2,500.00 ($2,200 grocery, $300 Eight Sites)
Cash Back, BlueCash	- 132.00 (This is 6% on grocery purchases)
Subtotal	$2,368.00
BlueCash Annual Fee	+ 95.00
Subtotal	$2,463.00
BlueCash Sign-Up	- 250.00 (The Smiths choose Preferred)
Subtotal	$2,213.00
Eight Websites Bonus	- 150.00
Total	$2,063.00

$437 saved, 17.5% off, but we aren't done yet. And can you even believe that we're like, "17.5% off, eh, well. I've seen better." I can't imagine what would happen if you tried to sell a Disney gift card for 17.5% off in any Disney group or on eBay. Sold to the first person who hears about it.

Additionally, I'm going to guess that the Smiths would be able to get the full benefit of the BlueCash 6% on groceries. They have used $2,200 of it above, so they have $3,800 left. That's $316ish a month. I bet most families spend much more than that. I point this out because it means that they'll save another $228 on their groceries. I don't want to add that to our count since it's not on Disney, but it would offset the $95 fee completely and still bring a profit. From another perspective, it may be savings that they have BECAUSE of Disney and so you might feel it's fair to include it. (If we included this as Disney savings, it would take the Smiths to 26.6% off.)

The Robinsons would need to either combine strategies or have both spouses get the BlueCash card. Or they could settle for just getting 6% back on $6,000 and maybe doing CardCash/Raise/Cardpool with Top Cash Back/CouponCabin/Kmart for the rest. I love having all these strategies at my disposal because it allows me to be flexible and take the right action at the moment.

For the sake of comparison, let's assume the Robinson's both signed up for the BlueCash:

Needed for Vacation	$9,500.00 ($9,200 grocery, $300 Eight Sites)
Cash Back, BlueCash	- 552.00 (6% from grocery purchases)
Subtotal	$8,948.00
BlueCash Annual Fees	+ 190.00 ($95*2: both spouses signed up)
Subtotal	$9,138.00
BlueCash Sign-Ups	- 500.00 ($250*2 both sign-up bonuses)
Subtotal	$8,638.00
BlueCash Referral	- 75.00 Spouse #1 refers spouse #2
Subtotal	$8,563.00
Eight Websites Bonus	- 150.00
Total	$8,413.00

The Robinsons would have saved $1,087 which is 11.4% and we're only in Chapter Five! Not too bad. But we can stack more in there, keep reading.

If you're inclined to include the rest of the savings from the American Express BlueCash, the Robinsons have $2,800 more that they can get the 6% back on. This would be $168 and would bring them to $8,245 or 13.2% off.

A couple other tidbits about the American Express BlueCash:
I do not use this card for gas. I have a different gas strategy which I'll share with you shortly, but if you do not have a gas strategy, 3% is better than 1%-2% or 0%.

I have also had this card offer me some really great deals. If you have an American Express, you may have these deals and not even realize (I didn't at first.) Login to your account online. Go to the "Home" screen for the card and scroll to the bottom of the page. You have to add the deal to your card and then use that card to pay to earn the deal.

Pro-tip: if you have more than one American Express registered to the same login, the deals that are offered and used will affect each other. They are tracking your actions to see what you find valuable. You may have a particular deal on both cards, but when you use it on one it vanishes from the other. A way around this is to open two browsers- I use Chrome and my backup is Safari. So, I login to one card with my Safari browser and the other with Chrome at the same time. I locate the deal that I want and make sure it is showing available for both cards. If it is, I can go ahead and add it to each card. That way I can use the deal twice.

Here are a few that might interest you as you're planning your trip:

>		Spend $175 or more, get $35 back Hampton by Hilton & Hilton Garden Inn	EXPIRES 1/31/2018
>		Spend $200 or more, get $40 back DoubleTree by Hilton	EXPIRES 12/31/2017
>	sunglass hut	Spend $200 or more, get $50 back Sunglass Hut	EXPIRES 12/31/2017
>	enterprise	Spend $200 or more, get $20 back Enterprise Rent-A-Car	EXPIRES 12/31/2017
>		Spend $175 or more, get $35 back Ray-Ban.com	EXPIRES 2/1/2018
>	OMNI HOTELS & RESORTS	Spend $300 or more, get $60 back Omni Hotels & Resorts	EXPIRES 2/28/2018
>		Spend $100 or more, get $20 back Undercover Tourist	EXPIRES 1/1/2018
>		Spend $500 or more, get $100 back World's Leading Cruise Lines	EXPIRES 12/31/2017

I just went on there at random and looked at what they offer right this minute. They have many different offers available throughout the year. If you're in the private Disney Within Reach Facebook group, I usually announce when I see offers on American Express cards that can be used for Disney.

I've taken advantage of some offers at Lowe's, Best Buy and Bed, Bath and Beyond. The Lowe's offer was buy $150 at Lowe's and get a $30 statement credit. I didn't need anything at Lowe's at that exact moment so I bought a Lowe's gift card and that qualified for the credit. They also have other gift cards that I could have chosen (Amazon, but no Disney), but that worked for me. The Bed, Bath and Beyond deal was spend $25 and get a $5 statement credit. I bought a $25 Disney gift card from them and got the $5. A quick 20% off. There have been other deals on this card that have helped me. This is one of the best cards in my wallet.

If you don't want to open the American Express BlueCash card, or if you need more than $6,000 and don't want to open two, or if you just want to save some serious cash on your groceries, I have a few more ideas for you:

- Both Chase Freedom and Discover sometimes give 5% off grocery stores, so keep that in mind if you are wanting to buy Disney from Kroger, Giant Eagle or your local grocery store. I track that just for regular grocery purchases too. When I have spent more than $6,000 on grocery purchases with the BlueCash card, these two are great back-up methods. If you're new to Discover, that 5% will double to 10% for your first year.

- Another back up I employ to save on grocery purchases once my $6,000 from the American Express BlueCash is used, is to buy Kroger gift cards from Raise at 1% off when they do bonus percentages off. They'll say, "5% Extra Off Site-Wide with Code [CODE]" and I'll buy Kroger at 1%, plus the 5% extra, plus I'll pay with my DoubleCash for 2% more so I'm at 8% off from Kroger. At most Krogers, these can be used to buy other gift cards. If you haven't maxed out the cash back from Top Cash Back you should be able to get another 1%-2% back there too.

We aren't done discussing grocery stores though. There are a few regional grocery store chains that I am aware of that can help you save even more in conjunction with your BlueCash card. The four that I know about are Kroger, Albertsons, Giant Food (Giant) and Giant Eagle. I'm going to break down Kroger and Giant Eagle separately because I know them well and their programs are easy to explain. I've used both of these.

Let's start with the other two:

Albertsons is a gigantic conglomerate with at least 15 different brand names (check: https://en.wikipedia.org/wiki/Albertsons#Chains   to see if you recognize any) and their programs vary by location. I can tell you that they are in the following states: Arizona, California, Colorado, Idaho, Louisiana, Montana, Nevada, Oregon, Texas, Utah, Washington and Wyoming. And you can go to: http://www.albertsons.com/rewards/ to see how their fuel rewards programs work near you.

Giant Food (commonly called Giant) is a smaller chain. They are located in Delaware, Maryland, Virginia and Washington, D.C. I've not used their program, this is one that a reader pointed out to me. The program looks good though. You can save up to $1.50 per gallon of gas and you earn $0.10 off for every 100 points. Points are good for 30 days. The savings is good on a maximum of 20 gallons of fuel. Now, I read in the terms and conditions that gift cards aren't eligible to earn points, but a reader swears that it works on gift cards despite that, so I'm just giving you the info and you can try it for yourself. I hope it works for you!

Note: If you know of any other regional chains with deals like this, email me and let me know. I'll include it in the next edition.
LJ@SmartMomsPlanDisney.com

So, next up, **Giant Eagle**. They have locations in Pennsylvania, Ohio, West Virginia, Indiana and Maryland. Their program is called FuelPerks. For every $50 you spend in Giant Eagle stores, you receive $0.10 off per gallon. In some areas, you receive $0.20 off per gallon. Giant Eagle also runs specials occasionally doubling the amount you receive. This doubling is unpredictable and should be considered a bonus if you can catch it. You can use your rewards on up to 30 gallons of gas at one time and up to the full price of a gallon of gas.

So, if you live in an area where you get $0.10 off per gallon for every $50 spent (which is most Giant Eagle areas), and you went to Giant Eagle and bought $1,000 in gift cards, you would receive $2.00 off per gallon. The math works like this: Since you get perks on every $50 spent, we'll divide $1,000 by $50: 1,000/50=20. This is the number of ten cent perks you would receive. 20 perks * 10 cents = $2/gallon Since you can get 30 gallons per transaction, this would be a savings of $60 ($2*30 gallons.) Effectively, this is a $60 savings on $1,000 spent. That's 6% off (60/1,000).

Obviously, this is much more of a hassle than the other savings methods. Unless you drive a truck with a big gas tank, you need to use gas cans to get the savings. I have heard of some people meeting up and using two cars, but this isn't technically allowed by the program.

You can make this more convenient by forgoing some of the savings: my small SUV will take 17 gallons of gas at a fill up. If I didn't want to use gas cans, I could just take the $34 ($2*17 gallons) in savings and call it a day. It would be 3.4%. Better than 0%.

But, I'm going to just pretend that the Smiths and Robinsons are as crazy as I am about saving money, and show this at the max capacity. I've been using gas cans for a long time. I'll do what I have to do to get to Disney more often. If you're reading this book, I'm going to assume that you feel the same way.

The Smiths:

Needed for Vacation	$2,500.00	($2,200 Giant Eagle, $300 Eight Sites)
Cash Back, BlueCash	- 132.00	(This is 6% on grocery purchases)
Subtotal	$2,368.00	
BlueCash Annual Fee	+ 95.00	
Subtotal	$2,463.00	
BlueCash Sign Up	- 250.00	
Subtotal	$2,213.00	
Eight Websites Bonus	- 150.00	
Subtotal	$2,063.00	
FuelPerks	- 132.00	($60 per thousand Giant Eagle)
	$1,931.00	

This is a savings of $569 which is 22.8% off. Now we're picking up some momentum. And remember the Smiths will also save another $228 on their groceries over the next year because of the BlueCash card.

Let's see how the Robinsons are doing now.

The Robinsons:

Needed for Vacation	$9,500.00	($9,200 Giant Eagle, $300 Eight Sites)
Cash Back, BlueCash	- 552.00	(This is 6% on grocery purchases)
Subtotal	$8,948.00	
BlueCash Fees	+ 190.00	
Subtotal	$9,138.00	
BlueCash Sign-Ups	- 500.00	
Subtotal	$8,638.00	
BlueCash Referral	- 75.00	
Subtotal	$8,563.00	
Eight Websites	- 150.00	
Subtotal	$8,413.00	
FuelPerks	- 552.00	($60 per thousand at Giant Eagle)
	$7,861.00	

So, the Robinsons paid $7,861 for $9,500, a savings of $1,639 which is 17.25% (7,861/9,500.) That is some pretty excellent savings! I get desensitized to it sometimes. I'm saving so much money that I stop being impressed by it. But look at it this way: the Robinsons get to enjoy the exact same vacation as other families in their shoes. But because they're smart and put in a little effort, they also get to pay $1,639 less for that vacation.

Kroger has a very similar program. This is one of my absolute go-to ways to save. This is because, like the Giant Eagle program, it's sustainable. I can do it every month.

Kroger is located in Alabama, Arkansas, Delaware, Georgia, Indiana, Illinois, Kentucky, Louisiana, Maryland, Michigan, Mississippi, Missouri, North Carolina, Ohio, Oklahoma, South Carolina, Tennessee, Texas, Virginia, West Virginia.

Kroger's Fuel Points program is as follows: you earn a fuel point for every dollar you spend in their store. You earn 2X Fuel Points on gift cards. At least every month, for all the while I've been doing this (18 months or so), they'll offer 4X Fuel Points on gift cards. Since this is predictable, I'll include it as a savings. For every 100 Fuel Points, you get $0.10 off a gallon of gas. The catch is that you can only get $1.00 off per gallon at a time, not like Giant Eagle where you can get your gas for free if you have enough

FuelPerks. You are allowed to get up to 35 gallons at a time with Kroger.

Let me show you this both with the regular 2X Fuel Points and with the 4X Fuel Points.

With 2X Fuel Points you would spend $500 to get $1 off fuel. This would save you $35 dollars if you got all the fuel you're allowed. 35/500: 7% savings.

With 4X Fuel Points, it's simply doubled: you would spend $250 to get $1 off fuel. This is still a savings of $35. $35/250: 14% savings. It's obviously worth it to plan and purchase when they are offering the 4X Fuel Points offer.

The good news is that this stacks easily. Pay for the gift cards with the American Express BlueCash card for an additional 6% off (or with another cash back credit or debit card.)

AND Kroger also offers a credit card that gives you $0.25 off a gallon when you redeem at least $0.10 in Fuel Points. When you do this, you'll pay $250 for the gift cards with the BlueCash, get $15 back in cash, then you'll get $1 off for the Fuel Points and $0.25 for the Kroger credit card, so $1.25 off 35 gallons= $43.75 off. So, you save $58.75 ($43.75+$15) off $250 for a savings of 23.5% (58.75/250).

So, I wait for the 4X Fuel Points and buy around $1,000 in gift cards. This gives me 4,000 Fuel Points. I need to fuel up four times with thirty-five gallons each time to maximize my savings. My car takes around seventeen gallons and then I put the additional eighteen gallons in gas cans. My husband uses that gas in his truck and around the farm.

I have videoed this strategy for you step-by-step so you can follow it easier (it's so much less complicated than it seems.) It's on my Instagram account under my highlights.
www.instagram.com/smartmomsplandisney

There is another strategy that stacks with this, but it has the feeling of being limited time. I'm going to put it in here, but just be aware that it may be fleeting.

Ask in the Disney Within Reach Facebook group if you want to know for sure.

But, if this works, it's quite a bit more savings.

What you're going to do is get Visa or MasterCard gift cards at the grocery store and take them to Best Buy. There will be an activation fee for these (around 6%, but look and you might find a deal), but we're going to offset it with the next step. We'll use Swagbucks at Best Buy to get a whole bunch more money off. (Note: if your Best Buy allows gift card to gift card transactions, you can buy Best Buy cards and flip them to Disney to avoid the 6% fee. Most Best Buys allowed this until recently, so try it with a small amount like $25 and see.)

Swagbucks is giving 2% cash back on purchases from Best Buy plus a bonus: $5 off $50, which is basically 12% off. That's an insane stacker.

You need to use your phone's browser to login to Swagbucks (you cannot use the Swagbucks app for this), choose shop, search for Best Buy, scroll down to find your QR code. Have the cashier scan that and buy $50. Pay with your Visa or MasterCard gift card that's already 17.5% off (23.5% off+6% activation fee.) You're paying $50, but getting $6 back from Swagbucks.

You need to generate a **new QR code for each** $50. Also, it says in the fine print that they don't pay on gift cards, but in store they do. I have seen many on Facebook who have successfully done several thousand dollars, $50 at a time and been paid on each. The truly annoying thing about this is that you can only earn the bonus once per day, so multiple trips are a must.

Here are the ads to look for on Swagbucks:

Best Buy Coupons & Cash Back

In Good Back
Earn 2% Cash Back
That's 2 SB per $1 spent

Shop Now

Special Terms

*Bonus SB will only be awarded on qualifying purchases of $50 or more that are also eligible for the standard SB per dollar reward. Bonus SB will only be awarded for an in-store purchase with your personal QR code or a purchase of items featured in the Weekly Ad (in-store or online). Offers cannot be stacked.

The following purchases are not eligible for SB: Apple-branded products (Apple Watch, Laptops, Tablets, Desktops, iPhones, etc), Mobile devices, Best Buy Business orders, Bestbuy.ca orders, gift cards, warranties, transactions on 3rd Party Websites, online photo center sales, digital downloads, Geek Squad Services, phone activations, long-distance and internet service sales and Reward Zone Purchases. Items eligible for SB are subject to change without notice.

Best Buy is the number-one retailer of consumer electronics, personal computers, entertainment software and appliances. With a huge selection of products available in all areas of consumer electronics at competitive prices

Best Buy Weekly Ad

Check back every Sunday for the latest deals from Best Buy.

Spend **$50** or more and earn 500 SB.

Find Deal

Let's pretend that the stars align for both the Smiths and the Robinsons. They are near Kroger, and Best

Buy and they can get 35 gallons of gas at a time. Here's where the Smiths would be:

Needed for Vacation	$2,550.00	($2,250 Kroger/Best Buy $300 Eight sites)
Cash Back, BlueCash	- 135.00	(6% on grocery)
Subtotal	$2,415.00	
BlueCash Fee	+ 95.00	
Subtotal	$2,510.00	
BlueCash Sign-Up	- 250.00	
Subtotal	$2,260.00	
Eight Websites	- 150.00	
Subtotal	$2,110.00	
Fuel Savings	- 393.75	($43.75 for every $250 at Kroger)
Subtotal	$1,716.25	
SwagBucks	- 270.00	($6 off every $50)
Subtotal	$1,446.25	
Visa/MC Fee	+ 133.88	($5.95 for every $100 grocery/Best Buy)
Total	$1,580.13	

They have saved $969.87 which is a savings of 38% We are getting ever closer to that 50% mark which used to be my Holy Grail of savings. I know now how to get much higher, but really 50% is something to celebrate. Paying less than $1,600 for a $2,550 vacation is AMAZING—and so do-able.

The Robinsons:

Needed for Vacation	$9,550.00	($9,250 Kroger/Best Buy $300 Eight Sites)
Cash Back, BlueCash	- 555.00	(6% on grocery)
Subtotal	$8,995.00	
BlueCash Fees	+ 190.00	
Subtotal	$9,185.00	
BlueCash Sign-Ups	- 500.00	
Subtotal	$8,685.00	

BlueCash Referral	- 75.00
Subtotal	$8,610.00
Eight Websites	- 150.00
Subtotal	$8,460.00
Fuel Savings	- 1,618.75 ($43.75 for every $250)
Subtotal	$6,841.25
SwagBucks	- 1,110.00 ($6 for every $50)
Subtotal	$5,731.25
Visa/MC Fee	+ 550.38 ($5.95 for every $100 grocery/Best Buy)
Total	$6,281.63

The Robinsons saved $3,268.37 which is 34%. $3,268.38! What a great savings. If they can get their next trip for the same amount (which should be mostly do-able), their savings on this trip is more than half of their next trip. This effectively means that the Robinsons would get one and a half trips to Disney for the same money that a family with no knowledge of these strategies would spend on one trip. Aren't you so glad you know this stuff?

Saving More with Cycling (also called Manufactured Spending)

At least once a month, someone asks me, "If I buy Visa/MasterCard/American Express prepaid gift cards, and get fuel points with them, can I then use them to buy Disney gift cards and get double 4X fuel points?" This is called cycling or manufactured spending. I include those terms because if you would like to look into this further, it's helpful to google those terms. Manufactured spending can be quite lucrative if you have time and the inclination to work on it.

I did not think that it was valuable enough to include in the first edition, but since the question keeps coming up and this could be helpful in certain instances, I want to cover it. Here's the process and then I'll tell you what circumstances it could be helpful for:

- wait for 4X fuel points on prepaid cards (this is separate from the normal 4x fuel points)

- buy $100 in prepaid cards (earning 14% in fuel savings, plus whatever cash back from the card you used to pay (BlueCash would be 6%), but paying 6% in fees so 14%ish net if you use BlueCash,

- take that $100, set up a pin number and use it to buy a new $100 prepaid card, earning 14% again.

- Rinse and repeat as many times as you can, up to the amount of fuel you can use.

- If your store won't let you use a gift card to buy another (most won't but some will if you use the pin number and debit option), you could just move right to Disney at that point. This would add 14% (plus whatever from your cash back card), but subtract 6% for the fee.

Yes, this can add to your savings, but I don't mess with it and the reason why is the 6% fee. I can only use so much gas and that fee is cutting into my ultimate savings. So, yes, I'm getting that specific card for a high percentage off when all is said and done, but I'm only getting 8% off from my Kroger rewards, instead of 14%.

Practically, it comes out like this for me: I can use four fill-ups per month. This is $1000 in gift cards from Kroger. Since I have multiple businesses, I don't have trouble hitting that $1000 since I buy Amazon, Lowe's, eBay, Home Depot, Target, Disney, etc. Without flipping I earn 14% ($140) back in fuel points. If I did $500 prepaid and then flipped to Disney (or whatever), I would earn the $140, but would also pay $30 in fees ($6 for each $100, so $6*5=$30). This reduces my overall savings by $30. But that's me.

That said, this would be a really good way to save if you can use more gas than you can buy gift cards OR if you only had a small amount of money to cycle:

- Say you have $500 seed money and your trip is 12 months away and you want to see how much you can make off that $500—this method would be a good one.

- It would also be good if you use more gas than you can buy gift cards for: say you fill up five times in a month, but can only allocate $750 a month to your Disney fund. $750 is enough to get $1 off a gallon, three times. So, to get the $1 off the other two times, buy $500 in Visa or MasterCard prepaid cards and use those to buy $500 in Disney. You'll end up getting 14% off in fuel savings (provided you use the full thirty-five gallons when you fill up), but losing 6% in fees. You're still winning in that situation. This is a bad idea if you need more $250 increments of gift cards (of anything: Disney, Amazon, Target, etc.) than fill-ups each month.

Meijer

Last, but certainly not least inside the grocery chapter is Meijer. Meijer is a grocery store trying to be a super store like Walmart, located in Michigan, Illinois, Indiana, Kentucky, Ohio, and Wisconsin. It seems to me that the Midwest has unfair advantages when it comes to grocery savings.

The great thing about Meijer is that you do not have to purchase fuel in order to save money on Disney. The savings isn't quite as high as with Kroger or Giant Eagle, but considering it's super easy, I'll go for it. And since fuel isn't involved, it actually doesn't interfere with my Kroger use. I can use Kroger AND Meijer each month, but you probably don't need to spend that much money each month (a big portion of my spending is for my businesses.) Let me tell you about this deal.

Around once a month or so, they will offer $5 back in mPerks when you purchase $50 in gift cards. An mPerk is to Meijer what Kohl's Cash is to Kohl's. You can use it to buy whatever they sell—with a few exceptions: most notably, gift cards. You can use your mPerks to buy groceries (or whatever you need from Meijer—they have everything, similar to Target) and put the money from your grocery budget back into your Disney fund.

Stack this with any of the other ways we've discussed to get cash back at grocery stores:

- American Express BlueCash- 6% back for a total of 16% off (there are reports of AMEX not crediting at Meijer when you purchase gift cards, so you may want to test this for your account.)

- Chase Freedom when grocery stores are the 5% category for the quarter- 15% off total.

- Discover when grocery stores are the 5% category for the quarter- 15% off total, and that doubles to 20% total if you are a new Discover user in the first year.

- CitiBank DoubleCash for 2%- 12% total

Here's what you'll see on your mPerks account when this sale is going:

$5 off

your next purchase for every $50 you spend on Gift Cards (Exclusions: Meijer Gift Cards, iTunes, Gaming, Sling TV, Google Play, HBO Now, Hulu, CBS All Access, Spotify, Amazon, Prepaid Debit, Visa, MasterCard, American Express, and Phone Cards)

You will not need to activate the coupon or do anything online—it is automatic. You just purchase the gift cards and earn $5 for every $50, up to $500. You do not need to check out with multiples of $50. I check out with $500 and get 10 $5 credits, which can then be used all in one transaction.

I videoed this whole transaction to make it easier for you to understand. It is in my highlights on my Instagram account: www.instagram.com/smartmomsplandisney

rip #54 One   Trip #54 Two   Meijer Deal   Rider Switch   Stitch F

This deal isn't the most advantageous out there, but it's EASY. There's so little to it. It's very little effort. So, if easy is your jam, this is for you.

Let's check in on the Smiths and the Robinsons.

Here's the Smiths:

Needed for Vacation	$2,500.00	($2,200 Meijer, $300 Eight sites)
Cash Back, BlueCash	- 132.00	(6% on grocery)
Subtotal	$2,368.00	
BlueCash Annual Fee	+ 95.00	

89

Subtotal	$2,463.00	
BlueCash Sign-Up	- 250.00	
Subtotal	$2,213.00	
Eight Websites Bonus	- 150.00	
Subtotal	$2,063.00	
mPerks	- 220.00	($5 for every $50 at Meijer)
Total	$1,843.00	

The Smiths have saved $657 which is a savings of 26%. Considering the little time and effort involved with this deal, this is a nice chunk of change to save.

The Robinsons:

Needed for Vacation	$9,500.00	($9,200 Meijer, $300 Eight Sites)
Cash Back, BlueCash	- 552.00	(6% on grocery)
Subtotal	$8,948.00	
BlueCash Annual Fees	+ 190.00	
Subtotal	$9,138.00	
BlueCash Sign-Ups	- 500.00	
Subtotal	$8,638.00	
BlueCash Referral	- 75.00	
Subtotal	$8,563.00	
Eight Websites Bonus	- 150.00	
Subtotal	$8,413.00	
mPerks	- 920.00	($5 for every $50)
Total	$7,493.00	

The Robinsons have saved $2,007—this is 21% off. Again, not the most we've seen, but a nice return for such a small effort. Meijer is a great asset in getting to Disney frugally.

All Summed Up:

Grocery stores, fuel programs and Best Buy can be a huge saver. Don't underestimate them. If you aren't willing to use gas cans, you can still save quite a bit of money. But if you are willing to use them, this can be an excellent sustainable strategy. It can help you get to Disney World again and again.

Remember, you don't HAVE to stack everything together. If you don't want to deal with gas, you might still want to get the American Express BlueCash card or Meijer. If you don't want to get a new credit card, you might still want to use the fuel programs or mPerks.

And if you don't have Kroger, Giant Eagle, Meijer or one of the other grocery stores with fuel programs, you may still be able to grab some savings with the BlueCash card.

Chapter Six:
Buying Disney at Big Box Stores

I mentioned Best Buy in the last chapter. We're going to discuss Best Buy again here and also Sears and Kmart. Using these stores is a less popular way of saving, but it can be a good option if you don't want to use credit or if you don't have access to Kroger, Giant Eagle, Meijer or one of the other helpful grocery stores.

Remember when we learned about CardCash, Raise and Cardpool? We're going to use them again with this strategy. If you need to, head on back to Chapter Two and Four for the ins and outs of the cash back websites and the gift card resale sites.

We'll also be using eBay in this chapter. Did you know that you can click through Top Cash Back to eBay for a little extra savings sometimes? It's usually 1% back, but they sometimes offer sales. Sign up for Top Cash Back's emails and favorite eBay and they'll email you with sales. Their terms say that they don't give cash back on gift cards, but in my experience, they do sometimes. This is getting a bit more hit or miss, but I still see them paying for some of my gift card purchases through eBay.

There are two processes for saving in this chapter. The first is to find Sears or Kmart gift cards at a discount and then take them in and purchase Disney gift cards with them. The second is to buy Disney gift cards at Best Buy using Swagbucks, as we discussed in the last chapter. I'm going to add that discussion here too, because I don't want anyone without access to a good grocery store deal to miss the Best Buy opportunity because they skipped the grocery store chapter.

Buying Gift Cards at A Discount and Flipping to Disney

Remember when we talked about buying Walmart gift cards and using them to purchase Disney gift cards at Sam's Club? Well, you can do something similar at Kmart too:

Go to Top Cash Back (TCB), Coupon Cabin, or eBates (whichever is paying the best) and click through to Raise, CardCash or Cardpool, then look for Kmart. When you find them at good percentages off, buy them! Take them in person (gift card to gift card sales are not allowed online) to a Kmart that allows gift card to gift card transactions and buy Disney gift cards with them.

To get better percentages off at Cardpool and Raise: watch and refresh. You should be able to get Kmart or Sears gift cards for 7% off pretty consistently. Cardpool has three at 6.5% off right now, just sitting there. But if you're finding that you are missing out on the higher percentages try these steps:

- Try using the Raise App. I'll just set my phone next to me, with the app up and on the Kmart page and refresh it every few minutes. You can't use Top Cash Back through the app so you lose that 2%, but you can only get that on the first $1,000 (according to them, though they paid me on at least $2,500 on each of my accounts...ahem, I mean on my account and my husband's account.) So, I set my standards a little lower on the website if I knew I was getting the 2%. I would buy at 6%. On the App, I'd hold out for 7% or higher.

- Make sure your credit or debit card is preloaded into Raise. I'm not a huge fan of letting places save my card info, but it's imperative at Raise. You will miss out if you're typing in your card info. I even tried with my Apple Wallet filling it in which is fairly quick and I still missed out. I don't find Cardpool to be as tough.

- Set up an alert. I have noticed that the good cards become available in waves. So, I set up an alert to be notified at a certain percentage (5%), and then I start stalking and refreshing when I get the alert. I usually miss that first one that I was actually alerted about. But, lots of time I'll be able to grab two or three more at a nice high percentage.

Raise verses Cardpool verses CardCash

Here are my thoughts on these platforms. I'm sure you'll develop your own opinion once you get used to using these, but this will give you somewhere to start.

Raise is my favorite because of ease of use. Cardpool has higher percentages. CardCash seems to have more problems with their cards, but always refunds them promptly. I use all three and I love all three. Raise is easier, because they deliver faster and have a one-year guarantee on any of their gift cards. When I've run into any issues with their gift cards (didn't arrive, didn't have the right amount on it, wouldn't work at all, was zeroed out, etc.) Raise has immediately refunded my purchase price. I have run more than $30,000 through Raise over the years for my businesses and they have taken excellent care of me. Once, I had a $450 gift card not work and they refunded it without a word.

Cardpool can take up to 24 hours to deliver a gift card to me. I usually don't have the patience for that. I don't plan ahead enough. I'm headed to Kmart THAT DAY, and want to roll to Disney. But I go to Disney often, and am usually paying for a trip that's coming up in only a few weeks or so. You may have more time and better luck with Cardpool. I have spent less with Cardpool, but still a significant amount and I've never had any issues with any of their cards. They've always been exactly as promised. That's pretty impressive.

CardCash is the newest of the three. I'd been using them for only a little while when I wrote the first edition of the book, and I didn't yet feel comfortable sharing about them. Now I've used them a lot more. I've run more than $5,000 through there, and though I have had some hiccups, I feel good about recommending them. I've had a few cards not work. It's been a higher percentage than at Raise. But they refunded the cards in an expedient and efficient manner. Still, one of them was for $750, and you get a little nervous when a card that's supposed to have $750 on it won't work. I don't like having that happen, but I get great deals over there and I have saved more than enough to make the risk worth it. But if this type of thing will be a stressor for you, you might want to stick to Cardpool.

Both CardCash and Cardpool are VERY (excessively) careful who they accept as customers. Your first order with them will take forever (maybe days), they might want to call you on the phone and they might cancel your order because they have some random security question that they won't even tell you about. To me, it was worth it to keep trying. Once I got the first order to go through, I've never had any other issues. So, if your order gets cancelled, try a different card, or just keep trying. Try with small amounts. Hopefully, it will pay off.

Coupon Cabin verses eBates verses Top Cash Back

Between Coupon Cabin, eBates and Top Cash Back (TCB), Top Cash Back wins almost every time. They are the more generous of the websites and they pay easier. eBates only pays once every quarter. You can have them PayPal you, but I sort of like getting a check in the mail. It feels more real that way. I think you can also choose from gift cards (not real useful ones, things like Ann Taylor Loft. Not knocking them, but I'm not real eager to have an Ann Taylor Loft gift card when I could have cash. P.S: I sort of love Ann Taylor Loft.)

Top Cash Back pays you whenever you want, they can PayPal you, or give you useful gift cards. Lots to choose from, but the best ones are probably Amazon or American Express. You get a small bonus for choosing a gift card payout, but it's not usually enough for me to do it. I usually get PayPal payouts.

Coupon Cabin is new to me. I've only been using them for a few months, but they have proved very useful. They may even overtake Top Cash Back as my favorite. No one else pays on CardCash, so that's a big plus. They also do these "$30 off $30" at Target, Best Buy, Kohl's etc. deals, but they are only for the first ten people, and I'm not about that inconvenient life of stalking deals like that. But if you have the time (and a little luck), you can score some good deals that way. They also have that Chrome Extension which helps me out quite frequently. They also pay on Etsy... which is big for me!

All this means I basically never use eBates, unless Top Cash Back or Coupon Cabin doesn't give any cash back in a particular situation. I did download the eBates pop-up bar. It comes up when I'm on a site that eBates gives cash back on. It usually goes like this: "Oh, eBates. Yes, let me go check Top Cash Back and see if they give more. Yes, they do." Top Cash Back should really pay eBates for that pop up because it's sent me to them a lot of times!

eBates has deals with more stores, but Top Cash Back's deals are better. Coupon Cabin seems to be leaning toward being the best of both worlds, but I'll be sure to update this as I learn more.

For me, I usually decide which gift card resale site I'm going to be using in a particular situation. It's usually Raise or CardCash, depending on percentages. Then I just go check eBates, Top Cash Back and Coupon Cabin to see which has the highest percentages back. That way I'm not checking all three sites (eBates, Top Cash Back, Coupon Cabin) for all three sites (Raise, Cardpool, CardCash). That's a lot to keep straight. *Brain melts*

Back to the Deal Discussion:

So, you're starting at Coupon Cabin/Top Cash Back/eBates, then you're going to Raise/CardCash/Cardpool. You're buying Kmart or Sears gift cards at around 7% off (hopefully). Then you're taking those to Kmart (in person—it won't work online) and using them to buy Disney gift cards.

And remember, you can pay CardCash or Raise or Cardpool however you want. I use my CitiBank Double Rewards card for Raise so I end up with 2% back on top of whatever percentage off I get.

So, let's check in on the Smiths and Robinsons. This is one of those general strategies that is hard to calculate with any level of surety. But I would like to calculate this at least once for you so you can see how it can add up.

I think it will be fair to calculate their percentage off from Raise and Cardpool at 6%. You could certainly do much better if you waited and stalked and had all the time in the world and nothing better to do with it.

And you could certainly do a lot worse if you just went and bought whatever was available without trying for the higher percentages. So, with a reasonable amount of effort you could bank 6%. I'm about reasonable amounts of effort. I don't do things that take too much time. But I realize that there are people who do have that time. You just have to balance what your time is worth vs. what your money is worth.

The Smiths:

Needed for Vacation	$2,500.00 ($2,500 from Eight Sites)
Saved via gift card site	- 150.00 (6%)
Subtotal	$2,350.00
Cash Back via cash back site	- 40.00
(2% on $1,000/spouse, but you should do better.)	
Subtotal	$2,310.00
Eight Websites Bonus	- 150.00
Total	$2,160.00

At this point, the Smiths have saved $340, which is a savings of 13.6%.

If the Smiths paid with a cash back credit card, they could also bank another $23.50 ($2,350*1%) on a 1% card or if they had the DoubleCash Rewards Card, they'd bank another $47 ($2,350*2%). This would bring their savings to 14.5% or 15.5%, respectively.

The Robinsons:

Needed for Vacation	$9,500.00 ($9,500 from Eight Sites)
Saved via Raise/Cardpool	- 570.00 (6%)
Subtotal	$8,930.00
Cash Back from TCB	- 40.00
(2% on $1,000/spouse, but you should do better.)	
Subtotal	$8,890.00
Eight Websites Bonus	- 150.00
Total	$8,740.00

At this point, the Robinsons have saved $760, which is a savings of 8%.

If the Robinsons paid with a cash back credit card, they could also bank another $89.30 (8,930*1%) on a 1% card or if they had the DoubleCash Rewards Card, they'd bank another $178.60. This would bring their savings to 8.9% or 9.9%, respectively.

This also highlights the difference between a 1% and a 2% cash back card (I told you I'd explain this.) Most people think it is such a small difference that it doesn't matter. But even if you just spend $1,000 a month with your regular everyday spending (groceries, gas, cell phone etc.), 1% is $120 a year (1000*12*.01), while 2% is $240 a year (1000*12*.02). To me, the extra $120 is worth having the right card in my wallet.

You could take this another step out and multiply this by ten years. In ten years, the 1% earnings on your normal everyday expenses would be $1,200. That's a heck of a lot better than if you were using a normal debit card and getting 0% back. You could basically take a long weekend at Disney on that decision alone. On the 2% card, you'd wind up with $2,400 over that ten-year period. That's pretty much what the Smiths need for their vacation—at full price. It's a little thing, but it adds up.

I do want to note here that Kmart could change their policies at any time. Corporate policy is to allow gift cards to be used to purchase Disney gift cards now, but they could change that. And some Kmarts do not follow corporate policy regardless.

I always feel fairly comfortable with the "risk" of ending up with a bunch of Kmart money when I really wanted Disney money. I figure worst case scenario, I grocery shop there for a couple weeks and then put the money I would have spent on groceries back into my Disney fund.

Funny story, once I was moving a bunch of money through quickly because I was about to pay for our big fall trip. My husband is not quite as Disney obsessed as I am (but he's getting there), so when he comes, I like to stay in better places and do bigger things.

So, anyway, I needed about $3,500. In this case, I was using Target not Kmart, back when Target's gift card policy was very lax. I had gone through Raise and had Target gift cards set aside to order Disney gift cards.

And then, Target changed their online policy. Suddenly, you couldn't order gift cards with gift cards online. I was a little panicky thinking maybe they had changed their entire policy, but I was able to go into the store and buy my Disney gift cards without a problem.

It would have been inconvenient to have $3,500 in Target gift cards and still need to come up with the $3,500 in Disney funds that I actually needed. But I did a little research and realized that because I had bought the Target gift cards so well, I could have sold them and lost little to nothing. But still, keep that in mind. If you have the savings to cushion you, it would be little impact, as you'd be able to unload them over time and not lose much, if anything. But if you don't have the savings, be more careful.

Examples:

Let me give you some real-life examples of how this would work. Right at this moment, Raise only has one Sears card and it's at only a half a percent off. No good. Let's check Cardpool. Cardpool has plenty available and they are all at a respectable 5% off. So, if you clicked through Coupon Cabin, Top Cash Back or eBates you'd get another 1% off and you'd probably at least use a 1% cash back credit card to pay. Now you're up to 7% off. This isn't anything to write home about, but it's sure better than 0%. If your previous go-to was Target's 5% off, this would save you an extra $20 per thousand. That could add up to quite a lot of money.

CardCash has Kmart at 2.5%. Raise has Kmart at 4.7% off. Cardpool has Kmart at 6.5%. You can't get ShopKicks with Kmart, but you can use Coupon Cabin, Top Cash Back or eBates (whichever is better at the time) and your cash back credit card to pay. That would add another 2-3%. Sears is at the same percentage on both Raise and Cardpool and it's not available on CardCash at this exact moment. You CANNOT buy gift cards with gift cards at Sears. However, you can buy gift cards with Sears gift cards at Kmart, but they have to be the plastic gift card. They can't accept the codes. When I've accidentally bought the codes in the past, I've gone into Sears and had them put them onto a plastic gift card and then I've taken it to Kmart to buy Disney. This is extremely time consuming and I do not suggest you do it! So, with this strategy, you should end up at 8.5%-9.5% off.

But I think we can do even better with this strategy if we head over to eBay. Right now, there are a couple attractive options on eBay. There is a private seller selling a Sears gift card for even more than 5% off. I have had very good luck in the past with Sears and Kmart gift cards on eBay. PayPal occasionally runs a sale for a $100 Sears gift card for $85. 15% right off the bat and you can still add the 2-3% from Top Cash

Back (maybe) and a cash back credit card. 17-18% is nice.

For the record, PayPal is not my favorite merchant to work with. They have a fair amount of fraud and they don't back up their gift cards the way that I think they should. They are huge and they can throw their weight around a lot. They are the only seller allowed to sell digital gift cards on eBay. I feel like it's odd that eBay has separate rules for them. AND their feedback is low for such a giant. You can look at the negative reviews and see what I'm talking about with the fraud. In addition to this, they are extremely picky about their customers and I've heard horror stories of PayPal closing accounts or locking up funds for months while you try desperately to prove you are who you say you are. Their customer service isn't very good and you will waste tons of time if you ever end up needing to talk to them on the phone.

So, does that mean that I steer clear of them? No. Maybe I should, but they offer such great deals and I'm not that risk adverse so I keep using them and so far, I've never been burnt. I've never had a fraudulent card and I've never lost any money. At this point, they've saved me close to a thousand dollars so even if I lost money here, I'd keep using them. I have had to prove my identity, had my account locked for a few days and spent several hours on the phone with them, but that was years ago. I feel like I know how to be careful and walk the line so that I don't get into any trouble with them and so I can still take advantage of their deals without putting much at risk.

Here are my best practices:

- Be ready to spend any gift cards you acquire from PayPal Digital Gifts. I usually give myself one day. So, if I can buy Best Buy today and turn it tomorrow, I'll do it. Any longer than that and I'll skip it. If the cards aren't digital, I don't worry as much.

- If your order gets cancelled, leave it alone. Do not try and order again or you're going down the path of getting your account locked.

- Know the maximum purchase amounts and order that exact amount in one order. So, if you're allowed to order three $100 gift cards for $85, order those three in one transaction, not one at a time. Ordering only one or two would be fine too, if that's all you need. But do not place multiple orders.

- If your husband or another close family member has an account with eBay and PayPal, they can also order the maximum. Make sure you're using the right eBay account with the right PayPal account. I switch devices as well, if I have the luxury. So, we order from my account with my laptop, my husband's account with his iPhone and my dad's with my iPhone or my dad's computer.

- If you start getting vague "won't go through" issues on a phone, switch to a computer for more information. If you are getting red error messages on a computer, stop trying. Give it 24 hours and try again and it may go through. Don't keep trying if you're getting error messages no matter what they are. If you miss the sale, you miss it. Give it to God.

- Finally, if your PayPal account gets locked, don't freak out. It's probably temporary. Your best course of action is to do nothing for 72 hours. The account will probably unlock on its own. Calling is usually a waste of time as they have no ability to shorten the lock time and they are not pleasant to deal with.

I know it sounds like a huge hassle to work with them, but I don't feel like it is now that I just follow these rules that I made up for myself. For over a thousand bucks in savings over the last few years, I'll keep doing it.

I do want to warn you again that Sears and Kmart can be a gray area. Have you heard the term "your mileage may vary?" It's used in the online community to convey that this isn't a sure thing. It's often shortened to YMMV. If you start researching this type of thing online, you'll certainly see it and now you'll know what it means.

Sears and Kmart are classic YMMV. I have access to several Kmarts and some will allow me to purchase gift cards with gift cards and some will not. No Sears (Searses?) in my area will allow purchases of gift cards with gift cards. I have gone around, tried and now I feel familiar with where I'll have success and I just go there for this strategy. I suggest you start with $25 or $50 and try it. Also, see if you have the nerves for this. Some of my friends say going into Kmart not knowing what will happen makes them feel jittery or like they are breaking the law. This doesn't affect me. What's the worst that can happen? They tell me no. They sell groceries, so I'll just spend my $50 on feeding my kids and I'm none the worse for the wear.

I want to underline that I spent zero time looking for these cards. I literally just pulled up the sites and checked what I could buy right this second. I didn't look at auctions, I didn't hit refresh at CardCash, Raise or Cardpool. If you had time and were strategic and enjoyed it (I kind of enjoy it, I'm sick!) you could get a much better deal. I've gotten 20% off from eBay. People just list gift cards wanting to be rid of them. I see a great Buy It Now and I add it to my Disney stash. You could probably do very well if you tried.

Disney Savings with Best Buy and Swagbucks

Before we get too far into this, let me say that I think this next deal is going to be temporary. It's working now, but I have this feeling that it's not going to last. Still, I want to make you aware. And ask in Disney Within Reach to see if it's still going if you want to use it.

Here it is: Swagbucks is giving 2% cash back on purchases from Best Buy plus a bonus: $5 off $50, which is basically 12% off. That's insane for such an easy deal.

You need to use your phone's browser to login to Swagbucks (you cannot use the Swagbucks app for this), choose shop, search for Best Buy, scroll down to find your QR code. Have the cashier scan that and buy $50. Pay with your cash back credit card (or a discounted prepaid Visa or MasterCard—see the previous chapter to learn how to get those at a discount.) You're paying $50, but getting $6 back from Swagbucks and maybe $0.50-$1 from your form of payment (or much more with the discounted prepaid cards.)

You need to generate a **new QR code for each** $50. Also, it says in the fine print that they don't pay on gift cards, but in store they do. I have seen many on Facebook who have successfully done several thousand dollars, $50 at a time and been paid on each. The most annoying part is that you can only earn the bonus on $50 per day.

Here are the ads to look for on Swagbucks:

Best Buy Coupons & Cash Back

4% Cash Back
Earn 2% Cash Back
That's 2 SB per $1 spent

Special Terms

*Bonus SB will only be awarded on qualifying purchases of $50 or more that are also eligible for the standard SB per dollar reward. Bonus SB will only be awarded for an in-store purchase with your personal QR code or a purchase of items featured in the Weekly Ad (in-store or online). Offers cannot be stacked.

The following purchases are not eligible for SB: Apple-branded products (Apple Watch, Laptops, Tablets, Desktops, iPhones, etc), Mobile devices, Best Buy Business orders, Bestbuy.ca orders, gift cards, warranties, transactions on 3rd Party Websites, online photo center sales, digital downloads, Geek Squad Services, phone activations, long-distance and internet service sales and Reward Zone Purchases. Items eligible for SB are subject to change without notice.

Best Buy is the number-one retailer of consumer electronics, personal computers, entertainment software and appliances. With a huge selection of products available in all areas of consumer electronics at competitive prices

Best Buy Weekly Ad

Check back every Sunday for the latest deals from Best Buy.

Spend **$50** or more and earn 500 SB.

Find Deal

All Summed Up:

Big box stores can save you money a couple different ways:

- Buying discounted gift cards and flipping to Disney
- Using Swagbucks $50 at a time.

Both of these options can be great without credit cards and they are open to pretty much everyone.

Chapter Seven:
Your Mileage May Vary Options

I really debated this chapter. For the most part, it'll be useless to many of you. But there may be someone out there who can use this information AND these are questions that get asked in the Facebook group so if I answer them here, they won't be a mystery to you.

You remember that Your Mileage May Vary (YMMV) is a term used in savings circles to mean that this is a risky maneuver. I have used all of these and they've all worked for me in some form or fashion.

1. Bed, Bath and Beyond: I mentioned before that I occasionally get coupons for $5 off of $25, and that's a great deal. But if you can find a cashier who will try, their system will allow gift card to gift card transactions. I have heard conflicting things about their gift card to gift card policy. I'm quite a good talker, so I can usually get the manager to let me, but I don't

push this or try to make it a regular strategy. For me, savings needs to be fun and easy. If you find a cashier or a store who doesn't care, Bed, Bath and Beyond gift cards are usually available at quite a discount.

2. Walgreens: similar story as BB&B. Their systems allow gift card to gift card, most stores allow it too, but some do not. Luckily, there are about 30 gazillion Walgreens in the world so if one doesn't allow it, another might. Just keep trying. One thing that will never work is a Walgreen merchandise card to a gift card. And if you buy discounted gift cards from Raise or one of the other sites, you might get a merchandise card. It's impossible to tell if you are going to get a merchandise card or gift card. If the discount is high enough, you might just roll the dice. You can always pick up some toilet paper if the gift card can't be used on Disney. Then use your toilet paper budget to refill your Disney fund.

3. ShopDisney: This one actually ALWAYS works for me, but it's not supposed to so maybe it won't someday. What you do is click through Top Cash Back to ShopDisney (which is the new name of the Disney Store) and then buy Disney gift cards. They have egift cards. I use my 2% cash back card, and so I end up around 7% off. This is super convenient if I need

something fast and don't want to leave the house. #disneywithoutgettingdressed

Another time when this comes in handy is with cashing in the Chase rewards points card. That card is annoying. I mean, I'd rather have money on it, verses not having money on it, but it's still not the most user-friendly thing in the world. You earn money on it by spending money with your Disney Chase Visa or by referring a friend. I sometimes run contests in Disney Within Reach that can result in your link being put on my blog, so you might be able to score some referrals that way.

Anyway, when they pay you, they put it on a card that's not a gift card, not a credit card. It's a weird "Rewards Card." It expires, it's weird if you need a refund. It's just not my favorite. But, redemption! You can use it to buy Disney gift cards from ShopDisney.

You can get egift cards or regular ones (I like to take the opportunity to buy cute ones) AND you usually get the 5% credited to you. I've never had it not work. Easy extra 5% and makes my life easier since I then don't have to deal with the Rewards card.

4. Ok, this one is way out there, but stay with me. We aren't even a quarter of the way into this book, but hopefully you've seen enough

value with me to hang in there. Have I impressed you enough that I can let a little of the crazy show? Hope so.

This strategy has actually been a really big saver to me over the years. But some people might think I'm bonkers. Oh well. Here it is: sharing rooms.

It all started with my mom. She got an annual pass two years ago, and I realized that when she came along we could split rooms and my costs were lower. But she's a teacher and couldn't always come along. So, I started asking my internet friends. It totally works. AND bonus, we've become completely real friends. That makes it sound like I was just asking them along to save money, but that's not the case. They were super cool and I wanted to hang out with them, but it was sweet that it lowered the cost of our trip too.

Hang out in the Facebook groups long enough and you'll get yourself some best internet friends. Then schedule a trip with them. Usually, I do me and one kid and another mom and one kid. We each share a bed with our kid and pay half the room. We come and go as we please, no pressure. Hang out sometimes, other times I don't see them at all.

I'm putting this in the YMMV chapter because though it's not about gift cards like the other options, it is YMMV. Is your friend a crazy person who stays up all night and then uses all the hot water in the morning? Only time will tell. Just make sure you feel comfortable with your friend though and I suspect you'll be just fine and will have made a friend for life.

Or you could just stay in the realm of normalcy (what's it like there? I've always wanted to go.) and invite grandma, grandpa or an uncle or aunt or your bestie (like one you've actually met in person before.) Either way, I wanted to bring it to your attention.

All Summed Up:

There are some lesser-known, lesser-tried ways of saving on Disney out there and they just might work for you. If they don't, no worries, you're a little smarter for having read this chapter.

Chapter Eight:
What Do We Do Without the DVA???

On July 25, 2017, Disney discontinued the Disney Vacation Account (DVA). I have received many questions regarding what to do now that it's closed. I originally was just going to remove the chapter from the book and move on, but I thought that wasn't giving you the tools needed to save. So instead, this chapter will focus on what to do now. It won't save you a lot of money (the Disney Vacation Account never really did either: 2%), but it will guide you and make it a lot easier and less frustrating to set some of the other strategies in place.

Let me back up just a second, because I'm sure we're leaving a few frustrated readers behind, especially those who didn't read the first version of this book. You may be asking, "What is the Disney Vacation Account?" It was an account with Disney where you could save your money and then use it to pay for your vacation. You didn't earn any interest, but you did get a 2% bonus whenever you used the money to pay Disney expenses. It was very helpful because the Disney Vacation Account accepted Disney gift cards and it helped with keeping them organized and secure. I wrote a complete blog post about the Disney Vacation Account that tells you a lot more about the account and the process and if you're curious, you can see that here: http://bit.ly/SMPD_DVA but for now we're going to focus on filling the gap the Disney Vacation Account left (in our wallets and our hearts.)

We have speculated about why Disney decided to do away with the Disney Vacation Account, but the reason that they gave was because it was underused. All I can say was that I was doing my part, using the heck out of mine!

The big problem that I see without the Disney Vacation Account is the convenience. It really made it quite a bit more convenient to use gift cards. It was easy to bring gift cards home from the store and just load them into the account and not worry about it. The account was secure (not all gift cards are), it was safe, it was easy. You could put as much into it as you wanted. To me, Disney has done away with something that made it easier to be their customer. I am sincerely hoping that they decide to bring it back as a courtesy.

But our real focus needs to be what to do from this point. The specific issues we're facing without the Disney Vacation Account are:

- No opportunity to earn 2% for saving with Disney

- Money put into the Disney Vacation Account stayed away from our regular funds and wasn't as likely to get pulled back in to pay a bill or cover an emergency

- Unable to combine many gift cards into one to make one payment

- Gift cards aren't as secure as the account

- Refunds go to some random gift card that you may not even have anymore

- Keeping track of gift cards and balances is now more important

Let me discuss each one of these and give you my best advice about how to make each of them less of an issue for you. And to my new readers, you may not know what you're missing without the Disney Vacation Account and that's all the better for you. But these strategies will serve you well if you are planning on using the gift card strategies that are discussed later on in the book. I suggest you just skim over the ideas in this chapter and don't worry about them at this point. Maybe put them in the back of your mind for when you find yourself up to your elbows in Disney gift cards. Then come on back and check this chapter out in detail. You have my blessing to skip ahead if you want.

Let me answer the first two at the same time because one solution handles both issues:
No opportunity to earn 2% for saving with Disney and **money put into the Disney Vacation Account stayed away from our regular funds and wasn't as likely to get pulled back in to pay a bill or cover an emergency:** We are never going to be as lucky as to find a savings vehicle that gives us 2% in interest just for having an account open for 120 days like the Disney Vacation Account did, but there are lots of accounts that do give SOME interest. And this also presents an opportunity to separate your Disney funds from your regular household budget.

Open an account at a separate institution from the one where you're banking for your regular banking needs. Take some time to look around and see where your money will earn the most interest. Every little bit helps. Look especially at credit unions and local banks. Credit unions are very similar to banks, but they are non-profit organizations. This means that they can't show a profit, they have to reinvest all of what would be their profit back into their members ("members" is a term they use instead of "customers.") Being a non-profit also shelters them from quite a bit of their tax liabilities. It's not hard to see that if you compare a bank who is taxed and who shows a profit with a credit union who is not taxed in the same way and who cannot show a profit, the credit union is the one who is in a better position to help its members/customers.

Small local banks often lose to credit unions, but they may win compared to the big banks because they aren't in the position to pay for lots of advertising, compete on such a large scale and to produce a return for shareholders. My local bank offers a checking account with a 3% return, without a lot of hoops to jump through.

Having said all that, if you don't have access to an awesome small bank or credit union, either locally or online, there are a few big banks out there who are being very competitive for your business. And it may not be convenient to use them for your everyday bank, but they may be just the ticket for your Disney savings, where you might even consider it a positive thing that the money is a little bit difficult to get to.

Start your search out by taking a look at these: Great Lakes Credit Union, Consumers Credit Union, PNC, Northpointe Bank and Discover (yes, the credit card people offer savings and checking accounts and their interest rates might surprise you.) These are the winners right now with percentages as high as 5%, but make sure you look around a little as this type of thing is somewhat volatile. I know that's annoying. You're always welcome to email me and ask my thoughts (LJ@SmartMomsPlanDisney.com) or ask in the private Facebook group.

By creating a separate account, you are earning some interest, but you're also putting yourself in the position to save money apart from your regular life. A few years ago, I wanted to start putting aside a monthly amount to cover some larger expenses that happen each year, so I opened a second checking at the same bank. How convenient. I scheduled a transfer from my main account into the smaller account each month. The idea would be that then when those larger expenses come around (my property taxes for my rentals), the money would be in there and ready to be used. Well... things didn't go according to plan.

I saved the money each month for a year or so. But then when the bills came, I paid them out of my regular account because I didn't have checks for the little one. No harm, no foul, I thought. I have the money. But then later when money was tighter, I saw that little account and thought, "Hmm, I did already pay the taxes. I could dip into that." So, I did. That little account has mostly lost its purpose. Now it's just another account that I sometimes like to spend time moving money in and out of. Hardly a helpful situation.

But I learned my lesson. The money needs to be in another place and it needs to be set up so that I can use it easily for what I intend to use it for, otherwise I might fall back into my old patterns.

All that to say, take the time to set up the account in a different place than your normal accounts. Decide how you'll use it for Disney when the time comes (and we'll talk more about that along the way.) Also decide how you'll fund it. Your employer may be depositing your checking into your regular bank account each pay period, but they may be able to split it between two accounts. Can you set up $50 or $100 or $500 or $10 or $5 (because everyone is in a different place financially and everyone has different goals) to go to your separate new account? You may never even miss it, if you never even see it.

Another note on this, if you are the type that has a very hard time saving your money for a big purchase, like a vacation, but you are committed to going to Disney, you may want to skip this account altogether. You may want to just buy Disney gift cards straight off, as regularly as possible. Every payday, buy a discounted gift card and make a payment on your vacation. It's hard to spend Disney gift cards on other things so that may well be a way for you to make the magic happen!

The next issue we can tackle is the **inability to combine many gift cards into one to make a**

payment. There is actually a solution to this, or at least a partial solution. Disneygiftcard.com will be your new best friend. You can create an account and save up to five gift cards in there at a time. Each gift card can hold up to $1,000. Disney is not responsible for your money the way that they were with the Disney Vacation Account, so you still want to be cautious about your gift cards. Personally, I do not feel like it's a good idea to leave money sitting on the disneygiftcard.com site because it's one more avenue for a hacker to have the ability to steal from you. More on that below.

Remember how I said that one of the problems now is **gift cards aren't as secure as the account?** Here's a way to mitigate that risk. Book a package with Disney. Conceptually, this should be the vacation that you intend to take, if that's possible. If it's not, like maybe if you are saving for Disney for three years from now and they won't allow you to book yet, or maybe if you just really haven't decided what you want to book, you can still book a package. Just book it for really far out (499 days is the limit, and that far out, you'll need to call vs. booking online I believe). Then when the date gets closer (before 30 days) or once you decide what you want, call and change the booking to the REAL reservation you'd like.

So, once you have a booking set up with Disney, you can secure your gift cards by paying them. Choose one gift card number that you are always going to use to pay Disney. Over the years, I have acquired a few cute Disney gift cards. Different characters, not just the red or purple Mickey ones. You obviously do not have to do this, but it was fun and made my life easier because I know I won't accidentally mix that one up with the other zillion red Mickey ones I have. You can get the cute ones at the Disney Store or on shopdisney.com (which is the new disneystore.com). I selected one of those that I'm going to use as my "pay Disney" card. So, what you'll do is go on to disneygiftcard.com and transfer whatever you want to pay Disney onto that card. Let's pretend it has Buzz Lightyear on it. Say you pick up a $50 Disney gift card at Target (at a discount, yay!) when you went to get milk and you would like to apply it to your account. Well, you could just log on to Disney's site and pay that $50 toward your package. That would achieve the security we are hoping for.

But we can solve another problem here too: **Refunds go to some random gift card that you may not even have anymore.** If we add the extra step of using disneygiftcard.com to transfer the balance to the "pay Disney" card (remember we said it has Buzz Lightyear on it?) then we are able to use the same card every time we pay Disney (or have our travel agent pay Disney.) Then, in the event we need a refund, they'll all go back to that same card. If it's more than $1000, Disney won't want to put it all on one card and they will likely issue you new cards which is also an acceptable solution. What we don't want to have happen is to have a refund of say $3,000 all go back to

60 random $50 gift cards that we threw away already. That extra step protects you from that fate.

The process we just discussed will also help with the final issue: **Keeping track of gift cards and balances is now more important.** If we do not use the gift card to actually pay Disney, there is no chance of a refund being sent to it, so as long as we transfer the balance to our "pay Disney" card before using the funds, the card can be trashed. (Full disclosure, I keep all of mine because I'm Type A to the core. But there's really no need to do so.)

I do have another solution to this issue as well. I found these little gift card holders that slip over the gift card and allow you to write on the back and keep track of your balances. I especially use one for the "pay Disney" card to keep track of what I paid Disney, and I also use it for gift cards that I intend to use in the parks. I have another character gift card that I use to actually take to the parks and pay my room charges (or for food/souvenirs/general costs at the park if I'm not staying on site.) I like to use a tracker for that one as well.

I found these trackers on Etsy (https://www.etsy.com/listing/169012923/credit-card-sleeve-with-ledger-debit or just search for gift card sleeves and the seller I like is TYVM. I believe that listing above is sold out because she couldn't get the colors again, but she has others. She's been great. They are around $1.50 each, but if you're in the Facebook group for this book, you might be able to win one.

I have a couple final thoughts on gift card security. There are only a few occasions where you should ever be giving out your gift card number:

- Directly to Disney over the phone or internet to pay off part or all of your booking

- To your travel agent over the phone or via a secure email connection

- If you are renting Disney Vacation Club points and are purchasing the dining plan, the member will need to call and add dining for you. You will need to give them some form of payment for that. We'll discuss this in later chapters.

Other than those situations, you should not be giving out your gift card number to anyone else. There are lots of scams these days, so I feel like I should tell you that. And I do want to caution you not to use your regular "pay Disney" gift card if you are renting points and need to have the member add dining for you. I like to use one of the regular red Mickey gift cards, and put as close as I can to the exact balance needed on it. Then I give them that card number to pay Disney with, and, once it's used I transfer any other amount off of it, write on it with Sharpie, "Dining plan for DVC Stay- Dates" then I hold on to it until the trip is over and then toss it in with the thousands of others that I could throw away, but I still keep. I'll probably need a psychiatrist to intervene at some point, when my old Disney gift cards are taking up an entire room in my home. #newsateleven

All Summed Up:

Disney's decision to do away with the Disney Vacation Account certainly makes life a little more complicated, but there are lots of ways to mitigate the risks and bring back a bit of the convenience and savings by following the advice in this chapter.

If you're new to the gift card game, skip this chapter and come back when you have a solid discounted gift card strategy in place and a need to protect your funds.

Part II: Account Bonuses

Opening credit card accounts is like Vacation Money 101. In fact, saving money on a Disney World vacation has a reputation of being "all about credit cards" and though it can be a lucrative part of anyone's strategy, it doesn't have to be part of yours if you don't want it to be. There is an appendix for you if you don't want to open credit cards. You can take a look at it: Appendix D.

And don't skip Part II completely, because though I am going to run through two credit cards that will help you, the first chapter doesn't require credit cards at all, and it can net you an easy $500-$1,000 (or more) every year.

Chapters in this section:

Chapter Nine: Checking Accounts to Disney

Chapter Ten: $500 Fast

Chapter Eleven: Chase Sapphire Preferred

Chapter Nine:
Checking Accounts to Disney

I'm really excited to add this chapter to the second edition because:

- it's something that anyone can do

- you don't need to have good credit and it doesn't affect your credit

- you can do it again and again

- this is totally stackable since the bonuses come in cash: cha-ching

The first time I ever used a checking account opening bonus, I was eighteen and starting my Mary Kay business. There was a local bank that was offering $600 to start a business checking account. I opened mine under the name: Lauralyn Johnson, Independent Beauty Consultant and bam! $600-- which I spent on my inventory. That business would go on to help me through college. Selling mascara to college girls? It went like hot cakes. And someone asked me if I was eighteen last month (I'm...um... twenty-nine) so I'm going to go ahead and say it: their skin care works. Not a pitch, I haven't sold it since college, I'm just saying.

But how does this checking account thing work and how can it be a lasting repeatable way to get to Disney World? Glad you asked.

There are lots of banks out there who want your business. They want it so badly that they'll pay for it. Uh-huh. I know you've heard of this. You've seen the advertisements. $300 for opening a checking account. $100 for opening a savings account. They are all around and you can totally take advantage. And then you can do it again.

In a nutshell, here are the steps:

- Locate a bank with an offer you would like to use

- Read through the terms and make sure you can meet them. Usually the most difficult are balance requirements, length of deposit requirements and direct deposit requirements

- Go ahead and take the steps to set up the account and earn the bonus

- Watch out for fees. It's ok to pay fees as long as you come out ahead in the end, just be mindful of them.

- After you've met the requirements and collected the bonus AND ensured you have met the requirements for the account to be open, close the account. You definitely want to take this step so you can use this account/bonus again as soon as possible— some banks have requirements about being a new customer or about how recently you closed an account.

- Keep your real checking account in place and don't mess with it more than you have to meet the new accounts requirements (for example: you may need to change your direct deposit, but set it up so your money goes into the new account and then transfers to your real account so you don't have to deal with changing your bill pay etc.)

- If you have a spouse who meets the requirements as well, you can usually qualify for the offer for both of you. Double the bonus.

Here are some of the offers that you should check out and remember, these are extremely volatile so please treat these just as your starting point—a place to begin your search:

Chase
- Premier Plus Checking: $300
- Total Checking: $200
- Savings: $150
- College Checking: $50
- Total Business Checking: $200

TD Bank: (for residents of: CT, DE, DC, FL, ME, MD, MA, NH, NJ, NY, NC, PA, RI, SC, VT, VA)
- Premier Checking $300
- Convenience Checking $150

PNC Bank: (For residents of AL, DC, DE, FL, GA, IL, IN, KY, MD, MI, MO, NC, NJ, NY, OH, PA, SC, VA, WI & WV)
- Virtual Wallet: $300

Suntrust Bank: (For residents of: AL, AR, FL, GA, MD, MS, NC, SC, TN, VA, DC & WV)
- Signature Advantage Account $500
- Select Checking $250

BMO:
- Personal Checking: $100
- Statement Savings $50
- Health Savings: $50
- eStatements: $50

Bank of America
- Interest Checking or Core Checking $300

Charles Schwab
- New account: $100 Cash Bonus

HSBC:
- Choice Checking: $200
- Advance Checking: $350
- Premier Checking: $750

CitiBank (targeted)
- CitiBank is offering either $400 or $600 to new customers with a targeted promotion.

KeyBank (AK, AL, CO, CT, FL, ID, IN, ME, MA, MI, NY, OH, OR, PA, UT, VT, WA)
- Key Express, $100
- Key Advantage, $200
- Key Privilege $200
- Key Business Reward Checking $300

Wells Fargo is also a likely candidate and one I've used personally.

The key here is to be savvy and read all the terms and to plan carefully to change your direct deposit as soon as you'd earned the bonus and get earning the next one!

I have a really clear memory of February 2017, I was at Disney's Boardwalk Resort (on DVC points that I'd rented from eBay— you'll learn about that soon.) opening our new checking accounts online, that would net us $1,000. We only applied for two accounts— one for each of us. We don't have any direct deposits, so we can't maximize this, but hopefully you can. Even without the direct deposits, this can be lucrative.

Take the bonuses you've earned and get discounted Disney gift cards from them to increase your Disney spending power even further. See Part I for details on discounted gift cards.

This is a pretty general strategy, but I'd like to show you the Smiths and Robinsons with it included. It's not specific enough for me to be able to say, "The Smiths saved $1,000 and the Robinsons saved $750." However, this is a predictable strategy. It's one that almost everyone can use in some form. Some can make this a lasting repeatable way to bank $1,000 or more a year. Some can save $250 once. Mike and I are on the low end since we don't have direct deposits and they are a frequent requirement, and we still do pretty well with this.

Just for argument's sake, let's say that most families can net $500 per year with this strategy. I think that's conservative. You may be able to do a lot more, or maybe a little less, but it's fair. Let's see the Smiths and Robinsons now. And remember, since this is completely stackable, the Smiths and Robinsons can do EVERYTHING else they were already doing. This vacation is getting cheap.

Needed for Vacation $2,550.00 ($2,250 Kroger/Best Buy $300 Eight Sites)
Cash Back, BlueCash -   135.00 (6% on grocery)
Subtotal $2,415.00
BlueCash Fee   +   95.00
Subtotal $2,510.00
BlueCash Sign-Up   -   250.00
Subtotal $2,260.00
Eight Websites   -   150.00
Subtotal $2,110.00
Fuel Savings   -   393.75 ($43.75 for every $250 at Kroger)
Subtotal $1,716.25
SwagBucks   -   270.00 ($6 off every $50)
Subtotal $1,446.25
MC/Visa Fee   +   133.88 ($5.95 for every $100 grocery/Best Buy)
Subtotal $1,580.13
Checking Bonus   -   500.00
Total $1,080.13

The Smiths are now paying $1,080.13 for a $2,550 vacation. So amazing! This is a savings of $1,469.87 or 57.6%. That is crazy talk. It's so good that I talk about it and people are like, "You're lying." Nope. Truth. And we're not close to done yet. Not even halfway.

And here are the Robinsons:

Needed for Vacation $9,550.00
($9,250 Kroger/Best Buy, $300 Eight Sites)
Cash Back, BlueCash   -   555.00   (6% on grocery)
Subtotal $8,995.00
BlueCash Annual Fees   +   190.00
Subtotal $9,185.00
BlueCash Sign-Ups   -   500.00
Subtotal $8,685.00
BlueCash Referral   -   75.00

Subtotal	$8,610.00	
Eight Websites Bonus	- 150.00	
Subtotal	$8,460.00	
Kroger Fuel Points	- 1,618.75	($43.75 for every $250)
Subtotal	$6,841.25	
SwagBucks	- 1,110.00	($6 for every $50)
Subtotal	$5,731.25	
MC/Visa Fee	+ 550.38	
Subtotal	$6,281.63	
Checking Bonus	- 500.00	
Total	$5,781.63	

The Robinsons saved $3,768.37 off a $9,550 vacation making their savings 39.5%. Mrs. Robinson is managing this and has tried to explain it to Mr. Robinson, whose eyes glaze over. Mrs. Robinson is ecstatic enough for both of them though. And she should completely go brag in the Disney Within Reach Facebook group because we totally get it.

All Summed Up:

Open checking, follow rules, earn bonus, close checking, get discounted Disney gift cards with bonus, rinse, repeat.

This can be a sustainable way to secure a sizable chunk of your vacation money.

Chapter Ten:
$500 Fast

If you've sleuthed around the internet about saving money for Disney, you've probably heard about the Disney Chase Visa. It's an incredibly easy way to grab a nice chunk of your vacation money.

And it's a card you really should have in your wallet if you're on the way to see The Mouse because there are a lot of perks at Disney.

These change occasionally, but right now you get:

- Exclusive character meet and greet at Epcot (usually 1-3 of the fab five: Mickey, Minnie, Goofy, Donald and Pluto)

- Exclusive character meet and greet at Hollywood Studios in the Star Wars Launch Bay (one of the Star Wars characters)

- 10% off any merchandise purchase totaling over $50

- 0% financing for 6 months on your vacation package

- 10% off select dining

- 10-15% off select tours and recreation

- 1% cash back on anything

- Frequent sales for card members only at the Disney Store and ShopDisney.com

- 20%-35% discounts from rack rate

- Advanced and increased availability on Disney resort discounts: you may get one or two days advanced notification and ability to book over the general public, and when the discounts are diminished for the general public, there may still be availability for cardholders.

Please note that there are two different Disney Chase Visas. The Premier and the regular. You want the regular. I usually encourage everyone to run their numbers and pick what works for them, but almost exclusively, you want the regular. The Premier has an annual fee and, in my experience, it's too much ($49). You should look at this yourself though.

Here is a comparison:
https://disneyrewards.com/compare-cards/

The Premier has a few extra benefits, the most important to consider is that it gives you 2% cash back on certain categories, while the regular card only gives you 1%. That still doesn't move me because I'd have to spend $4,900 in these specific categories to make back my $49. I can just use my DoubleCash Rewards card and not have any fee. Plus, the categories are things I can easily save more than 2% on (gas, Disney etc.)

Now, they'll try to entice you to go with the Premier by offering you a $200 statement credit while the regular card only gives a $50 statement credit, but don't listen.

If you click through the link on this post: https://www.smartmomsplandisney.com/chase-visa-link-explanation/ you can get the $200 on the regular Chase Disney Visa. But as usual in this book, there's more to come.

Here are the steps to get $200:

1. Sign up for the Chase Disney Visa through the link on the post above. Chase changes this somewhat frequently, so having you go to the post allows me to update that link when Chase pulls the rug out. Sorry for the extra step, but

I'd rather that vs. leaving you hanging with a outdated URL in this book. Do not add an authorized user at this time.

2. Spend $500 on the new Chase Visa

3. Receive a $200 statement credit

Simple enough. Let me comment on the $500 you need to spend. I see people using their card to charge their trip on. Sure, that's a quick way to get the $500 charged. But we can save WAY more on our trips with the other strategies in this book. So, I suggest you find other ways to spend the $500. Gas, groceries, and your cell phone bill are good predictable ways that you can spend $500. Or maybe your kids need shoes or you need a new suit for work. Use the card for those things that you can't get as discounted as Disney gift cards.

Or if you're using one of the stacking strategies, you could use this as your 1% cash back card. Two birds with one stone: Coupon Cabin or Top Cash Back> CardCash, Raise or Cardpool> Buy Walmart> Pay with Disney Chase Visa> Turn Walmart gift cards into Disney gift cards at Sam's Club (as one example).

Also, keep in mind that Chase has been changing the way they give the $200 payout. It was originally a Disney gift card, but more recently it's been a statement credit. Check your specific offer to see what you are going to get because it could change. Also, some people were sad when it wasn't a Disney gift card any longer, but my number crunching brain was excited. A statement credit is basically cash (literally, if you don't owe Chase anything and they give you the statement credit, they'll send you a check after one billing cycle.) So, if you have that cash, you can turn it into much more in Disney gift cards with our tricks.

Now let's earn $400.

Here are the steps:

1. Sign yourself and your spouse up through the link on the post above. Do not add an authorized user at this time.

2. Spend $500 on each of the Visas

3. Receive $400 in statement credits.

The reason that I say not to add an authorized user is because Chase sometimes offers bonuses for adding a user. It's usually $50. If you add your hubby and he adds you, that's an easy $100. You need to make sure that you have the offer to add the authorized user before you add them. This has been much more unpredictable than it was in the past. Do not count on it if your trip is soon. I haven't seen it in the last six months or so, but it's still worth looking for. I'm not including this as predictable savings, it should be considered a bonus if it happens.

To get the final $100 (for a nice round $500 towards Disney) you have to have plenty of time. If your trip is still at least two to three months away, you can earn another $100 by taking these steps:

1. Sign yourself up through the link on the post above (and thank you because that's our referral link.) Do not add an authorized user at this time.

2. When you receive your card, check if you have an offer attached to it to share with a friend and earn $100. I have usually had this offer available shortly after I've opened the account. Make sure that you receive $100 and your referral still receives $200. You can check if you have the offer here: https://www.chase.com/referafriend/

3. Use your referral link to sign your husband up for the Chase Disney Visa.

4. Spend $500 on each card.

5. Receive $400 in statement credits.

This is a nice little addition to the other strategies that we've built on. And since this is a statement credit, it's completely stackable. Yay, my favorite kind of savings!

Here's how this looks for the Smiths:

Needed for Vacation $2,550.00 ($2,250 Kroger/Best Buy $300 Eight Sites)
Cash Back, BlueCash -   135.00 (6% on grocery)
Subtotal $2,415.00
BlueCash Annual Fee +   95.00
Subtotal $2,510.00
BlueCash Sign-Up   -   250.00
Subtotal $2,260.00
Eight Websites Bonus -   150.00
Subtotal $2,110.00
Fuel Savings   -   393.75 ($43.75 for every $250 at Kroger)
Subtotal $1,716.25
SwagBucks   -   270.00 ($6 off every $50)
Subtotal $1,446.25
MC/Visa Fee   +   133.88 ($5.95 for every $100 grocery/Best Buy)
Subtotal $ 1,580.13
Checking Bonus   -   500.00
Subtotal $ 1,080.13
Disney Chase   -   500.00
Total $580.13

At this point, the Smiths are paying $580.13 for a $2,550 vacation. And we're not halfway through this book. Do you think they might make money on this by the time we're done? Maybe! I've done it. This is 77% off—a savings of $1,969.87

And here are the Robinsons:

Needed for Vacation	$9,550.00	($9,250 Kroger/Best Buy $300 Eight Sites)
Cash Back, BlueCash	- 555.00	(6% on grocery)
Subtotal	$8,995.00	
BlueCash Fees	+ 190.00	
Subtotal	$9,185.00	
BlueCash Sign-Ups	- 500.00	
Subtotal	$8,685.00	
BlueCash Referral	- 75.00	
Subtotal	$8,610.00	
Eight Websites	- 150.00	
Subtotal	$8,460.00	
Kroger Fuel Points	- 1,618.75	($43.75 for every $250)
Subtotal	$6,841.25	
SwagBucks	- 1,110.00	($6 for every $50)
Subtotal	$5,731.25	
MC/Visa Fee	+ 550.38	($5.95 for every $100 grocery/Best Buy)
Subtotal	$6,281.63	
Checking Bonus	- 500.00	
Subtotal	$5,781.63	
Disney Chase	- 500.00	
Total	$5,281.63	

I hope you're as excited as I am. Probably not possible, honestly. I just had a conversation with a friend in which I had to say, "I am getting the feeling that you are not as jazzed about tax deductions as I am."

I just love saving money. I think it's because I have a fundamental understanding that saving money means that your life is better. I am one of Walmart's harshest critics and still I love their slogan, "Save money, live better." It's just so true. If I can pay $5,281.63 for something that I would have paid $9,550 for, I have $4,268.37 to do something else. I could invest it or put it on my mortgage, or put it in an emergency account, or go to Disney World again with it (I'm probably going to do that last one, if you want the truth.) The Robinsons saved 44.7%

Can we step away from Disney for just two seconds? Trust me, we're going right back, but I am really passionate about this so here goes: if you are living paycheck to paycheck, probably the single biggest thing you can do to make your life significantly better is to have an emergency fund. Even a small one can be a huge benefit. I remember when we were younger, if anything happened like a tire getting a leak or the washer giving out, it felt like the entire world was crashing down. There was so much stress involved.

Recently, our hot water heater gave up the ghost. Suddenly and without warning, it just died. Now, I wish that hadn't happened. I wish I didn't have to pull $500 out of my savings to pay for a hot water heater and installation, but it did happen. And here's what I did. I called someone to bring us a new hot water heater and to put it in. He did so immediately, and I had hot water again about three hours after the first tank died. I paid for the tank and installation out of savings and then made a mental note to add some more money to savings over the next few months.

Almost zero stress. And our water is so nice and hot now. Bonus.

Ok, back to Disney: let's take stock of our credit card openings too. The Smiths opened four cards: two Disney Chases, American Express BlueCash and the Kroger Visa. The Kroger Visa isn't a huge savings so you can skip that one if opening credit cards is a challenge.

The Robinsons opened five credit cards: two Disney Chases, two American Express BlueCashes and one Kroger Visa. You may be thinking that this strategy involving opening multiple credit cards isn't for you. That's ok. You can use the other strategies in this book if you'd rather not open credit cards. But before you decide that's the path you want to take, think it through and do your research. I have opened six new credit cards in the last two years and have only seen my credit score improve as a result. I don't carry balances on any of them. They don't cost me any money.

I'm not a credit expert by any means— but I've been around it a lot. I worked at credit unions and in banking for several years, then in leasing for a large corporation and then I was the General Manager of a car dealership— a gig that included overseeing the finance department. My knowledge is the practical kind, not the kind they teach you in classes where they certify you to help people fix their credit. I don't have those credentials and so I can only tell you my experience.

And my experience has been that the credit cards that you open are not the problem. It's only the bills that you don't pay that get you into trouble. But do your own research and be especially careful if you are thinking of making a large purchase that you'll need to finance, like a car or house. You don't want to save $500 on a Disney trip and then pay a higher interest rate on your house for 30 years because of it.

All Summed Up:

The Chase Disney Visa can easily and predictably save you $200-$500. You may even be lucky enough to add another $50 or $100 to that if Chase gives a bonus for adding an authorized user. That can be a nice amount to put toward your vacation—and it's in cash (statement credit), so you can stack that savings with some of our other methods.

The Disney Chase Visa also offers several perks while on Disney property, so there are multiple reasons to add this card to your wallet.

Chapter Eleven:
Chase Sapphire Preferred

Gosh, I'm scared to put more about credit cards in this book. Let's make a deal though— if you can't use them, skip this chapter and don't let it stress you out. Look in the workbook if you'd like to raise your credit score. If you can use credit cards, read on.

Chase is the company that offers the Disney Visa. They offer many different credit cards and several of them can help you get to Disney. They offer the Southwest cards as well (we'll talk about those in the chapter on airfare.) Their sign up and referral bonuses are among the best in the industry. And they are a good solid company. There are some companies out there that I wouldn't mess with even to get a bonus, but Chase isn't one of them. They are excellent.

For my trip to Disneyland in 2013, flights were steep. I was flying from Cleveland to San Diego and the cheapest I could find was around $600. I was terrible with money back then and basically didn't have any. But a girlfriend had a few weeks off and I wanted to go see her and go to Disneyland for the first time. So, I got online and did a little investigating. I found that I could get my entire flight paid for by signing up for the Chase Sapphire Preferred card.

Now, I placed this chapter after the Disney Chase Visa chapter for one reason: the amount you have to spend to get the bonus. It's four grand and you have three months to spend it. This may be easy for some of you, and hard for others. But it's significant enough to make me feel like the Disney Visa is a better option for many of you. That $4K makes this a little tougher. Towards the end of the chapter, I'll give you some strategies to hit $4,000 if you need help getting there. The workbook pages for this chapter can be a big help to you too.

Why do we want this card in the first place? Well, because they offer 50,000 bonus points as a sign-up bonus after you spend $4,000 with them in the first three months. These points equate to $500 in cash if you take them that way, but you can get even more for them. You get a 25% bonus on your points when you spend them through their portal. I've found their pricing through their portal to be good for flights and rental cars. You can also book your Disney Resort stay through their portal, but I haven't found their pricing to be as attractive.

You also earn 5,000 points for adding an authorized user if they use their card in the first three months. That's another $50.

You can also refer your spouse like we talked about with the Disney Chase Visa. You earn 10,000 points for referring your spouse ($100 cash). They also earn the 50,000 points ($500) and they can add you to earn the additional 5,000 points ($50).

Let's add all of this up:

- You sign up for the Chase Sapphire Preferred: 50,000 ($500) http://bit.ly/ChasePreferredMJ (This is case sensitive if you are typing it in, and thanks for using it because it's a referral link.)

- You add your spouse: 5,000 ($50)

- You refer your spouse: 10,000 ($100)

- Your spouse gets the bonus points: 50,000 ($500)

- Your spouse adds you: 5,000 ($50)

- You've just earned $1,200

You can combine your points with your spouse's points to use them all together to pay for a big chunk at a time. You can NOT combine points with anyone who doesn't live with you. It's against Chase's rules. They don't want people buying and selling points. Chase is getting a little weird about combining so if that's important to you be sure to check into it— they are allowing it right now, but I have the feeling that it may be different soon.

And if you use the points through Chase's portal, they give you 25% more.

So, spent through Chase's Portal these points are worth:

- You sign up for the Chase Sapphire Preferred: 50,000*1.25=62,500

- You add your spouse: 5,000*1.25=6,250

- You refer your spouse: 10,000*1.25=12,500

- Your spouse gets the bonus points: 50,000*1.25= 62,500

- Your spouse adds you: 5,000*1.25=6,250

150,000 total— $1,500 towards travel!

Using the portal means that you would have 30,000 more points to use which is another $300 towards travel. You signed up for two credit cards and you have $1,500 to use for your flights, your rental car, or your Disney Resort. I could stay at Disney two or three times on that many points.

But alas, you cannot add the dining plan when you book through Chase. You also cannot take advantage of specials that Disney offers, like room only discounts or free dining.

I always make sure to check whether booking with Chase with the extra 25% is a better deal vs. getting the cash from Chase and then booking directly with Disney. Stacking comes into play here. I usually do best to get the cash from Chase run it through my discounted gift card machine (Kroger for me) where I end up with 23.5% or more for it, then I book a room using my Annual Passholder discount and pay with discounted gift cards.

This also allows me to get the dining plan and use the strategies in the dining chapters. For me the $1,200 gets turned into $1,482 and I can book at a discount, so it's a no brainer. But if your discounted gift card strategy yields you less or if the Disney discount isn't as high for you, AND you don't want the dining plan, booking through the Chase Portal might be the way to go.

Chase just made a change in July of 2018 that makes this deal even better: you can now buy Disney tickets alone, without a room, through their portal. This means that you can get tickets with your points at essentially 25% off. I say "essentially" because you'll pay full price for them, but with points that are worth 25% more. Then you can still book a Room Only reservation with Disney (we will talk a lot more about that soon) and add the dining plan. You can pay Disney with discounted gift cards. What a super easy way to maximize this. I was glad that I've been hoarding my points.

You can't get Annual Passes through Chase, but you can upgrade your tickets. So, you could buy ten day tickets with Hoppers to get pretty close to the price of Annual Passes and then just upgrade to passes when you're at Disney.

If you have flights or a rental car to book, it may make sense to book those through the portal as well. I've found the pricing to be good on both. My only complaint is my local rental agency isn't listed. So, when I want to rent a vehicle to drive to Disney (saving miles on my car or upgrading to something more comfortable), I have to drive about half an hour further to the local airport to pick up a vehicle. I don't know if this is common.

You can also transfer your points from their portal to Southwest, British Airways Executive Club, Flying Blue, AIR FRANCE KLM, Korean Air SKYPASS, Singapore Airlines KrisFlyer, Southwest Airlines Rapid Rewards®, United MileagePlus®, Virgin Atlantic Flying Club, IHG® Rewards Club, Marriott Rewards®, The Ritz-Carlton Rewards®, and World of Hyatt.

There is an Annual Fee of $95, but it is waived the first year. AND you can step down to the regular Chase Sapphire and avoid the fee after the first year. I even forgot to do it beforehand and when I saw the $95 fee on my statement, I called in to see what could be done and they switched me to the regular card AND refunded the fee since I was within 30 days of it being charged. Like I said, they are a stand-up company.

All in all, this is a very good travel card to have in your wallet. They give 2% back on travel and dining, they offer coverage on travel, and they allow you to participate in the Refer-a-Friend program. Just like you referred your spouse, you can take this to the next level by referring your mom, dad, siblings, or your Facebook friends. You can make 50,000 ($500) per year on each card by referring people. If you're in Disney Facebook groups that allow referral links, you may be able to scoop up a couple that way too.

I read in a Facebook group where someone opened the card at the tail end of a calendar year, got the 50,000 points for signing up, then referred 5 people before the close of the year and then another 4 in the beginning of the next year. Between the sign-up bonus, the 9 referrals, and the points from spending the $4,000, it came to 146,000 points which is $1,460 in cash or $1,825 through the Chase Portal. Wow! And that was on one card- they didn't even open the card for their spouse. She could have referred him too, earned another 10,000 in referral points and his 55,000 for signing up and adding her, plus 4,000 more for spending the $4,000 requirement. 215,000 That's $2,150 in cash OR $2,687.50 if used through the Chase portal. Double wow!

While we're on the subject of referrals, I just saw someone with their link posted below their email signature line. Every email she sends to anyone says: Sign up, spend, get $500 [her referral link]. Tacky? Maybe. Genius? DEFINITELY.

Another idea in this same vein, is putting your referral link in a public post on your timeline. Then, you can easily refer people to it. Type up a nice basic explanation of this deal and post it, making sure that it's public. Then you can send people there easily: something like, "I made $1,200 in cash toward my vacation by opening two credit cards. I explained it all in a post. If you click my name it should be the top post you see." It will be the top post if it is the most recent public post you've made and the person looking isn't your friend. They won't see all your other posts because they aren't friends with you, and the public post will show as first. You could also do this with eBates or any other referral link you'd like to share.

Feel free to grab this and post it as your "basic explanation" post. Don't forget to make it public. Also, to get your referral link, just google "Chase refer a friend" and you'll find the page to put your details in and get your link.

"I just made an easy $1,200 and you can do it too. Here's what to do:

- You sign up for the Chase Sapphire Preferred and hit the minimum spend in three months: earn 50,000 points ($500) [insert your referral link here]

- You add your spouse: 5,000 ($50)

- You refer your spouse: 10,000 ($100)

- Your spouse gets the bonus points: 50,000 ($500)

- Your spouse adds you: 5,000 ($50)

- You've just earned $1,200"

Now, let's talk about the $4,000 you need to spend in 90 days to earn the bonus. Plan to open the card when it makes the most sense. You may not want to open your account and your spouse's account right at the same time. You may want to wait 90 days in between so that you can put all your spending toward one, and then all towards the other and have the maximum amount of time to reach the threshold. You can put your trip on the card if you must do so. I don't recommend this, but I understand that you may need to in order to spend enough to hit the threshold. At the very least, you could use the card to buy gift cards at BJ's, Sam's Club, Raise, Cardpool, eBay, CardCash and stack a little more savings in.

I recommend that you use it to pay for things that you can't save on by paying for them another way. Your utility bills, your cell phone bill, food if you don't have the American Express BlueCash Card. Put it in your wallet and pay for everything with it. If you just don't spend that much, you always have the option to go to a grocery store and stock up on gift cards for things that you can spend in the future. Amazon, eBay, grocery stores, Target, Walmart. Most stores let you use a credit card to buy those visa or American Express prepaid/gift card/debit cards. If you found one that would allow that, you could just charge whatever you needed on to a few of those, and then use those in the months to come. There is an activation fee with those, but it would pale in comparison to the money earned. In fact, I saw Meijer has $500 with only a $5-$6 activation fee. That's not bad. You can do it. Where there's a will, there's a way!

Chase does have a rule to weed out those who are signing up for credit cards just for the bonuses: they will decline you if you have opened more than five credit card accounts in the past two years. This is ANY credit card, not just with them. They count store cards as well, so be strategic about what you're signing up for. My brother is planning a destination wedding, so I wanted to do the Southwest Companion Pass strategy (you'll learn about that later.) I thought for sure I hadn't opened five credit cards in the last two years. I was wracking my brain and could only count three. But I pulled my credit report and there were six! So, I am waiting until December to apply for the Southwest Cards because I don't want to apply only to be declined.

You can pull your credit for free on any of the three credit bureaus websites: Experian, TransUnion, or Equifax. Don't let them trick you into paying for anything. You don't need your credit score, just the report. You DO NOT need to put your credit card info in to get this. It is 100% free, so make sure you just get the report and aren't signing up for anything that you don't want. They can be tricky that way. It's sleazy, in my opinion.

Now, I've struggled with how to show you the savings here. It may not be practical for you to open ALL the cards in this book in order to stack the cash back and the sign-up bonuses. I don't even have them all yet (waiting to do the Southwest cards—you'll learn about them in the flights chapter) and I've been at this for four years and many, many Disney trips (fifty-three Disney trips at the time of this writing!) So, to say that the Smiths or Robinsons used the Disney Visas and the Sapphire Visas may be a stretch. They should look at what will work best for them and take that avenue.

But there may be no reason that they couldn't use all these. Chase is the only company that I'm aware of with a hard and fast rule about opening accounts- you can open five in two years (they call it the 5/24 rule.) And to use every strategy in the book, they'd be opening six each: two Southwest, one Disney, one Sapphire, one American Express, one Discover. As long as they opened the Chase cards first, and sprinkled the others throughout a year, and their credit was good, they should be able to do this. Full disclosure: I haven't done this. I wish I'd been as organized, but I didn't know about these strategies all at once. I learned them a piece at a time. But I have opened more than 6 credit cards in a year and not had any issue.

So, let's continue to do the math as though the stars were in complete alignment, the Smiths and Robinsons had access to everything we've discussed and they had the credit to take advantage of it. Let's just see where they fall.

As I calculate this for the Smiths and Robinsons, I had to decide about how to represent the bonus from the Sapphire Preferred cards. I could count it as $1,200 (cash) or as $1,500 (through the Chase Portal.) I believe that most people will find that if they run $1,200 through their "discounted gift card machine" (whatever it is for them at that moment) and then book with Disney at a discount, then get the dining plan and use it to the max, they'll do better than the

Chase Portal. Look at this for your specific situation though (especially if you have flights, because Chase wins on flights often for me.) For our purposes, I'll assume the Smiths and the Robinsons got the cash from Chase and then used it to buy discounted gift cards.

The Smiths entire trip is covered. Yep, they are paying nada. Here's how this looks for the Smiths:

Needed	$2,550.00	($2,250 grocery/Best Buy $300 Eight Sites)
Cash Back, BlueCash	- 135.00	(6% on grocery)
Subtotal	$2,415.00	
BlueCash Fee	+ 95.00	
Subtotal	$2,510.00	
BlueCash Sign-Up	- 250.00	
Subtotal	$2,260.00	
Eight Websites	- 150.00	
Subtotal	$2,110.00	
Fuel Savings	- 393.75	($43.75 for every $250 at Kroger)
Subtotal	$1,716.25	
SwagBucks	- 270.00	($6 off every $50)
Subtotal	$1,446.25	
MC/Visa Fee	+ 133.88	($5.95 for every $100 grocery/Best Buy)
Subtotal	$1,580.13	
Checking Bonus	- 500.00	
Subtotal	$1,080.13	
Disney Chase	- 500.00	
Subtotal	$580.13	
Chase Sapphire	- 1,200.00	
Total	-$619.87	

In case math isn't your thing, that negative sign in front of the $619.87 means that the Smiths are making money on this trip. They have everything paid for and they have $619.87 to keep. Souvenirs—or maybe they can go again in a little while.

The Robinsons can go the whole way and open both cards if they would like.

And here are the Robinsons:

Needed	$9,550.00	($9,250 grocery/Best Buy $300 Eight Sites)
Cash Back, BlueCash	- 555.00	(6% on grocery)
Subtotal	$8,995.00	
BlueCash Fees	+ 190.00	
Subtotal	$9,185.00	
BlueCash Sign-Ups	- 500.00	
Subtotal	$8,685.00	
BlueCash Referral	- 75.00	
Subtotal	$8,610.00	
Eights Sites Bonus	- 150.00	
Subtotal	$8,460.00	
Kroger Fuel Points	- 1,618.75	($43.75 for every $250)
Subtotal	$6,841.25	
SwagBucks	- 1,110.00	($6 for every $50)
Subtotal	$5,731.25	
MC/Visa Fee	+ 550.38	($5.95 for every $100 grocery/Best Buy)
Subtotal	$6,281.63	
Checking Bonus	- 500.00	
Subtotal	$5,781.63	
Disney Chase	- 500.00	
Subtotal	$5,281.63	
Chase Sapphire	- 1,200.00	
Total	$4,081.63	

This means the Robinsons paid $4,081.63 for a vacation that cost $9,550. They saved $5,468.37.

57.3% this is creeping up and up and up. Can they get this vacation for free??

We're over halfway, but we are coming ever closer to where the savings stops being super quantifiable. We have a couple more chapters where we can really add up the savings, but after that a lot of the savings is hard to see.

I get people who say, "I can't open credit cards and that's where a lot of the savings is." But that's not actually the case. Sure, opening a few cards and earning those bonuses can be a huge help the first time around. But I'm well past being able to earn sign-up bonuses and I'm still seeing tons of savings, it just may not be as visible at first glance. I'm saying this to encourage you if you can't or don't want to open a card, or if you maybe just don't want to do it right this minute because you want to buy a house or car in the next few years and want to be super careful about your credit. Or maybe you have these cards, or are getting them now, but are concerned about next year's Disney trip. Don't get disheartened if you can't partake in these bonuses for whatever reason. There are lots of options for you to come! And an entire Appendix that tells you what's repeatable.

Before we finish off this section on account bonuses, I want to briefly mention another card and another strategy. This is not something that I have personally used, but it is used by many and explained well in a recent blog post by the Richmond Savers. I don't know them personally, but they seem like a nice family who are making a killing referring credit cards to Disney people. So, that's what's in it for them. But that doesn't mean their information isn't good and I want you to have it so you can make the best decision for you. One note- the card they are initially talking about isn't the one that works. That one isn't open for new applicants. The one you want to get is the Capital One Venture. You can see info on that in the recent comments on the blog post.

Here is the post:
https://www.richmondsavers.com/strategy-free-disney-world-park-tickets

If that helps you, take it. If not, leave it. ☺

All Summed Up:

The Chase Sapphire card can fairly easily get your family $500-$1,500 towards your vacation. If you are successful with referring friends, family or random strangers from Facebook, you could earn $500/year for both you and your husband = $1,000. This would turn into $1,250 if used through the Chase portal.

Part III: Staying Onsite for Less

So far, everything we've talked about has been things that don't really involve Disney World. This is good if your reading this book for Disneyland, Adventures by Disney, Aulani or the Disney Cruiseline. Everything to this point will work for you. Not much in Part III will help you though, so skip on to Part IV. If you're thinking of Disneyland Paris or anywhere else overseas, only the cash stuff will help as they don't accept Disney gift cards.

If you're a Disney World go-er, get excited because you're about to learn a boatload of helpful stuff. I mean a ton. Enjoy!

Chapters in this section:

Chapter Twelve: Disney Resort Basics

Chapter Thirteen: Disney Resort Discounts

Chapter Fourteen: Disney Resort Hacks

Chapter Fifteen: Agency Exclusives

Chapter Sixteen: Deluxe for the Price of Moderate? Or

Value?!?!

Chapter Seventeen: Renting DVC Points Wisely

Chapter Eighteen: Military Discounts

Chapter Twelve:
Disney Resort Basics

I am a big believer in staying onsite at Disney. I was a hardcore off-siter for years. But then I stayed onsite and couldn't believe the difference in the experience. There are still times that I stay offsite, but they are few and far between. Out of 10 stays in 2016 (I usually go to Disney every month, but I took two months off to have Cyrus), only 2 were offsite. One was because I had a large party (at the time I didn't know how to make large parties on Disney property affordable) and the other was because it was extremely last minute and all affordable Disney options were booked up. And honestly, if I knew what I know now about large parties, I'd have stayed onsite for that one.

Out of my 15 stays in 2017, only one of them was offsite. That's because we booked at only two weeks out (for Thanksgiving! Eek!) In 2018, I stayed onsite in January, February, March (x2), April, May, June and

July already and am booked onsite for August, September and October already too.

When I used to stay offsite, it was because I believed it was less expensive and because you got more for your money. And at a glance, that is true. If you just compare Disney rack rate (non-discounted room rates) to prices for hotels on I-Drive, I-Drive probably wins every time. This is compounded when you think about the fact that you may be able to score an entire vacation home for a similar cost to stay in a moderate or deluxe (or sometimes even a value).

So, what changed my mind? First and foremost, gift cards. When you can pay for Disney at 10% off, 15% off, 25% off or even more % off, it really closes the gap. When I'm comparing apples to apples, discounted gift cards along with the Disney discounts that are available make Disney resorts less expensive than staying offsite nine out of ten times.

Second, the dining plan. I'm going to explain later how to maximize the dining plan. For now, I'll just say it's a huge saver for me and my family. I pay more for food when I can't use the dining plan, even if I have a full kitchen and buy food at the grocery store. You'll learn about this later. One thing that I feel like I need to say every time I mention the dining plan: you can buy the dining plan anytime you're staying onsite. You do not have to be buying tickets. You do not have to be a DVC member, Florida Resident or Annual

Passholder. You only need to be staying on site. I get that question a lot, and it's a recent change.

Third, I mentioned that the experience is much better onsite. Obviously, this is opinion, but it's one shared by many. You're at Disney World the entire time you're on vacation. You're in the cocoon of Disney's customer service. They have almost no crime. I always feel safe even if it's just me and my baby. I don't always feel safe traveling without my husband elsewhere. To get those low prices offsite, you sometimes have to stay in sketchy places. I've stayed close-by-- off Disney property in years past and felt uncomfortable coming back to the hotel after dark: peaking around corners to make sure no one was waiting to ambush me. It's not a good experience. The onsite perks are nice too, but the main thing for me is that you're always in the Disney bubble.

Let me give you an example of the Disney bubble-when we stayed at Fort Wilderness recently, the splash pad was closed due to a burst pipe. Disney waived my golf cart rental fee because of the inconvenience. At $60 a night, that was a nice gesture!

Compare this to staying in a vacation home over Thanksgiving. The pool light was out and we couldn't swim after dark. Considering it got dark at 5:30pm, and the fact that my family are huge night owls, this was a huge inconvenience. We called to let the caretaker know and he sent someone out to look at it. We had to deal with the repair person and he couldn't fix the issue so we didn't have a light in the pool area for the entire trip and we couldn't swim after dark. No apology was given, no refund issued, nothing. And believe me, I gave them more chances to make it right than should have been necessary. Disney takes care of their customers. Period.

But this book isn't about how to enjoy the best time at Disney World so I'll move along. I just wanted to give you a reason to even try to save money to stay onsite. Hopefully, I gave you enough to research onsite vs. offsite more.

In this chapter, I'm going to talk about the types of discounts, and discount categories. The next chapter will tell you about the resort discounts and the one following that will give you some different "hacks" I've discovered in my research and used to great success. All three of these chapters will arm you to save a ton on Disney accommodations.

I want to mention **discounted gift cards** again because I want you to realize that those savings come off the final number that you agree to pay Disney. Rack rate may be $100, but after discounts you're at $84 and then you paid with a discounted gift card to save another 10-25% off. Suddenly, you're paying $63-$75 a night onsite. It's hard to find a decent offsite hotel that low.

Let's dive in and talk about the **discounts** that Disney offers. Now, everyone loves free dining. I get asked about free dining all the time. People love free. But it's not the best discount that Disney gives. They offer promotions almost year-round. If you choose the right time of year to go, you can save even more. Disney charges less when fewer people want to stay with them. Supply and demand. We'll discuss them here, but you can always see the current promotions here: https://disneyworld.disney.go.com/special-offers/

In the last edition of the book, I left the specific discount information out because I thought it was pretty easily accessed elsewhere and because it changes rapidly. I also came to the (wrong) conclusion that I couldn't add anything to your knowledge about Disney's resort discounts. I've realized that I know a lot that isn't apparent on the Disney sites. I know when they usually come out, how to make sure you get the discount you want, and lots of other stuff that I took for granted. But when the same questions were asked again and again, I realized, "Hey, I know the answers here and I should put them in Disney World Within Reach!"

And now that I've come to grips with the need to update this book every year, I'm much more comfortable sharing the information that is available now, and speculating about what's coming later. I'm going to use historical information to make some educated guesses about when other offers will come out, what they'll be and who will qualify for them. Just remember that I'm going to do my best to make this accurate as of now, and make good guesses, but don't hold it against me if I'm not 100% dead on. This is not a science, but an art.

Let's first talk about the main types of discounts that Disney usually offers, then I'll explain each in greater detail. In the next chapter, I'll go over to whom they offer those discounts and we'll move into discussing individual discounts.

Main Types of Discounts:

- **Packages**— these include at minimum a room and ticket combo (or less commonly room and dining), but some specific deals also require that a dining plan be purchased as well (sometimes even specifying which dining plan.) Some examples:
    - Free Dining
    - Ultimate Disney Christmas
    - Play, Stay and Dine
    - Summer Meals

- **Room Only**— these deals don't require that you purchase anything else to receive the discount, but you are still able to add tickets and/or a Dining Plan. That turns the discount into a package, but generally doesn't change the discount. This may be good for you if your work offers discounted tickets as many large companies do or if you have tickets already (or Annual Passes) or can procure them at a discount elsewhere. You may save a little money by buying from an Authorized Reseller (discussed later in this book), but I generally find that I do best with discounted gift cards straight from Disney.

I defined Room Only and Packages above for you, but they follow different rules and I want you to have that info too. Here are the rules for each:

Cancellation

- Room Only reservations can be cancelled with no penalty up to the five nights before check-in. If cancelled after that, the penalty is the cost of one night's stay.

- Packages can be cancelled with no penalty up to thirty days before check-in. If you cancel with under thirty days to go, but more than one day before check-in there is a $200 penalty. If you cancel a package one day before check-in, you will forfeit the entire package. I speculate that the tickets would stay on your account. I couldn't find information to that effect, but it doesn't make sense to me that Disney would take your tickets just because you cancelled your room reservation.

Pro-Tip: When I've needed to cancel a reservation within thirty days and would normally owe the $200 penalty, I've instead just called and changed the reservation to another date (more than thirty days out.) I've kept the reservation then, but I assume that you would be able to cancel without penalty at that point. I have heard of others doing it. There could be a change fee for this... and that brings me to Changes.

Changes

Changes are things like switching, adding or removing dining plans, changing resorts, adding or removing guests, adding or removing tickets or changing the number of tickets, etc.

- Room only reservations can be changed with no penalty up to six nights before check-in if you booked online, up to five nights before if you booked via phone. No penalty is listed for changing at say four nights, but you could speculate that it might be the same penalty as the Packages ($50). However, I have definitely made changes within five days and have never been charged anything.

- Packages are subject to a $50 change fee and a $15 processing fee after you have made final payment. Timeframe doesn't matter here- if you pay in full 6 months before check-in and then need to make a change, this fee is supposed to be charged. Moral of the story: don't pay in full until you have to do so.

- o I have never been charged this fee, but I have heard that Disney is becoming more and more strict about it.
- o One thing that seems consistent is that it is waived if your change makes the package more expensive, but not when it makes your package less expensive.
- o If you are being charged this fee, ask for it to be waived. They may just accommodate as a courtesy.

Deposits

- Room only reservations require the cost of one night's stay as the deposit.

- Packages require a $200 deposit. Sometimes this is less or more than one night's stay. Generally, with a Value the $200 deposit would be higher, while with a Moderate, the two would be very close and with a Deluxe, the cost of one night's stay would be higher.

Payment in Full

- Room Only Reservations require payment in full at check-in.

- Packages require payment in full 30 days before check-in. They will usually offer you a few days' grace before cancelling your reservation. Some travel agencies will ask for payment in full at 45 days.
    - If you need a few extra weeks to get your discounted gift cards together, you can book a room only reservation and then switch to a package. This would affect your ability to book FastPasses because you won't have tickets on the account, unless, of course, you are an Annual Passholder.

Extras

- Room Only reservations receive MagicBands for each member of the party.

- Packages receive:

1. MagicBands,

2. Luggage tags: and at the risk of straying from the topic just a bit, let me give you some info that you may find helpful. Your luggage tags

182

correspond in color to the MagicBand you order. So, if you pick green, you're getting Goofy. Pink, you're getting Daisy. Below is a picture of all the luggage tags available so you can make an educated choice. For my kids, sometimes they care more about the character on their luggage tag than they do about the color of their MagicBand. Here's a list of the characters and colors if you're viewing this picture in black and white:

Green: Goofy
Blue: Donald
Pink: Daisy
Orange: Pluto
Red: Minnie
Gray: Minnie kissing Mickey
Yellow: Mickey
Purple: Mickey and Minnie with the scooter

3. Four tickets to Mini-Golf at one of their two courses (side note, my daughter thinks it's Minnie Golf. I've tried to explain, but it's just too hard. Because Minnie is indeed at mini-golf. Asher has a similar confusion with the Minnie Vans at the resorts and regular minivans that we rent. He was sorely disappointed that our rental van "isn't a Minnie van like you said. It's just stupid gray."),

4. Four tickets to ESPN's Wide World of Sports,

5. And discounts too numerous to name here (and not super helpful if I'm being honest.) You can find those here: https://disneyworld.disney.go.com/guest-services/vacation-package-magical-extras/

Note: if you want the extras but aren't booking a package, you can buy the luggage tags on eBay, and usually can score the mini-golf or ESPN tickets from someone who isn't using theirs. Ask in the Smart Moms Planning Disney Facebook group (www.facebook.com/groups/SmartMomsPlan Disney) and I bet someone will hook you up.

Okay, now that we know what a Package is and what Room Only is and what rules they each follow, let's move into the discussion on actual discounts.

All Summed Up:

It's completely worth it in my opinion to stay onsite with Disney. So many reasons why, and not the least of these is: you should be able to actually pay LESS for onsite vs. offsite if you follow the advice in this book.

Packages and Room Only are the two different types of Disney reservations and they follow different rules. Knowing these can help you make decisions on what will save you the most money.

Chapter Thirteen:
Disney Resort Discounts

Continuing from our last chapter, let's dig into the discounts Disney offers: first question, who is eligible?

You probably already know that Disney gives better discounts to their Annual Passholders, Florida residents and Disney Vacation Club members (learn more about DVC soon). But almost any member of the general public can score a room below rack rate. It just depends on when you're going and when you book. So, be smart.

Groups of people who qualify for discounts with Disney:

- Annual Passholders
- Florida Residents
- Disney Vacation Club Members
- Disney Chase Visa Cardholders

- People from certain countries (usually Canada and the UK. If they do offers for other countries, they may be marketing them only in those countries because I haven't seen them.)

- People currently on vacation at a Disney resort

- Active, Retired, or 100% Disabled Military Members-- this will be discussed at length in its own chapter because it is so long and detailed and not of any use to the majority of the population. I didn't want you slogging through it here if you aren't military. If you think you may qualify, check out the military discount chapter.

- General Public- this seems obvious, but I want to point out that if you fall into any of the other categories, you can still book the deals that are available for the general public. This can be good to keep in mind, because if availability for say the Chase discount is gone on your dates, ask if there is a discount for the General Public. Good Cast Members will know to do this, but some will not.

Historical Offers

If you aren't ready to think about your dates, or if you already have them selected and don't want to consider changing, feel free to skip to the end of this chapter.

As I'm writing this, it's the tail end of 2017 and there are still a few offers that cover 2017. It's likely that you'll be reading this after these offers have passed, making these historical. But I think they still have some value if you're thinking of booking in late 2018 or late 2019 because Disney rarely changes their discounts entirely. They may tweak them, but it's an exception, not the rule, for them to change completely. This info can also be helpful as you are deciding when to book.

- Annual Passholders can receive 10%-20% off Disney rack rate from now until Christmas Eve 2017. This can be booked as a room only reservation, or package with tickets and/or the dining plan. This discount can be booked up until Christmas Eve.

- Florida Residents can receive 15%-25% off Disney rack rate from now until Christmas Eve 2017. This can be booked as a room only reservation, or package with tickets and/or the dining plan. This discount can be booked up until Christmas Eve.

- Finally, anyone can book the Ultimate Disney Christmas package. I thought you might like more information on this package, especially since it has lots of moving parts (party tickets, Christmas Eve dinner etc.) Here are the details:

Celebrate the magic of the holidays in the most magical place on earth. Arrive on December 21, 2017 and depart on December 26, 2017, and enjoy an itinerary full of festive fun— including exclusive experiences just for Guests on this package!

Take a look at all the unique Yuletide offerings included in this offer:
- Tickets to Mickey's Very Christmas Party at Magic Kingdom park on December 21, 2017
- Exclusive nighttime access to Pandora – The World of Avatar at Disney's Animal Kingdom park on December 22, 2017
- An exclusive holiday Character experience at Disney's Hollywood Studios on December 23, 2017
- An exclusive Christmas Eve dinner celebration at Epcot on December 24, 2017
- A special holiday gift delivered to your Disney Resort hotel room on December 25, 2017

This offer also includes a 5-night stay at a select Disney Moderate, Deluxe or Deluxe Villa Resort hotel, plus 4-day theme park tickets with a Park Hopper Option. Starting at $139 per person, per night, a family of four can stay in a standard room at Disney's Coronado Springs Resort for a total package price of $2,775.

Book now through December 10, 2017 and start ushering in a new era of holiday traditions with your family!

View sample rates based on a 5-night stay in a standard room or studio with 4-day Magic Your Way tickets with a Park Hopper Option for a family of four—2 adults, 1 junior (ages 10 to 17) and 1 child (ages 3 to 9)—within the chart below.

Sample Resorts Valid Travel Dates: 12/21/17 – 12/25/16 (Arrival: 12/21/17 and Departure: 12/26/17)	Sample Package Prices
Disney's Coronado Springs Resort	Starting at $2,775
Disney's Saratoga Springs Resort & Spa	Starting at $3,721
Disney's Animal Kingdom Lodge	Starting at $3,777

Priced based on 2 adults, 1 junior (ages 10 to 17) and 1 child (ages 3 to 9). The number of rooms allocated to this offer is limited. The number of packages available for purchase is limited. Valid theme park admission required to attend theme park events included with this offer. Theme park tickets with Park Hopper Option must be used within 14 days of first use. First use must be by December 31, 2018.

Early 2018, Historical Offers
(helpful if you're booking for early 2019):

- The general public can book the Play, Stay, Dine Vacation Package. Here are the details:

Kick-start the new year by making incredible memories together in the middle of the magic. Play, stay, dine and save up to $500 on a 5-night/6-day room, Magic Your Way base ticket and dining plan package for a family of 4 at select Disney Resort hotels.

This special offer is valid at select Disney Resort hotels for arrivals most nights from January 1 through March 10, 2018 when you book now through December 22, 2017.
View sample rates based on a 5-night stay in a standard room or studio with 6-day Magic Your Way base tickets for a family of 4—based on 2 adults, 1 junior (ages 10 to 17) and 1 child (ages 3 to 9)—within the chart below.

Resort Category	Save on Stays Most Nights
▶ Select Disney Deluxe Villas	Save $500
▶ Select Disney Deluxe Resorts	Save $500
▶ Select Disney Moderate Resorts	Save $500
▶ Select Disney Value Resorts	Save $300 For stays most nights 1/7 to 2/5/18, 2/9 to 2/20/18 and 2/25 to 3/10/18

- The general public can receive a 15%-25% discount from rack rate on stays from January 1 through April 14, 2018. This must be booked by January 2, 2018. This can be a room only reservation or a package with tickets and/or the dining plan. This is called the "Gift of Magic Room Offer" if it's Room Only. It's called the "Family Gift of Magic Package" if it's booked as a package.

191

- Disney Chase Visa Card Holders can receive a 25%-35% discount from rack rate on stays from January 1 through April 14, 2018. This must be booked by January 2, 2018. This can be a room only reservation or a package with tickets and/or the dining plan.

- Annual Passholders can receive a 25%-35% discount from rack rate on stays from January 1 through April 14, 2018. This must be booked by April 14, 2018. This can be a room only reservation or a package with tickets and/or the dining plan.
  - Note that this is basically the same deal as offered to Chase Disney Visa Cardholders, but there will be greater availability for Passholders, and they don't have to plan so far ahead.

Fall and Winter 2018

- Free Dining:

Book through July 7, 2018 for arrivals most nights August 20 through September 29, November 24 through November 27 and December 7 through December 23, 2018.
Explore Disney Resort hotels included in this non-discounted 5-night/6-day room and ticket package and the eligible Disney dining plan.

Note: packages for other lengths of stay may be available.

Resort Category	Dining Plan
▶ Select Disney Deluxe Villa Resort Hotels	FREE Disney Dining Plan
▶ Select Disney Deluxe Resort Hotels	FREE Disney Dining Plan
▶ Select Disney Moderate Resort Hotels	FREE Disney Quick-Service Dining Plan
▶ Select Disney Value Resort Hotels	FREE Disney Quick-Service Dining Plan

- Soak Up Some Fun and Sun: With this offer, you can save up to 20% on rooms at select Disney Resort hotels, valid for stays most nights from April 15 through June 10, 2018 when you book through May 12, 2018.

Resort Category	Resort Savings
▶ Select Disney Deluxe Villas	Save up to 20%
▶ Select Disney Deluxe Resorts	Save up to 20%
▶ Select Disney Moderate Resorts	Save up to 15%
▶ Select Disney Value Resort Hotels	Save up to 10%

- Incredible Summer (can also be booked as a package with tickets.)

With this offer, you can save on rooms at select Disney Resort hotels for stays most nights June 11 through August 1, 2018:
- Save up to 25% on rooms, when you book by May 22, 2018.
- Save up to 20% on rooms, when you book by August 1, 2018.

Find other great rates when you check availability for stays most nights May 28 through June 10 and August 2 through August 30, 2018.

This special offer is valid for the Disney Resort hotels listed below. View the chart for a breakdown of savings within each Resort category.

Resort Category	Resort Savings
▶ Select Disney Deluxe Villas	Save up to 25% for stays most nights 6/11/18 to 8/1/18
▶ Select Disney Deluxe Resorts	Save up to 25% for stays most nights 6/11/18 to 8/1/18
▶ Select Disney Moderate Resorts	Save up to 20% for stays most nights 6/11/18 to 8/1/18
▶ Select Disney Value Resort Hotels	Save up to 20% for stays most nights 6/11/18 to 8/1/18

- Free Kids Dining: Valid for arrivals most nights from May 28 through August 30, 2018 when you book through August 1, 2018. Kids get the same dining plan as adults in the party, but for free.

- Enchanted Escape: With this offer, a family of 4 will enjoy a package that includes a 4-night stay in a standard room at a Disney's All-Star Resort hotel and 4-day Magic Your Way base tickets for as low as $2,067.

Sample Resorts Most Sunday through Thursday Nights	Sample Package Prices
Disney's All-Star Resort	Starting at $2,067
Disney's Coronado Springs Resort	Starting at $2,338
Disney's Animal Kingdom Lodge	Starting at $2,876
Disney's Saratoga Springs Resort & Spa	Starting at $2,923

- Play Big:

Jump on the chance to save up to 25% on rooms at select Disney Resort hotels for stays most nights, August 2 through October 7, 2018 when you book through September 7, 2018! This special offer is valid for the Disney Resort hotels listed below. View the chart to explore savings within each Resort Category.

Resort Category	Resort Savings
▶ Select Disney Deluxe Villas	Save up to 25%
▶ Select Disney Deluxe Resorts	Save up to 25%
▶ Select Disney Moderate Resorts	Save up to 25%
▶ Select Disney Value Resort Hotels	Save up to 20%

• Big Fun Awaits:

For as low as $1,009, a family of 3 can enjoy a package that includes a 3-night stay in a standard room at a Disney's All-Star Resort and 2-day Magic Your Way base tickets. Sample package price is valid for stays most Sunday through Thursday nights, August 12 through October 4, 2018 when you book through September 7, 2018.

Planning a longer stay or have more people in your party? Check availability for packages that can accommodate other lengths of stay and party sizes.

Sample Resorts Most Sunday through Thursday Nights	Sample Package Prices
Disney's All-Star Resorts	Starting at $1,009
Disney's Coronado Springs Resort	Starting at $1,212
Disney's Animal Kingdom Lodge	Starting at $1,614
Disney's Saratoga Springs Resort & Spa	Starting at $1,649

• Celebrate Fall and Holiday Excitement

With this offer, you can save up to 20% on rooms at select Disney Resort hotels.

- Book through October 7, 2018 for stays most Sunday through Thursday nights October 8 through November 8, 2018.
- Book through December 24, 2018 for stays most nights November 11 through December 24, 2018.

Resort Category	Resort Savings
▶ Select Disney Deluxe Villas	Save up to 20%
▶ Select Disney Deluxe Resorts	Save up to 20%
▶ Select Disney Moderate Resorts	Save up to 15%
▶ Select Disney Value Resort Hotels	Save up to 10%

• Passholders Enchanted Escape

Passholders can enjoy stays for as low as $89 per night, plus tax in a standard room at a select Disney's All-Star Resort most Monday through Wednesday nights from August 27 through September 25, 2018.

So, that's what we know at the time of this writing. I wish I could look at your exact situation and run it through my knowledge base and tell you, "Based on history, your best bet is to book three months in advance and get the [Play, Stay and Dine Package]." But I simply cannot do that.

What I can do is give you the tools to do it for yourself. Below is a list of the discounts available for the general public. You can easily look up your dates and see which discount would have been best for you in 2017 and see when it came out and when it expired. This should allow you to have an edge on 2018 and 2019. The Disney discounts won't stay exactly the same, but they will be similar. If you don't know your dates, that's ok. Keep reading.

Announced   **Stay Dates**
September 30, 2016   January 1-April 8, 201
Book By: December 21, 2016
Discount offered: 15-25% off room rates. Play, Stay, Dine also offered (discounted package.)

Announced   **Stay Dates**
December 28, 2016   February 20-June 10, '17
Book By: March 30, 2017
Discount offered: 10-25% off room rates. Bookable as a package as well.

Announced   **Stay Dates**
December 28, 2016   May 30- August 24, '17
Book By: February 12, 2017
Discount offered: Summer Meal Package (1 free quick service meal per night.)

Announced   **Stay Dates**
March 27, 2017   May 28- August 31, '17
Book By: July 14, 2017
Discount offered: 15-25% off room rates. Bookable as a package as well.

Announced   **Stay Dates**
April 24, 2017   August 1- October 7, '17
Book By: August 31, 2017
Discount offered: 15-30% off room rates. Bookable as a package as well.

Announced   **Stay Dates**
April 24, 2017   August 21- Dec. 23, '17
Book By: July 7, 2017
Discount offered: Free Dining. Blacked Out 10/1-11/13, 11/21-11/24, 11/28-12/7)

Announced   **Stay Dates**
July 17, 2017   October 8- Dec. 24, '17
Book By: October 7, 2017
Discount offered: 10-20% off room rates. Bookable as a package as well. Blacked Out October 8, 13, 14, 20, 21, 27, 28 November 3, 4, 10, 11, 22, 23, 24. (Friday

and Saturday nights and the Wednesday, Thursday and Friday of Thanksgiving.)

Announced   **Stay Dates**
October 16, 2017   December 21 -26, 2017
Book By: December 10, 2017
Discount offered: Ultimate Disney Christmas (discounted package.)

Here is some more info that might calm your nerves and help you know what to expect as we head into the future:

In 2017, there were only nineteen nights that were not discounted for the general public at some point. That leaves 346 nights of the year that were discounted by at least 10%, but sometimes up to 35% for certain resorts. That means that only 5% of the year was not discounted, while 95% was discounted. Annual Passholders and Florida Residents only had three days in the entire year that weren't discounted. (Find out more about the historical Annual Passholder discounts in the Annual Pass Savings Strategies chapter.)

For your reference, the nineteen nights in 2017 that were not discounted were as follows:

- Fridays and Saturdays October 8th through November 11th (comes to eleven non-discounted nights: October 8, 13, 14, 20, 21, 27, 28 November 3, 4, 10, 11)

- November 22nd through November 24th (the 23rd was Thanksgiving Day)

- December 27th through December 31st (these were the three days that were also not discounted for Annual Passholders and Florida Residents.)

In 2016, there were only twenty-one nights that were not discounted for the general public at some point throughout the year. 5.7% of the nights were not discounted while 94.3% of the time was discounted in some way. In 2016, the lowest percentage off discount was also 10% and it went up to 30% off for certain resorts.

The twenty-one nights that were not discounted in 2016 were as follows:

- January 1
- November 5th - 12th
- November 23rd-25th (November 24th was Thanksgiving Day)
- December 23rd – 31st

LAURALYN "LJ" JOHNSON

So, we've learned that the vast majority of nights will be discounted. This makes me chuckle at the folks who say you need to go during a certain time of year to save money. I hear it all the time and I'm baffled by it. The discount might be slightly higher during some months, but not enough to plan your trip around, in my opinion.

Almost all dates are discounted at one time or another. The problem is the timing. If you were booking just a few months out during certain times, you would have been out of luck as the discounts had already come and gone for the time of your visit. We don't want that to happen to you!

Availability is another issue. There may be a discount over a certain time period, but not all the rooms in all the Disney resorts are going to be discounted. They only offer certain numbers of each of the room types at each resort (unless they aren't included, as in the case of the Little Mermaid rooms which are often excluded.) You may be booking at a resort during a period that offers a discount, in a resort that's not excluded and you still may not be able to have the discount applied. Nearer to the end of the chapter, I'm going to give you some tools to make sure you turn over every rock if this ever happens.

So, here is my suggestion on strategy when you're first booking. If you have exact dates or a general idea of when you want to go, book early and watch in the

200

Facebook group for when the new discounts are dropping. Each time new discounts come out, you can check if they are better than your current rates and, if so, you can switch to the lower rate providing that there is availability. This is your best strategy to get your room at the lowest possible price.

If you are looking to pick your dates based on the lowest cost, I honestly just wouldn't start there. I'd choose based on the weather and crowds first and then look at cost. This is because the discounts usually only vary by 5%. To put that in perspective, if a Value room is $120, 10% off is a $12 discount, while 15% off is $18. $6 more per night over a seven-night stay is $42 total. If you get discounted gift cards at 10% off, the $42 becomes only $37.80. I don't know about you, but if I'm spending a bunch of money on a vacation, I'm not cutting out $37.80 and ending up going at a bad time weather wise. I bet those rained out by the hurricane last September agree with me.

If you're doing deluxe that difference in savings was historically as high as 10% so it means a bigger difference in cost. If the room was $400, 10% savings is $40 a night. Across a seven-night stay, that's a difference of $280. But if you're about to drop $2,800 on a hotel room for seven nights, I still wouldn't choose bad dates to save $280. In fact, if you're trying to do Deluxe on a budget, my best advice for you is to stop thinking about Disney discounts and skip right to the Agency Exclusive chapter. If you can make that

Labor Day deal work for you, it will be the BEST savings on deluxe for anytime of the year. It's magical.

This isn't really about saving money, but while we're on the topic, my favorite months at Disney World (and remember, I go every single month so I know what I'm talking about!) are February and October. My third and fourth choices are March and April (just watch out for Spring Breaks) and fifth is December, but only if you go the first or second week. Here's a complete list of the months in order of my favorite times to go to my least favorite. These are all based on crowds and weather.

- October (October beats February for me because I enjoy the fall decorations, Halloween and Mickey's Not So Scary Halloween Party.)
- February
- March
- April
- December (but go early in the month.)
- September (the Labor Day Sale! Discussed in the Agency Exclusive chapter.)
- November (but go early in the month. Very busy closer to Thanksgiving.)
- May
- June
- August (The heat/crowds can be bad, but the Labor Day deal starts in August!)

- January (I have been freezing in Disney wearing tons of layers. Go late in the month for better weather.)
- July (but I do love Independence Day at Disney)

You can find out a lot more about crowds if you go take a look at Touring Plans (http://bit.ly/SMPDTouringPlans   Note: this link is case sensitive if you're typing it in.) Their crowd calculator is amazing and helps me out a lot when I'm picking dates.

These days, I go every month so I don't have to pick a month, but I suggest you start there- think about what kind of weather is going to most behoove your enjoyment on your vacation. Think about the holidays. If you sort of hate Halloween, don't go in October. Disney goes ALL out over the holidays, so think about what décor you'd enjoy. Between weather and holidays, that should narrow it down to maybe a couple months. Then go look at the crowd calendar and decide from there. Once you have the month, look at flights (more about that in the chapter about travel) and compare with the crowd calendar. That should help you narrow it down to exact dates.

I try to remain flexible in case I can get a better deal by adjusting just a couple days before or after, so keep that in mind too. You can stay flexible by multi-booking any hard to get must-dos like Be Our Guest,

Cinderella's Royal Table, and Bibbidi Bobbidi Boutique. I often call this the #bookeverythingmethod For instance, book two or three BOGs over the ten-day period around when you think you might go. Then if you end up needing to jog over by a few days to save on plane fare or to qualify for a Disney discount, you can do so without losing your precious BOG. Just be sure to cancel in a timely manner so that someone else can book it and so you don't get charged a no-show fee.

Cinderella's Royal Table requires full payment at the time of booking unless you have a Dining Plan booked that will cover it. That doesn't mean you can't book it and then cancel, you still can, you just need to know that they'll charge you're card for it and then refund it after cancelling, so definitely a lot less clean.

And be aware that there are some holier-than-thous out there who frown on this practice of booking multiple reservations knowing that you'll only keep one. To me, you aren't breaking any rules and it's strategic, so I don't see any problem with it. Just don't advertise it or you might get an earful from someone who thinks they get to have an opinion about your life (so cute that they think we care about their opinion! 😄)

If you aren't booked yet, consider booking with a Smart Moms Recommended Travel Agent. I'm picky about who makes this list. They have to have enough

Disney experience and be able to help you with the strategies in this book. I've worked with them to create a lot of resources that we provide free for those booking with Smart Moms TAs. These tools use my strategies to make your Disney experience as magical as possible. If you think I'm good with money, you should see me manage a Disney World vacation. You can check into the possibility of working with a Smart Moms Travel Agent here: http://bit.ly/SMPDTA Note that this is case sensitive, if you're typing it in.

Annual Passholder Room Discounts

Annual Passholder discounts typically range from 20%-35% off. In case you aren't familiar with how the discounts work, when the discounts are listed as a range (like 20%-35% off) the first number is usually for most Values and the second number is usually for most Deluxe Resorts. Moderates will fall somewhere in between (probably around 30% in this example.) Sometimes some resorts or room classes will not fall into the usual category and those will be noted on the offer. Art of Animation and Fort Wilderness Campground are the two resorts that will usually have some sort of exclusion. You can find the current Passholder Offers here:
https://disneyworld.disney.go.com/special-offers/?type=passholder-offer

Looking at history to try to see the future, there were only three nights in 2017 that weren't covered by an

Annual Passholder discount at some point. Comparatively, there were nineteen nights that weren't discounted for the general public.

Obviously, for those sixteen days that were covered by an Annual Passholder discount, but not discounted for the general public, being a Passholder was a huge benefit. But even for all the other days where there was a discount for both, Passholders had an edge in two ways:

- First, the Passholder discount is 10%-15% HIGHER than the discount offered to the general public. (Passholder discount is usually 5% higher than the discount offered to Florida Residents as well.) For example, the discount offered to the general public for stays May 28th-August 31st 2017 was 15%-25%. For Annual Passholders it was 30%-35%.

  o To put this in perspective, if a Value is $120 the general public will save $12 a night with a 10% discount. Over a seven-night stay, that's a savings of $84. A Passholder received 30% off during this time which would be $36 off a night, for a total of $252 on a seven-night stay. This is a savings of $168 more than a member of the general public.

  o This gap is somewhat intensified if you stay Deluxe. The general public would save 25%

on a room that's around $400 a night. That's $100. $700 over a seven-night stay. Annual Passholders would save 35%: $140 a night or $980 over the same time period: an additional $280 in savings over a member of the general public.

- Second, Passholders receive a lot more flexibility in booking. I believe that this is because Disney counts on being able to fill their rooms at the last minute with Passholders dropping in for a few days. Passholders don't have to plan so far in advance to be able to receive discounts (provided there is availability.) The Passholder and general discount do not usually run exactly on the same timelines so this is a little hard to quantify but look at these examples.

  o Members of the general public had to book by December 21, 2016 for a discount on April 8, 2017 while Passholders could have booked up to April 7, 2017 for a discount on that same date.

  o Members of the general public had to book by July 14, 2017 for a discount on August 31, 2017 while Passholders could have booked up to August 30, 2017 for a discount on that same date.

○ Members of the general public had to book by October 7, 2017 for a discount on Christmas Eve, 2017 while Passholders could have booked the day of and still receive the discount.

To wrap up Annual Pass resort savings for now, let me say that this has been a great benefit for our family. It's one of the things that has enabled us to travel to Disney so often, as the Value rooms are now maybe $84 for us. Then we pay with discounted gift cards at 23.5% off and that room only costs us $64.26 a night. For a four-night stay (which is what we normally do when I take one-on-one trips with the kids), the resort costs us $257.04 while it would cost a member of the general public $480 at full price, $432 if they received the 10% discount. You can see how this easily becomes a core part of my strategy.

Adding a Discount

Ok, last thing before we close out this chapter: when a discount comes out that you think you qualify for and you'd like to have it applied to your reservation, you need to call Disney or have your travel agent handle it for you. If you call in, just follow the prompts to modify a resort reservation and when you get a person on the line, tell them that there have been new discounts and you'd like to see if your stay qualifies for a discount. They will usually match up your reservation with the discount and tell you how much you're saving. If the Cast Member tells you there is no discounted availability try these things:

- If you qualify in any other categories ask about those. So, if you have a Disney Chase Visa, or an Annual Pass, ask to check in those discount pools. Conversely, if you are calling about a Disney Chase or Annual Passholder discount and it's sold out, make sure you ask if there is a similar discount for the general public.

- Ask if there is a different room type that may still have availability. You may be able to switch from a Garden View to a Pool View and get the discount.

- Ask if there is another resort in the same class that may have availability with the discount.

- Ask if there would be discounted availability if you changed your dates just a little bit forward or back.

- Ask the Cast Member if they can think of any other way for you to qualify for the discount. You never know— you may even get a little bit of pixie dust! (In case you don't already know, pixie dust is when Disney gives something for free as a courtesy.)

All Summed Up:

Disney offers discounts to many different groups of people. They offer many different discounts throughout the year.

Disney discounts the vast majority of nights at some point during the year and the discount amounts do not vary that widely (usually within 5%-10%). This means that it's not that important WHEN you go, it's only important that you book enough in advance to get the discount when it's available.

Chapter Fourteen:
Disney Resort Hacks

The last chapter focused on the discounts offered directly by Disney. There are a lot of rules to follow to be able to use them: eligibility, dates of the promotion, whether you need to buy tickets or the dining plan, etc.

But this chapter is going to focus more on things that everyone can use. These are ideas that I've used to bring the costs of my trips down, while not missing out on premium experiences. And they are ideas that I would have never thought of on my own. It took me lots of research to stumble upon these. They just aren't something that would come to mind, but I know they can help you save!

In this chapter, we're going to cover **Split Stays, Booking More Than One Room, Onsite + Offsite, Bounce Backs, PIN codes** and the **DVC Tour**. Now, I'll be honest. I struggled with whether to put Bounce

Backs and PINs here in this chapter where we talk about hacks, or in the last one where we talked about discounts. This is because these are discounts that Disney offers, so they could go in the last chapter, but to me they feel a lot more like little-known secrets, so I ultimately decided they belonged here with the Disney resort hacks.

First up, one of my favorite hacks: I'd like to tell you about **Split Stays** and how they can be used strategically. "Split Stay" is a commonly used term in the Disney community for a trip that includes a change of resorts. You might do this for many reasons. Maybe your preferred resort is booked for some of the time you want to stay, but only has half the days available. You can take them and then spend the other days elsewhere.

My good friend, Beth, and I had a trip where we spent three nights at Pop Century and three more nights at Bay Lake Tower. We did this because we aren't independently wealthy, but we want to have the experience of the Bay Lake Tower. We also did it because it was our foodie trip (#BestFriendsEatDisney) and we wanted to maximize dining plans.

I'll talk in the Dining Plan chapters about how you can use this strategy to help with the cost of food as well. For now, let's focus on how this can save you money on your resort stay.

Many families love the convenience of the monorail resorts. They can hop on the monorail and arrive at the Magic Kingdom in minutes. And as a stroller mom, I concur. The monorail is the height of convenience. But that convenience does not come without a cost. The monorail resorts are the most expensive. It would be very difficult for my family to afford a seven-day vacation at the Polynesian, Grand Floridian or the Contemporary.

It would be much more do-able to enjoy four nights at the Poly and three at a value. Or three at the Poly and four at a value. The monorail resorts are very convenient for visiting Magic Kingdom and Epcot, but they don't help you much for Hollywood Studios or Animal Kingdom. So, you could plan your Magic Kingdom days for the time you are spending at a monorail resort and then go to Hollywood Studios or Animal Kingdom on the days you're at a value.

My genius friend, Lauren, is doing a split stay coming up. She's staying at Beach Club and the Poly. She's doing Epcot and Hollywood Studios on the days that she's at Beach Club (you can walk from Beach Club to Epcot and HS) and then doing MK on the days she's at the Poly. SO smart! This probably isn't *much* of a saver because Beach Club is still a Deluxe resort (and so worth it; that pool!) But from a convenience standpoint, Lauren is on to something!

You can do a Split Stay with any resort for any number of days for any reason. The sky is the limit. I spoke with a woman once (coincidentally, we were in the Beach Club pool at the time) who was staying at four resorts over a week-long vacation. She said she wanted to see them all. I would feel like moving that much would be a hassle, but moving once really isn't bad. Disney makes it easy. And you can prepare yourself to make it even easier:

- Pack your bags according to stay, not according to person. This way you can open fewer bags and have less to pack up when it's time to switch resorts.

- Use packing cubes http://amzn.to/2n4O3xr and pack your clothes according to days. During a split stay, I like to pack all our clothes together for Monday, then all our clothes for Tuesday are together, etc. My husband doesn't participate in this nonsense. He packs his own bag and manages it himself. But with five outfits to plan (me and four kids), packing cubes are a lifesaver—perfect if I want coordinating outfits too.

- Pack your bags and leave them with Bell Services before you head off to the park on moving day. They will "magically" arrive at your new location...as long as you tell Bell Services where you're headed.

It really is very easy to switch resorts. For a half-an-hour's worth of hassle packing up your stuff and moving it, you can see two resorts, enjoy the convenience of one and the economy of another.

Pro-tip: I like to stay in the Value resort first and then move up in the world, rather than staying Deluxe and then stepping down. You really notice the huge difference in amenities when you go from Value to Deluxe (more room, better linens and pillows, nicer furniture, better bathroom etc.) and I'd hate to go the other way. Plus, this gives you something to look forward to as the trip goes on. When we stayed at All-Star Movies and then moved to Beach Club, we very much enjoyed All-Star Movies, but we also talked about how fun the Beach Club pool would be and it made that "vacation is ending lull" that sometimes happens on the last few days completely non-existent. We were so excited to move to our next home!

Another way to save also involves two reservations. If you have a large party, offsite is usually more attractive, but make sure you consider **booking more than one room** before you decide that offsite is cheaper. Many parties of six think that their only option is the Cabins or a Family Suite. But this isn't true. You can book two adjoining rooms at a value resort and many times this will be less expensive than a larger room. Run the numbers.

We stayed off-site in February 2016 with my brother-in-law, his two kids, my in-laws and my family of five (at the time- I was pregnant with Cyrus.) If I'd have been wiser, we could have booked two values and stayed under occupancy even with ten because two of the kids were under 3. With two rooms, we could have added one baby to each room and fit.

We would have been able to take advantage of the 60-day booking window for FastPasses, which is a HUGE benefit to a large party. Seriously, have you ever tried to get eight or ten FastPasses together at 30 days? It's bonkers. We also could have skipped the TWO rental cars we needed (one of them a mini-van and expensive) because we could have used Magical Express and the Disney buses. My in-laws also had no MagicBands so we needed to buy four bands (mother-in-law, father-in-law, brother-in-law and my nephew) at a cost of around $60.

The accommodations themselves would have been a savings as well, even booking two rooms. We had booked a five-bedroom home for the ten of us and it cost about $220 a night plus pool heat at $25 a night: $245 total/night. Two rooms at Disney would have been around $80 a night each with the Annual Passholder discount. So, $160 a night vs $245 a night? Not actually, because we could have used discounted gift cards to get another 25% off at Disney, making it

$120 vs $245. $125 per night savings times seven nights is $875.

We also could have been really strategic with the dining plan and the children. You'll learn a lot more about this in the dining plan chapters, but we could have put all the children together on one room with just one adult, bought the Quick Service or Deluxe Dining Plan for that room and shared with the other room. It's a huge savings. Instead we spent around $600 on groceries and then didn't get to use a lot of them. But you live and you learn! I estimate I could do that trip about $1,500-$2,000 less expensively than we did if I'd have known more. Please let my learning curve save you money!

Another way to save is to break up the party or the stay into **onsite and offsite**. This affords you some flexibility. If you have a party of 8 you could easily break it up so that four are onsite and four are not. This would give you the ability to get the onsite perks for those four people as well as the dining plan.

Or you could do a few days onsite and a few offsite. This allows you to get the onsite perks when you want them (plan accordingly) and the offsite "savings" (I say that in quotes because there's really only savings in certain situations.) Again, you could the use the dining plan strategically as well.

Next let's talk about **Bounce Back Offers**: these deals require that you are currently on vacation with Disney. There is a special phone number (407-939-1923) to call. They will verify your reservation and that you are indeed still on vacation (or on the day of check-out) and then they'll book for you. These can be room only or packages.

Let's dive in and give you all the info you'll need to take advantage. Let me say first that Disney doesn't call these offers "Bounce Back Offers." That's something we, the Disney community at large, started calling them and it just sort of stuck. So, don't call Disney and ask about the Bounce Back Offer because they will not know what you are talking about. Actually, don't call Disney about this offer at all. Only call the Bounce Back Offer line (407-939-1923).

So, like I said above, you have to be currently on a Disney resort stay to book the Bounce Back. If you checked out earlier that day, you'll be ok to book it, but if you wait until the following day, you'll be out of luck.

Everyone who is on a Disney Resort vacation is eligible for the Bounce Back. You do not have to be special. You don't have to have the offer in your room to be eligible. The offer is usually in your room, but it doesn't have to be. If you don't have it, you can still call the number listed above and get the deal. Don't let anyone tell you differently, because they will (especially CMs who don't know better). Below is a picture of the magazine that usually has the offer and also a photo of the offer.

Am I getting obnoxious adding the phone number everywhere? I hope not. I just really want to make sure that you know to call (407) 939-1923 instead of the main number.

You will need to be ready to book while you're there, so bring an extra $200 on a gift card (you can use a credit or debit card, of course, but I like to use a discounted gift card whenever possible.) You can also put it on a credit card to start and then call later (same number as above, not the main one) and have the credit card refunded. This is a bit of a hassle and takes up quite some time so when I can avoid it by paying with a gift card directly, I do.

Each adult can book one Bounce Back per visit. So, when the Bounce Back is super good, I'll book a trip on Mike's account and I'll book one on mine. They've never asked to speak with him, he's just needed to be on the reservation.

After you're booked, you can always call and change your reservation anytime via the Bounce Back Line. So, when in doubt, book the Bounce Back and then call and change it as needed. I often don't have any sort of idea on dates, but I just randomly pick dates and a resort and book it, knowing I'll call and change it as it gets closer. You still have access to the offer when you change it as long as you were originally on property when you booked it. You can also cancel with no penalty (following the rules discussed in the last chapter for packages and room only.)

The current offer as of this writing is as follows:

Get a Free Dining Plan when you purchase a non-discounted 5-night/6-day Walt Disney Travel Company package that includes a room at a select Walt Disney World Resort hotel and ticket with a Park Hopper Option.

For arrivals most nights:
May 28, 2019- June 4, 2019
June 28, 2019- September 7, 2019
December 6, 2019- December 24, 2019

Book Through October 31, 2018.

Free Disney Dining Plan (Regular/Table Service) when you stay at a select Deluxe Resort or Deluxe Villa.

Free Disney Quick Service Dining Plan when you stay at a select Moderate or Value Resort.

Room Types Excluded: campsites, 3-bedroom villas, Bungalows at Polynesian, Cabins at Copper Creek, and The Little Mermaid Rooms at Art of Animation.

Blacked out dates:

June 5, 2019- June 27, 2019

September 8, 2019- December 5, 2019

Black Out Dates

*Skip this section unless you're booking around blackout dates. Because it's confusing and there's no need to tax your brain that hard if you don't need to do so.

If your stay includes blackout dates and you're booking a package, you can receive the discount on the days that are not blacked out, but you'll pay regular price during the blackout dates.

If your stay includes blackout dates and you're booking a room only reservation, your reservation will have to stop at the blackout date. You could then re-book for the rest of your stay using another discount or at regular price. If another part of your stay is during the Bounce Back offer you can book that too, but you'll need to book while you're on property either in another adult's name OR wait until you're on property again and book in your own name.

I feel like this is confusing so let me throw in an example:

If I want to stay April 4th- April 11th on the Bounce Back, and I'm booking a package (so with tickets or the dining plan), I'll receive the discount on the 4th,

5th, 8th, 9th, 10th, and 11th, but I'll pay full price on the 6th and 7th. This can all be one reservation.

If I want to book that same trip, but as a Room Only reservation, it will have to be three separate reservations. I'll book April 4th, 5th with the Bounce Back discount in my name. The 6th and 7th will be a regular booking through a TA or on My Disney Experience. Then the 8th, 9th, 10th and 11th will be a second Bounce Back reservation. I will have to book this in Mike's name on his account, or wait until I'm at Disney again and am eligible to book another Bounce Back.

If you are not planning to book another stay while you're at Disney (and honestly, just bring the $200, because you may change your mind) you can still use this information to your advantage. The dates that Disney offers the Bounce Back are dates that they are trying to attract attendance. That means that these will likely be low crowd dates to attend AND that these dates may be targeted for higher discounts that don't require you to be on property to book. Just something to keep in mind as you plan.

Let's move on to **Pin Codes**. You'll want to make sure that Disney has your information on file to have a chance at this one. They are constantly sending out special offers to specific individuals. These are commonly called PIN Codes because they have a special number that you have to give to Disney to book these. How to get Disney to send you a PIN is the stuff of Disney lore, but these things seem to help:

- Putting a vacation in your cart on the Disney site and not checking out
- Ordering the Disney World informational DVD
- Opting-in to promotions
- Opening an account for your spouse and never using it to book a vacation

Like I said, we don't really know the algorithms that Disney uses to assign PINs, these things only seem to help with the likelihood of receiving one. I have never received one. I think Disney is thinking, "She's coming anyway, we don't need to send her any discounts." My only hope is on my husband's account. Maybe someday.

A friend just received a PIN and it was a significant savings. The offer was for a Value for $59 a night when the Passholder Discount was $79 and rates offered to the public were nearer to $100. Remember, then you can pay with discounted gift cards and maybe get this into the $50 or $45 a night range. Beat that, I-Drive hotels!

The last thing that I want to mention in this chapter on reducing resort costs is the **DVC Tour**. You're going to learn ALL about DVC soon, but for now I want you to know that they will usually offer you a gift card for taking their tour. It is usually a $25 or $50 Disney gift card, but I've heard tell of them giving $100 occasionally.

Many timeshare resorts offer discounts or bonuses for watching their marketing pitch. I have a friend, Lorena, who takes full advantage of these and has stayed many times for free or almost free. I've not done this and wouldn't necessarily advise it. To me, there are just too many moving pieces. I think if you're very savvy and strong-willed (like my friend!) you'd be fine, but for most people, it's not worth the risk. I don't believe that the DVC tour is this way. Disney doesn't have to pitch so hard. If you get the offer to take a tour for a gift card, it can be a quick and interesting way to make your vacation a little more affordable.

All Summed Up:

Thinking outside the box when it comes to resorts can be a big saver. Don't be afraid to change resorts mid-vacation. Some of these lesser known ideas can score you huge savings. Being flexible is a big help.

Chapter Fifteen:
Agency Exclusives

One way I've found to make Deluxe Accommodations fit my budget is with the use of Agency Exclusive pricing. An Agency Exclusive Offer is a deal that you can only get through a specific travel agency. Because I like to understand why things are the way they are, I'll share with you how this works.

The travel agency works with Disney to buy a set amount of rooms at a discounted price. Disney agrees to offer this discount because the agency is agreeing to buy them all at once in a block. The agency bears the risk of any vacancies.

The agency then offers their specific block of rooms to the public. In my experience, these discounts can be quite attractive. I have booked The Grand Floridian at about $260 a night when Disney was over $500 a night. I also booked the Polynesian at $237 per night when Disney was over twice that.

These offers are somewhat difficult to find, except for two. Most of them are smaller and they change from year to year. They might have a tiny availability or only a small window of dates. I search for them occasionally, but I usually don't find much savings.

The two that I've found to be the most advantageous are through Magical Vacations Travel and Pixie Dust and Pirate Hooks. Here is the URL directly to their agency exclusive pages:

http://www.magicalvacationstravel.com/agency-exclusive-offers

http://www.pixiedustandpiratehooks.com/offers/exclusive-offers

They usually offer many deals each year that cover a wide range of dates. And in my experience, those do save some money and they have greater availability than Disney might have left. So, if I want to book and Disney says they're full, I head over to Pixie Dust and Pirate Hooks or Magical Vacations Travel. Remember, their room blocks are already sold according to Disney, so even though Disney says, "sold out" both or either agency may have availability.

But by far the best deal is their Labor Day Deal. It is for specific dates each year.

- Pixie Dust and Pirate Hooks' dates are August 20, 2018 – September 1, 2018
- Magical Vacations Travel's dates are August 15, 2018 – September 5, 2018

The deal is also for specific resorts and views. This year these are available with Magical Vacations Travel:

- **Disney's Polynesian Resort** - Standard View and Garden View/Club Level, Lagoon View/Club Level

- **Disney's Contemporary Resort** - Standard View/Garden Wing

- **Disney's Yacht Club Resort** - Standard View

- **Disney's Beach Club Resort** - Standard View, Standard View/Club Level, Lagoon View/Club Level

- **Disney's Grand Floridian Resort & Spa** - Garden View/Outer Building

- **Disney's Boardwalk Inn** - Standard View and Standard View/Club Level

- **Disney's Animal Kingdom Lodge Resort** - Standard View and Savanna View

And these are available with Pixie Dust and Pirate Hooks:

- **Disney's Polynesian Village Resort,**
- **Disney's Grand Floridian Resort & Spa,**
- **Disney's Animal Kingdom Resort** – Savanna View
- **Disney's Boardwalk Inn**

You generally cannot purchase the dining plan with these deals. You can purchase tickets with the deal, but they are convention tickets- they cannot be upgraded at all.

This deal won't help the Smiths at all. Their resort doesn't qualify for the deal, but the Robinsons can take advantage since they are staying at the Grand Floridian.

Their original price of $9,500 included their stay, tickets and the dining plan. With some Agency Exclusives, you can't include the dining plan so we need to back that out to compare:
The dining plan accounts for $1,805.65 of the original $9,500. This means that their room and tickets would come to $7,694.35 ($9,500-$1,805.65). With the Labor Day deal, they would pay $3,823.75 for the same room and same tickets (except that the tickets can't be upgraded, of course.) This would be a savings of $3,870.60

You could make the argument that they might pay more for food since they are off the Dining Plan. And it's true. If they eat the exact same food off the Dining Plan as they would on the dining plan, they'll pay more for it when they are off the plan. But in my experience, I don't eat as much when I'm off the dining plan. We usually end up very close to the same cost, but we do get less food. I'm not sure why this is. I don't feel deprived either way. But I do prefer to be on the plan when possible, so I think that says something about its value.

For our purposes, let's add $500 extra to the cost of dining off the plan. I don't think the Robinsons will spend that much, but this will make the comparison very conservative. So, the Robinsons new total will be: $6,129.40 ($3,823.75 for the room +$1,805.65 for dining +$500 for an extra buffer due to not being on the Dining Plan) I rounded to $6,300 below.

Ready to hear the best part?

YOU CAN PAY WITH DISCOUNTED DISNEY GIFT CARDS!

This makes the deal crazy good. We can still use everything that we've learned from the other chapters. I'm going to show this using the Discover/Sam's deal because though it's not the very best deal, it's the best deal that most people can easily replicate. Not everyone has access to the other options.

So, here they are:

Needed for Vacation:	$6,300.00	($6,000 Sam's, $300 Eight Sites)
Saved via Sam's	- 280.80	(40*7.02)
Subtotal	$6,019.20	
Cash Back, Discover	- 571.92	(6,000-280.80)*10%
Subtotal	$5,447.28	
Discover Sign-Up	- 100.00	(One spouse will need to apply.)
Subtotal	$5,347.28	
Eight Websites Bonus	- 150.00	
Subtotal	$5,197.28	
Disney Chase Bonus	- 500.00	
Subtotal	$4,697.28	
Chase Sapphire	- 1,200.00	
Subtotal	$3,497.28	
Checking Bonus	- 500.00	
Total	$2,997.28	

The Robinsons are now paying only $2,997.28 for a vacation that would cost a similar family $9,500. This is a savings of $6,502.72 or 68.4% AND I rounded up—giving them $170.60 for souvenirs. That means that this is really a 70% savings.

Just for fun, let's pretend like the Robinsons can maximize what we've talked about so far. They live near Kroger, their Best Buy is kind and gentle and lets them buy gift cards with gift cards, they use Swagbucks and gas cans. These are my kind of people.

Here's where they would be if everything worked for them:

Needed for Vacation	$6,300.00	($6,000 Kroger/Best Buy $300 Eight Sites)
Cash Back, BlueCash	- 360.00	(6% on grocery)
Subtotal	$5,940.00	
BlueCash Fees	+ 95.00	(Only one spouse needs to get the card.)
Subtotal	$6,035.00	
BlueCash Sign-Ups	- 250.00	
Subtotal	$5,785.00	
Eight Websites	- 150.00	
Subtotal	$5,635.00	
Kroger Fuel Points	- 1,050.00	($43.75 for every $250)
Subtotal	$4,585.00	
Swagbucks	- 720.00	($6 for every $50)
Subtotal	$3,865.00	
Checking Bonus	- 500.00	
Subtotal	$3,365.00	
Disney Chase	- 500.00	
Subtotal	$2,865.00	
Chase Sapphire	- 1,200.00	
Total	$1,665.00	

$1,665 for a $9,500 vacation. That's just absolutely amazing. Totally awesome. Nice job, Robinsons. Save your $7,835 or 82.5% for something else. AND I rounded up—giving them $170.60 for souvenirs. That means that this is really a 84.3% savings.

One final note before we move on:

Agencies that offer exclusives do not tend to offer the level of customer service that a good travel agent will. If you are comfortable with booking your own dining and FastPasses, it can be a good option for saving money. If you would like more help and guidance, I would steer clear of these agencies. They rely on their lower prices to win your business rather than their service: think Walmart as opposed to Macy's.

If you aren't booking at a much lower rate, as in the Labor Day deal, I would recommend you go with a different agency. The Smart Moms Recommended Agents would be happy to have you. You can learn more here: bit.ly/SMPDTA This URL is case sensitive.

All Summed Up:

Agency Exclusive Offers can be a way to save quite a bit during certain times of the year. Other times of the year, they may still be a minor saver or may offer vacancy that isn't available elsewhere.

Chapter Sixteen:
Deluxe for the Price of Moderate?
Or Value?!?!

I stay Value often. I really like the Value hotels. They are great for my family. My kids are little and they like the theming. So do I; I am Disney to the core. But I also enjoy luxury. I like a little more space. And if my entire family comes, we can't fit in one Value any more. I also want to do a massive blog post comparing the resorts from the perspective of someone who has done them all. So, I needed to find a way to get the Deluxe Resorts into my price range. I have stayed at every resort now.

You're about to hear my secret to accomplishing this: renting DVC points.

What is DVC?

DVC is short for Disney Vacation Club. DVC is Disney's version of a timeshare. Basically, DVC'ers pay a certain amount to "buy-in" to a property and they get a certain number of points to use each year. They also pay dues each year. There is a certain period of time for the points to be used or banked. Owners can borrow from next year's points.

What are points?

Points are the tracking system Disney uses for DVC members to use and keep track of their stake in the property. When the member signed up, they will have purchased a set number of points per year. Maybe they bought 50 or 100 or 576. Any number at all. And they will get that same number of points each year. They also pay dues on that number of points each year.

When a DVC member is ready to stay at a DVC resort, they can use their points as currency for their stay. They have access to a site that tells them what DVC resorts are available, and how many points a given stay will cost.

Fictitious DVC member, Jane, owns 100 DVC points. She can use those to book her stay at any DVC Resort. She'll need more points for more expensive resorts. She will need more points for more in-demand times. Just like cash in that regard.

What is renting points?

Renting points is when a DVC member charges someone and in return allows that person to use their points one time. This is different from buying points, which would be purchasing for the rest of the contract. Renting is for this one time only.

Where can you rent points?

There are two well know points rental brokers. They basically collect a fee for matching up people who want to rent with people who have points to rent. You work directly with the broker though, not the individual. This would be the safest way to rent, as these companies are well known and provide good customer service.

These two companies (in no particular order) are The DVC Rental Store and David's Vacation Club. I believe that David's is larger with more points availability, but they are also harder to work with. They make you pay just to check availability and if there is availability you have to book it or lose your deposit. I'm not a fan of that. I like to play around and see what's available. But I guess David's doesn't want me wasting their time that way.

Disclaimer: I do want to say that I have not used The DVC Rental Store, and I've only used David's Vacation Club once despite having rented points many, many times. I rent from individuals, and I'll explain that. But like I said, these two companies are widely respected and I would feel good about recommending them.

Renting from Individuals

You can skip the middle man and save some money by renting directly from individuals. This is riskier and possibly more work, but I have found it to be a good fit for me. I'm not risk averse (I did tell you about that time we left our only source of income to move 350 miles away from our family and start a farm, right? With no insurance, 4 months pregnant, and with two kids and two mortgages? God saw me through that and I figure He'll see me through it if something goes wrong on a DVC reservation!) I also own a real estate company and have a pretty good understanding of contract law so I feel good about my ability to write-up an enforceable contract, though I hope they never get tested in court.

You basically find an individual through one of the channels mentioned in the next chapter and work out a deal with them. You can offer less than they're asking, and you can ask them to check availability. You work out the terms with them and set up payment. You have little to no recourse in these instances if you were to find yourself working with a scammer (more on that later). This is 2.0 level DVC renting and I advise you to know what you're doing or to stay on level 1.0 (renting from the brokers.)

Confirmed Reservations

One of my favorite ways to rent points is to rent Confirmed Reservations. This means that a DVC member has already booked a reservation with their points and now for whatever reason, they can't or don't want to use it. There are also enterprising DVC'ers out there who book the most in-demand times and then sell those reservations at a premium. I wouldn't be their target market since I wouldn't be willing to overpay for those weeks, but I say more power to them! We all have to find a way to earn a living and if they have a market, I wish them well.

But I am interested in the Confirmed Reservations that are not over-priced. Sometimes points are about to expire and the member can't use them, but they book a reservation and then offer it at a discount because if it doesn't get rented they'll lose it. This creates a very motivated DVC member. My favorite kind. This is how I stayed at the Treehouses for $158/night.

Here's how much the Treehouses are with Disney (before tax, while my $158 included tax.)

Treehouse Villa

View Photos
Views of Woodlands
2 Queen Beds and 1 Bunk Bed and 1 Twin-Size Sleeper Chair and 1 Queen-Size Sleeper Sofa
Sleeps up to 9 Adults

Standard Room Rate
$969.00 USD
Avg/Night Excl Tax
Added to Cart

View Cart

How much does it cost to rent points?

This depends on where you rent them from. The brokers are on the high-end at $15-$16 a point or even higher, with an additional $1 per point charge for bookings between seven and eleven months in advance at the more in demand resorts. This seven to eleven month window is significant. Let me explain why:

When DVC Members buy their points, they buy them at a specific resort. That's their "home resort." They can book reservations at their home resort up to eleven months in advance. This means that if someone owns at the Grand Floridian, they can book there eleven months in advance. But they cannot book at any other resort with those same points until they are seven months out. This gives those who own at any particular resort an advantage in booking.

So, when the brokers charge that additional $1 per point during that time frame, they are giving a nod to those owners who have points at the more valuable resorts and are putting them up for rent so far in advance.

But back to how much points are worth: I have rented from individuals for under $5 a point, but I had to go that same week, and I was also taking my chances as discussed above. I find that it's pretty easy to get points for $12-$13 from individuals without needing to go super soon or anything like that. In fact, those prices are so common that they don't usually motivate me. I wait for a better deal, but I'm very flexible and don't need to book in advance, while you may want to budget for $12-13 so that you can book further in advance.

David's prices are $16 with an additional $1 for prime resorts and other situations. You can find the details here: https://www.dvcrequest.com/faq.asp#price-per-point Here are DVC Rental Store's prices (you can find these here: http://dvcrentalstore.com/faq-frequently-asked-questions/#006

Price Per Point: All Resorts (Booked Less Than 7 Months Prior to Check-In)

Price Per Point:	Amount of Points Rented:	Time until your Check-In:
$17.00/Point	Reservations of 50+ Points Reserved >>>>>>>>>>>>>>>>>>>>>>>>>>>>>>>>>>	0-7 Months Prior to Check-In
$18.00/Point	Reservations less than 50 pts Reserved >>>>>>>>>>>>>>>>>>>>>>>>>>>>>>>>	0-7 Months Prior to Check-In

Price Per Point: Non-Premium Resorts** (Booked 7-11 Months Prior to Check-In)

Price Per Point:	Amount of Points Rented:	Time until your Check-In:
$17.00/Point	Reservations of 50+ Points Reserved >>>>>>>>>>>>>>>>>>>>>>>>>>>>>>>>>>	7-11 Months Prior to Check-In
$18.00/Point	Reservations less than 50 pts Reserved >>>>>>>>>>>>>>>>>>>>>>>>>>>>>>>>	7-11 Months Prior to Check-In

Price Per Point: Premium Resorts*** (Booked 7-11 Months Prior to Check-In)

Price Per Point:	Amount of Points Rented:	Time until your Check-In:
$18.00/Point	Reservations of 50+ Points Reserved >>>>>>>>>>>>>>>>>>>>>>>>>>>>>>>>>>	7-11 Months Prior to Check-In
$19.00/Point	Reservations less than 50 pts Reserved >>>>>>>>>>>>>>>>>>>>>>>>>>>>>>>>	7-11 Months Prior to Check-In

**Non-Premium DVC Resorts: Disney's Old Key West Resort, Disney's Saratoga Springs Resort & Spa, Disney's Hilton Head Island Resort, Disney's Vero Beach Resort

***Premium DVC Resorts: Disney's Animal Kingdom Villas, Disney's Aulani Resort and Spa, Bay Lake Tower at Disney's Contemporary Resort, Disney's Beach Club Resort, Disney's BoardWalk Resort, Villas at Disney's Grand Floridian Resort, Disney's Polynesian Villas and Bungalows, Boulder Ridge Villas at Disney's Wilderness Lodge, Copper Creek Villas & Cabins at Disney's Wilderness Lodge, Villas at Disney's Grand Californian Hotel and Spa

Because you don't know how many points you'll need for a stay, these $12, $13, $15, $19 numbers probably mean very little to you at this point and that is ok. Don't worry about it. You'll start to understand later, but for now, let's talk about how renting points compares to Disney. That will make this process easier to understand.

How does the price of renting compare to Disney's resort prices?

This is also an "it depends" answer (which I hate, but it just is), since packages can be booked with different discounts, it's hard to compare. I will give an example below to show you some real numbers, but I'll also say that the general consensus is that renting points is a good way to get a Deluxe at the price of a Moderate. I have even been able to rent points and stay Deluxe at a cost lower than I would have been able to book a Value.

Example:

Let's look at a random week, and pretend like we're planning our vacation. I've selected July 23-29.

Prices from Disney:

- All Stars $138 per night,
- Moderates between $205-$230 per night,
- Deluxes between $325 and $595

Renting Points for a Deluxe through David's (broker randomly chosen):

- $200 per night for the cheapest (Animal Kingdom Lodge Studio)
- $417.50 per night for the most expensive (Bay Lake Tower Magic Kingdom View)

So, you can see, you'll still pay more than a Value, but may be able to book a Deluxe for the cost of a Moderate, quite easily.

I see rentals from individuals available at $12 a point quite often and I can usually book a room fairly easily if I'm willing to pay $12/point. Here are those same two reservations we looked at with David's, but at $12 a point from an individual:

- $164 per night for AKL
- $316 per night for BLT Magic Kingdom View

That puts AKL just $34 more per night than normal people pay for the All-Star Resorts. And remember, if you are flexible and persistent you can do even better than $12 a point. This takes a bit of acumen and skill, but if you keep at it, you make be able to get points for $8 or $10. Like I said before, I've been able to rent points for less than $5 a point on occasion. I have certainly booked Deluxe rooms for less than I would have been able to book Value rooms through Disney, but those are the rarer instances.

Let's move into talking about the differences between a DVC reservation and a Disney reservation. There are a few things you really need to know before you rent.

How does the reservation differ from normal?

Well, as the renter, you don't truly "own" the reservation until you check in. The DVC member still owns it and he or she is the only one who can make changes to it if needed. This is a tiny bit frustrating and is what makes renting risky.

The frustrating part: I frequently change my mind about who is coming with me. It might be one kid or two or a friend. Or, I might plan to take the whole family and then Mike can't go because of something on the farm. I have to three-way call with the DVC member and Disney to change anything. And if I want to add the dining plan or Magical Express, the DVC member has to do it.

The risky part: The DVC member could potentially take the reservation back from you. I have heard legends of horror stories (though I've never heard of it actually happening to anyone first person) where someone arrives in Orlando and goes to check in and the DVC member has taken back the reservation and the renter has little to no recourse. If you had a contract in writing, you'd have more recourse, but who wants to go to court over a vacation?

You also have to give your payment information to the DVC member if you want to add the dining plan. This also presents an element of risk. I like to three-way call with them to Disney and pay directly. I pay with a gift card with just the right amount on it (or I grab the rest off quickly) to limit the risk. I've never had an issue.

How does the resort differ?

DVC resorts are off to the side, behind, or otherwise tucked in near the parent resort. The exceptions include Old Key West which is a standalone DVC resort and Saratoga Treehouse Villas (which is waaaayyyy off to the side). This means you may walk a little further to the lobby or main pool, but it's not far enough to be upsetting. The amenities more than make up for this. DVC resorts usually have their own quiet pool. Laundry services are free in DVC resorts. And Boulder Ridge at Wilderness Lodge has an AMAZING workout room and lobby area that I took full advantage of when I was there. It went like this, "Babe, watch the kids, I'm going to go sit in front of the fireplace and write."

The vibe of DVC resorts is different and suits me better. The hustle and bustle is gone. The resorts are quiet. People enjoy their surroundings. People are relaxed. I put it down to the fact that these people come to Disney often and they have seen and done a lot and just want to enjoy their trip in their own way. It's not a mad dash to choke down a bagel and get to rope drop. I see people playing board games with their families in the lobbies. And I've had long chats with people who have nowhere to be and all day to get there. Just my speed, if I'm being honest.

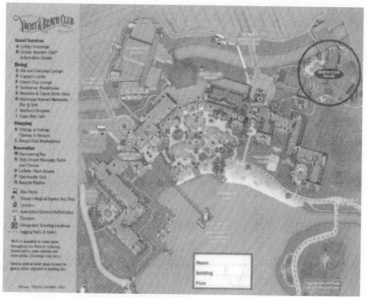

It's really not that much farther...

How do the rooms differ?

You are probably familiar with standard Disney hotel rooms. Even in the Deluxe Resorts, they are the same. Two Queen beds, and a very common layout.

The DVC equivalent of a Standard Room would be a Studio. These are the least expensive DVC rooms available. Everything in these rooms is more home-y than the standard hotel rooms. You will find a kitchenette in these rooms. It will have a small fridge, sink, microwave, coffee maker; along with dishes and common items. The other big difference is the second bed. In a DVC room, there will be one queen bed and a pull-out couch. This is fine for us; our kids will sleep anywhere. But it may not be desirable for everyone.

Other Room Sizes

Studios book up the fastest, since they are the least expensive, so you may need to consider a one or two bedroom. There are even larger rooms at some of the resorts. Grand Villas sleep twelve and Treehouses at Saratoga Springs sleep nine.

We stayed in a One Bedroom not long ago and it will be very hard to go back to a Studio. I'm hoping we win the lottery or something because seriously... it was amazing by comparison. The room was set up so that there was a full kitchen, a living room, a balcony, a bathroom with two separate sink areas and both a shower and separate whirlpool tub, and the master bedroom. There was a small stacked washer and dryer in a closet. The bed was a King which felt very luxurious for us (we had plenty of real estate for us and our co-sleeper baby.) The three big kids slept in a dog pile on the pull-out couch which works for now, but won't as they get older. I enjoyed that One Bedroom and honestly, we could have moved in and been happy with the space.

Example Floor Plan of a One Bedroom

Occupancy Questions

Most Studios and One Bedrooms sleep 4, but there are some that sleep five. However, all of the Studios and One Bedrooms are allowed to sleep five if the fifth person brings their own linens (and maybe a blowup mattress) towels, and pillows. You may read conflicting accounts about this rule, but when I've asked Disney they did confirm. You can also bring one child under three-years-old. So, our family of six can still fit in the DVC standard rooms because Cyrus is only one. When he turns three OR we have another baby, it's sayonara standard rooms and hello suites or two Value Rooms. Eek. But this is where DVC can make a HUGE difference in price. If you have a family of five (or six with one under three), you can't stay in the Values any more without getting two rooms, but you CAN all still fit in a Deluxe (and a few moderates offer occupancy up to five.) By renting points instead of paying Disney directly, you can keep the cost down and keep Disney affordable.

Two Bedrooms sleep eight or nine, and you can also bring one additional child who is under three years old. This can be a really good option for two families staying together.

What resorts have DVC?

Here are the DVC resort names and which resort they're located in/next to/near.

Bay Lake Tower-Contemporary Resort

Animal Kingdom Villas- Animal Kingdom Lodge

Beach Club Villas- Beach Club

Boardwalk Villas- Boardwalk Resort

Polynesian Villas & Bungalows- Polynesian Village Resort

Treehouse Villas at Saratoga Springs Resort and Spa

The Villas at Grand Floridian Resort and Spa

Boulder Ridge Villas and Copper Creek- Wilderness Lodge

Old Key West Resort (stand alone) And it's worth mentioning that Studios at OKW have two queen beds, not a pull-out sofa.

Things You Should Know

Ok, a couple more things that are worth noting:

- You cannot pay to rent points with gift cards since you aren't paying Disney directly. (Side note, if you were a DVC owner you COULD pay your dues with gift cards.) If you are renting from an individual, you can always ask if they will take Disney gift cards. Some will because they go to Disney often enough that it makes sense for them. If they say no, I'll even ask, "Would you consider accepting them if I paid you 5% more?" I know that I'm getting my gift cards at over 20% off so even if they wanted 10%-15% more to accept them, I'm still ahead. It is amazing what you can get in this world if you just say what you want. My mom taught me that and it's served me well.

- Mousekeeping is completely different with DVC. They don't come every day. They come after four nights and do a "Trash and Towel" which is exactly what it sounds like: empty the trash and leave new towels. And they do a full cleaning on night eight. You can also pay for a cleaning if you'd like more help. I believe it was around $40 for the one bedroom. They do leave cleaning supplies so you can do what you need to yourself. They also charge for extra wash cloths and the like. There is free laundry service in the DVC resorts so you could just wash your washcloths and towels if you need to, or you could bring some extras from home. We are usually fine on towels since you can just hang them up to dry and reuse them, but I like to bring extra washcloths so I have a fresh one when needed.

Let's check this out for our old friends the Robinsons. This really won't help the Smiths, except for the fact that they might just decide to stay Deluxe if they can get it for the price of Moderate.

The Robinsons original price of $9,500 included their stay, tickets and the dining plan. Renting DVC points only effects the stay so what we'll do to compare is hold the tickets and dining plan constant and just look at the resort stay.

The dining plan accounts for $1,805.65 of the original $9,500. This means that their room and tickets would come to $7,694.35 ($9,500-$1,805.65). Their tickets are $2,566.65. This means that their room is $5,127.70 ($7,694.35-$2,566.65).

That same room via DVC points would cost about $1,728. I got this figure for a seven-night stay with David's. You can look at the calculator here: http://www.dvcrequest.com/cost-calculator.asp

Now, their costs are: $1,728 with David's and $4,372.30 ($1,805.65+$2,566.65) with Disney for the tickets and dining plan (note that they'll actually pay David's for the dining plan and David's will pay Disney, but gift cards are allowed through David's for that purpose.) This brings their new total to $6,100.30

The ability to use gift cards for dining and tickets means we can still use everything that we've learned from the other chapters. I'm going to show this using the Discover/Sam's deal because though it's not the very best deal, it's the best deal that most people can easily replicate. Not everyone has access to the other options. They will buy twenty-seven $150 packs of Disney gift cards, saving $7.02 on each and one $50 gift card, saving $1.49 on it.

I'm going to assume they would pay David's with their Discover card as well. They earn 1% cash back with Discover and that doubles to 2% in the first year. That's really the most discount you can hope for on a purchase from David's. So, here they are:

Needed for Vacation:	$6,100.30
($4,100 Sam's, $300 Eight Sites, $1,728 to David's)	
Saved via Sam's	- 191.03
(27*$7.02+$1.49 on the final $50 with Sam's)	
Subtotal	$5,909.27
Cash Back, Discover	- 390.90
Subtotal	$5,518.37
Discover Sign-Up	- 100.00
Subtotal	$5,418.37
Eight Websites Bonus	- 150.00
Subtotal	$5,268.37
Disney Chase Bonus	- 500.00
Subtotal	$4,768.37
Chase Sapphire	- 1,200.00
Subtotal	$3,568.37
Checking Bonus	- 500.00
Subtotal	$3,068.37
Cash Back, David's	- 34.56
Total	$3,033.81

So, they are paying $3,033.81 for a $9,500 vacation, saving $6,466.19. This is 68% off.

I don't know if you remember, but the Robinsons paid only $2,997.28 when they did the Labor Day Agency Exclusive. With DVC, they only paid about $30 more. This means that with renting DVC, you can get the equivalent of the Labor Day Deal, all year round.

All Summed Up:

Renting DVC points from a broker is a really easy way to stay at a Deluxe resort for the cost of a Moderate resort. Mostly, this is the same as staying with Disney directly, but there are a few things to consider:

1. It's somewhat risky, although you can take steps to alleviate that risk.
2. The rooms may not be comfortable to your family since they have a Queen and pull-out couch.
3. You don't get Mousekeeping every day.
4. You can't use Disney gift cards to pay.
5. The DVC resort may be a few steps further away from the lobby/transportation.
6. Confirmed Reservations may not work with your schedule.
7. It is a tiny bit harder to compare pricing and get quotes/see availability.

Chapter Seventeen:
Renting DVC Points Wisely

As I'm writing the second edition, and thinking about what I can add to the DVC discussion to make it even better, two things come to mind. I didn't originally intend for this to be a "how to" on renting points, just a place for you to get the pertinent information and become aware of this option. But over the past year, I've realized that I have a "way" of getting my points as cheaply as I do and it's not obvious. You won't find it out there. So, I'm going to go into that here and I'll answer the two most common questions I've been asked. Which are:

1. How do I find cheap reservations?

2. What is the process when renting with brokers?

Let me answer those for you.

There is a video in the course (Disney World Within Reach: Made Easy) where you can see my screen that shows you exactly what I do when I'm searching for a cheap reservation, but I'll also describe it here for you.

First, I have searches running on **eBay** constantly. All my search terms are listed in the workbook so you can set up your eBay search exactly as I have mine. Not that it's the only way to find the reservations, but I did go through a lot of trial and error to get the search terms set up so that I am getting the results I want (and probably more importantly— not getting the results I don't want.)

I get an email every day (you could get one every week if you wanted, but I like to stay in the loop) of the new stuff that hits my search terms. I look over the email briefly. I can usually tell at a glance that it's nothing interesting to me and I delete it. But if it is interesting, I'll go in and watch it. Here are the two biggest indicators that this might end up being a good deal:

1. It's an auction.

2. It's beginning with a low enough starting bid.

If it's an auction, but it has a reserve or it's already too high, I don't pay any attention. If it's a Buy It Now, the price is usually too high to start with. I have occasionally found Buy It Nows that were a good deal and those were super easy to scoop up.

If it fits my criteria, I'll "watch" it on eBay, and make a note on my calendar of when it ends. Then the day it ends, I check it again and if it's still pretty decent in price and I'm hoping to nab it, I'll set an alarm for about two minutes before the end of the auction.

When the alarm goes off, I pull up the auction and take a look. If it's still in my price range, I'll plan to bid at the last second. I decide what I'm willing to pay for this thing beforehand and I put that amount in as my first and only bid. At about 30 seconds before the end of the auction, if the price is still below my threshold, I'll type in my bid amount and then watch the seconds tick by. My connection is pretty terrible so I have to hit "bid" at about 9 seconds out for the bid to squeak in at 2-3 seconds before the end of the auction— any more than that and you're risking someone bidding again and sniping it from you.

You can time your connection out by bidding on some cheap stuff that you really don't care about to see if you do it at five seconds out you can squeak it in, or is seven better or maybe nine like me. Some people can clearly get their bids in in under three seconds because of their speedy connections. Hopefully, that's you because it gives you an edge.

Recently, I stayed at Old Key West for incredibly cheap. Here's how it went down: I first noticed the auction about four days out. Put it on my calendar, then day of, I set the alarm. Log on and it's still in my price range so I watch and bid my best offer 9 seconds out. I get it! Yes! $499 for five nights at Old Key West. But I don't stop there. eBay takes gift cards. My Best Buy sells them and at that time, they allowed gift card to gift card transactions. Yep. So, I get Best Buy gift cards from Kroger (review the grocery chapter for details—you can still make this work even without Best Buy) and flip them to eBay and then pay for my reservation with them. Those eBay cards ended up at 23.3% off so I got the reservation for $382.73 in actual cash. That's $76.55/night for a Deluxe. Normal people would be rejoicing if they got a Value for that amount.

Note that Best Buy is extremely your mileage may vary now on gift card to gift card buying, but back then it was no problem. My grocery store sells eBay as well, so I can do that directly, instead of involving Best Buy. I could also buy Visa or Mastercard prepaid cards then go to Best Buy with those or I could get eBay from Meijer—tons of options.

A few notes on eBay gift cards: you can only use eight of them per transaction. You can't buy gift cards with them (bummer!) They usually come in $25s, $50s, $100s and $200s. I've never seen $500s but there are rumors they exist. So, if you can get eight $200s, that's $1,600 you can use in a single transaction. Lots of times, I can't find the $200s, so keep that in mind. I think eBay tries to limit them in the market place. Meijer usually has them, but they are sometimes scarce elsewhere.

Anything over the gift card paid portion would have to be paid by PayPal. Rules say you can only use $1,000 in gift cards in a single transaction, but usually it will take more for me. Sometimes, it does stop me. You have to have PayPal to use eBay gift cards. Also, if you use a gift card on an eBay account, it is forever connected to that account. So, if you use a gift card on your husband's account to buy a chicken feeder and then try to use that gift card on your account to pay for a Disney reservation on your own account, it ain't gonna work. #Iveheard

Ok, enough about eBay. The next thing that I do is check the brokers for **Confirmed Reservations**. I just cruise over a few times a month and see what they have. I probably miss things because I don't look as often as I could, but honestly, their prices just do not get me that excited so I don't pay a lot of attention. I've only rented from a broker one time and it was a confirmed reservation. It was a good deal: six nights at Boardwalk, pool view for $1,375 so $230 a night, which is what most people would expect to pay for a Moderate. But for me it was higher than I'm used to. I have a soft-spot for Boardwalk though so I'll pay a little more for it. I invited a friend and her daughter and I took my daughter and we had a blast. Side note:

splitting a room is a big saver too. Review the YMMV chapter.

Next stop: Mouse Owners. I find better deals than the brokers on the Mouse Owners board. Link/URL is at the end of the chapter. I've rented several times from individuals on their site and I've not had any issue. I look specifically for confirmed reservations and then if I find something that suits me, I'll email and ask for a lower price. It's just what I do. Even if the price is pretty good, better is always better so I just say something like, "Interested in your reservation. Is your price firm?" Most of the time, they will lower it some.

Then, I ask if they'll take Disney gift cards. There are always things you can ask. You can always do a little better. If they say it's firm, ok fine. I still ask if they'll take Disney gift cards and if not I'm not out anything for asking. In the interest of clarity, let me explain that if they take Disney gift cards, they are just pocketing them, not paying Disney for anything. They would have already paid Disney for their points and dues and when they rent, they are recouping that. But lots of DVCers are Disney nuts and don't mind being paid in Disney gift cards because they know they'll spend them easily. I've also offered MORE if they take Disney gift cards. If my gift cards are discounted to 20% off and I offer a DVC owner 10% more if he or she takes Disney gift cards, I'm up 10% from paying cash. Also, it's handy to know that they are able to pay their dues with Disney gift cards, so I mention that when I make the offer too.

I am regularly able to book several months in advance at a great savings. Heading to Animal Kingdom Lodge for three nights in just a few weeks for less than $150 a night and I booked that five months out. Usually, I will then look at flights and maybe add a day or so at the beginning or end to make the stay work with cheap flights. We are actually going to drive this time so I didn't care about flights, but I don't like to go down just for three nights, so I added a couple nights at a Value beforehand. Split stay—just like we talked about before. You'll learn in the dining chapter that this has a lot of extra benefits to it as well. We are doing the first two nights with the quick service plan and then the second three nights with the deluxe plan and I have the kids strategically listed on the reservation. Good food, cheaper! You'll learn soon.

So, that's how I do it. Maybe that will help you some with coming up with a process for your search. Let me know if it is helpful or not, because I left it out of the last edition thinking that I'm not typical (flexible, going every month, can drop everything and go next week, etc.) But some aspects of it may help you and I kept getting the question, so here we are.

Now, let's move into talking about the process with brokers. I think for a lot of you, this is a really nice and easy way to ease into renting DVC points. It's a lot more secure, it's tried and true.

Two ways to do this: **Confirmed Reservations** or just **renting points**. Confirmed Reservations are less complicated so I'll explain that first.

So, you found a reservation that will work for you. It's listed under DVC Rental's or David's Confirmed Reservations. But is it actually available?

Step 1: Confirm availability.

- With David's you'll put all your info in and actually pay the deposit. If the reservation is still available, they'll email you back and ask you to pay the full reservation within 48 hours or you forfeit your deposit and lose the reservation. If it's not available, they'll just refund your deposit and apologize for wasting your time.

- With DVC Rental Store, you don't have to make a payment to check availability. You can just put in a request to see if it's still available. Then if they email back that it is, they'll explain how to go ahead and book it.

Step 2: Make your payment.

- Again, with David's they'll email you and you'll have 48 hours to make your payment. They are holding the reservation for you at this point because you've already put your deposit down.

- When the email comes confirming availability, you'll be able to go ahead and book the reservation. This is NOT your reservation until you pay for it, so don't delay.

Step 3: Make sure all your information is entered properly.

You'll have put information in when you're requesting to see if the booking is still available. Sometimes I don't really know who is coming with me so I only put one or two of my kids or my best guess. You can usually change the guest info except for the lead guest so make sure that's right!

Step 4: Confirmation Number

They'll send you a confirmation number and you can then link that to My Disney Experience. As long as you have tickets or an Annual Pass you will then be able to make your FastPasses at 60 days out. And you can book your Magical Express through the broker.

Step 5: Dining Plan

If you are getting the dining plan, the broker will take your payment and have the owner of the points call in to pay for the dining plan. You need to do this as soon as possible because the brokers have rules about when they can guarantee it will be added. I think it has to be at least 10 days before the trip, but don't quote me on that.

So, that is the process for booking a confirmed reservation. Now let's talk about what happens if you prefer to choose specific dates.

Step 1: Check availability.

Both brokers will start by having you fill out a form to check availability. David's will make you put a deposit down, while DVC Rental Store will not. You will be able to give your dates and then say whether or not they are firm. You can also give multiple resorts if you're flexible, so if you're first choice is unavailable, they can check your second and third choices for you.

Step 2: Confirming

If the reservation you're requesting is unavailable, you'll just get an email saying so. In my experience, the Rental Store will try to match you up with something close or will give you some helpful options. And they will reply to your emails from that point, so you don't have to re-fill out the form every time you want to check availability. David's just sends an auto-generated form that will tell you it's unavailable and advising on a refund of your deposit.

If the reservation is available, with David's you have to pay in full within 48 hours or lose your deposit. With the Rental Store you need to put your deposit down right away as the reservation isn't held until you do.

From there, everything will be the same as it is for the Confirmed Reservations, so I'll spare your time and won't make you re-read the whole process.

I do want to say that I've never booked anything except Confirmed Reservations because I don't find their prices to be THAT attractive compared to the other deals I can usually get. So just bear in mind that I may be slightly off.

I want to reiterate that using the brokers can be a great way to rent points with very little risk. I don't want you to feel negative about them because I don't find the deals to be that good. They are SUPER good when compared to Disney itself and I'm in a unique situation of being able to go on short notice, so these other deals I find may not be for you.

URLs

Big DVC Rental Companies:

http://dvcrentalstore.com/ (Easier to work with, less availability.)

https://www.dvcrequest.com/(More cumbersome to use, more availability.)

Confirmed Reservations:

Mouse Owners:
http://www.mouseowners.com/forums/forumdisplay
.php?f=63 Also check out their post on scammers:
http://www.mouseowners.com/forums/showthread.
php?t=114451. It's pretty enlightening. And scary.

DVC Rental Store's Confirmed Reservations:
http://dvcrentalstore.com/discounted-points-
confirmed-reservations/

David's Confirmed Reservations:
https://www.dvcrequest.com/available-
reservations.asp David's also has a mailing list that you can join to be informed if they have any good deals.

Also, don't forget: eBay Search "DVC" or by specific resort: "Old Key West Disney". Look in the workbook for more info on setting up your searches. My best deals have been from eBay.

Calculators

This is my favorite calculator for figuring out how many points you need: https://www.dvcrequest.com/cost-calculator.asp And the same link can also help you with occupancy (just click "Show Occupancy") You can also look by cost. It's David's calculator so they show his pricing, so keep that in mind. I find that it's easy to use their pricing as a ballpark as I'm strategizing.

I would like to show you this for the Robinsons, but I need to make sure you understand the liberties I'm taking here. I rent points from eBay quite regularly. In fact, less than two hours ago, I scored Boardwalk for $187 a night. I'll use discounted gift cards to pay eBay and bring that down to about $149.60 per night. That doesn't mean that this will work for you. The dates might not work. Or it might be the wrong resort. But if it does work for you, this can be AMAZING.

So, as I calculate this, I want you to understand that this is the outlier. I'm not going to show you the cheapest I've ever rented, because that would just be silly. That happens once in a blue moon. I'm going to show you something that would make me move. This is modeled after a resort stay that we've had. We've done better, we've done worse. This is a middle of the road, good deal.

You remember this from calculating the Robinsons from the previous chapter: The Robinsons original price of $9,500 included their stay, tickets and the dining plan. Renting DVC points only effects the stay so what we'll do to compare is hold the tickets and dining plan constant and just look at the resort stay.

The dining plan accounts for $1,805.65 of the original $9,500. This means that their room and tickets would come to $7,694.35 ($9,500-$1,805.65). Their tickets are $2,566.65. This means that their room is $5,127.70 ($7,694.35-$2,566.65).

I was able to book the Wilderness Lodge for seven nights on eBay for $1,300. Let's pretend like the Robinsons were able to get that same deal.

Now, their costs are: $1,300 with eBay and $4,372.30 ($1,805.65 and $2,566.65) with Disney for the tickets and dining plan. This brings their new total to $5,672.30

The ability to use gift cards for dining and tickets means we can still use everything that we've learned from the other chapters. I'm going to show this using the Discover/Sam's deal for the Disney gift cards and a grocery store for the eBay gift cards to the $1,000 limit.

So, here they are:

Needed for Vacation: $5,672.30
($4,100 Sam's, $300 Eight Sites, $1,300 to eBay)
Saved via Sam's   - 191.03
(27*$7.02+$1.49 on the final $50 with Sam's)

Subtotal	$5,481.27	
Cash Back, Discover	- 390.90	Sam's($4,100-$191.03)*10%
Subtotal	$5,090.37	
Discover Sign-Up	- 100.00	
Subtotal	$4,990.37	
Eight Websites Bonus	- 150.00	
Subtotal	$4,840.37	
Disney Chase Bonus	- 500.00	
Subtotal	$4,340.37	
Chase Sapphire	- 1,200.00	
Subtotal	$3,140.37	
Checking Bonus	- 500.00	
Subtotal	$2,640.37	
Meijer/BlueCash	- 160.00	
16% off $1,000 at Meijer for eBay, with BlueCash		
Total	$2,480.37	

So, they are paying $2,480.37 for a $9,500 vacation, saving $7,019.63. This is 74% off.

It's funny. I was typing this all out and I actually paused after this chapter to pay for my Boardwalk reservation that I'd just won on eBay and it made me realize that I forgot a couple things in this calculation: Top Cash Back and eBay Bucks. Top Cash Back is paying 1.5% on eBay right now. Sometimes eBates is higher, but rarely. eBay Bucks is a rewards program with eBay where you get 1% of your purchase back to spend on eBay. So, the Robinsons would get $19.50 back from Top Cash Back and $13 back from eBay Bucks. $32.5 more in savings—bringing their total to $2,447.87, $7,052.13 or 74.2% off.

And this was nowhere near being the best deal I've gotten on DVC. The Robinsons could get even luckier.

All Summed Up:

I love renting DVC. It's so awesome that it's hard to justify actually becoming a DVC member (I still want to though, just on principle.) It can be an easy way to stay Deluxe on a tight budget. It's not going to help you stay as inexpensively as possible though. The Smiths wouldn't be helped by renting DVC, but the Robinsons can save this way.

Chapter Eighteen:
Military Discounts

The Armed Forces Salute is a great discount if you can use it. I put this chapter last in the original Disney World Within Reach because it's the hardest to qualify for by far. You can't have just been in the military (which would be hard enough #amIright), but you have to be ACTIVE, RETIRED or 100% DISABLED. Having a DD214 with honorable discharge does not qualify you for the promotion. If you have questions about your eligibility, the best resource is Shades of Green. This is a military resort which is on Disney property. http://www.shadesofgreen.org/
Here is some more info on eligibility:

Eligible Current or Retired Military Members:

- Active
- Reserve
- National Guard
- Coast Guard

- Commissioned Corps of the Public Health Service (PHS)
- Commissioned Corps of the National Oceanic and Atmospheric Administration (NOAA)

Members who are **100% Disabled** must have a military issued ID with the DAVRPM code.

The good news is that if you do qualify, it's one of the best discounts that Disney offers and a military spouse is allowed to use the offer as well. That makes it significantly easier to take advantage of this offer, especially if the military member is deployed. However, it is important to note that the military spouse doesn't qualify to use the discount *in addition* to the military member, just *in place* of the member. If both spouses qualify they may both use the discounts to the limit.

The offer that is outlined here is valid until December 15, 2018. It has been renewed for the past nine years, since 2009. If continued, look for the renewal to be announced in the fall of 2018. It will likely be very similar to the current offer.

There are two parts to the Armed Forces Salute: **Hotel Discounts** and **Armed Forces Salute ticket vouchers**. We are going to go through everything, but if you would like to see the discounts on Disney's site you can do so here:

- Military Resort Discounts: https://disneyworld.disney.go.com/special-offers/military-hotel-rates/

- Military Ticket Discounts: https://disneyworld.disney.go.com/special-offers/military-multi-day-tickets/

Hotel Discounts: Each eligible person may book up to three rooms with the military discount. The eligible military member or their spouse must be a registered guest in one of the rooms. This means that your military uncle can't book for you, unless he's coming along (or at least checking in.) The other two rooms can be booked separately. They will have their own reservation numbers, and they can be paid for separately. This makes it easier for extended family or friends to enjoy the discount.

There are a specific number of rooms of each room type and at each resort that can be booked with the discount. You aren't guaranteed the discount just because you are an eligible military member. Rates can be sold out just like any other offer. Of course, if they are sold out, you can always keep trying just as you would with another offer, because cancellations happen all the time.

The military discount is considered a Room Only discount. This means that it can't be used with a package promotion (like free dining). You are able to buy tickets and the dining plan yourself though, just like with any other room only reservation. The dining plans are not discounted.

If you want the most bang for your buck, don't add tickets to your reservation through Disney. See the section below about tickets. Together the two discounts will likely put you under any other promotion that Disney offers, but of course, run the numbers to be sure. Especially consider that you can't use gift cards on military tickets, so if you have a great discounted gift card machine, you might be better off using those to purchase tickets at full price.

Here are the room discounts offered with the Armed Forces Salute promotion:

> Value Resorts (note that The Little Mermaid rooms at Art of Animation are excluded): 30% off
> Moderate Resorts (including the Cabins at Fort Wilderness): 35% off
> Deluxe Resorts and DVC properties: 40% off

Armed Forces Salute Vouchers: You can buy discounted park tickets at military bases and at Shades of Green. Look for a discount of four to five percent. You'll receive a voucher which will act as a ticket. It can be linked to My Disney Experience so that you can set up your FastPasses. But you're not quite done yet. When you arrive at Disney you will need to activate the vouchers at any Guest Relations. You will need your military ID to activate them. If you buy your vouchers from Shades of Green, you can skip this step as they will already be activated.

The vouchers expire December 19, 2018. A great advantage to them is that they do not expire 14 days after you first entry into the park. They can be used at any time throughout the year, up until December 19, 2018. This makes weekend trips suddenly more affordable.

Eligible military members are allowed to purchase either six Armed Forces Salute tickets OR enough for their immediate family's usage, whichever is greater. So, if you are a family of eight, you can buy eight tickets, but if you're a family of four you can buy six.

The Salute tickets (sometimes called vouchers) come as four-day tickets or five-day tickets. There are two types.

Park Hopper tickets are $226.00 for four days and $246.00 for five days.
Park Hopper Plus tickets are $266.00 for four-day tickets and $286.00 for five-day tickets.
Sadly, these cannot be paid for with gift cards. (Why doesn't Word let me use the crying face emoji?? I NEED it whenever I say you can't use gift cards.)

Park Hopper Plus tickets allow for entrance into Disney World's two water parks. They are able to be used in addition to the park tickets. So, if you purchase four-day Park Hopper Plus tickets, you would be able to go to the parks for four days and ALSO be able to go to the water parks four times. Now notice I said you could go to the parks four DAYS and the water parks four TIMES? That's because the water parks count each entry as a use of the ticket. If you enter, and then leave, and then come back, that's two entries, not one ticket as it would be with a Disney park.

This really means that the 5-day option with the water parks added could keep you busy for ten days. I would be comfortable planning a two-week trip with those tickets. Lots to do at the resorts on the off days. Remember too, that the tickets don't expire like normal tickets (they just expire completely on December 19, 2018), so you could enjoy four days at the parks and then come back two months later for a water park vacation.

Another option to stretch the tickets a little further is to purchase **Mickey's Not So Scary Halloween Party** tickets with the military discount. Ticket information hasn't yet been released as we go to publishing, but I'm comfortable sharing information based on past military offers. In the past, discounted tickets have been available to military members for some September Not So Scary Party dates. They were not available for preorder and had to be purchased on Disney property. They were around $50. Another thing to keep in mind is that military members are sometimes able to purchase tickets for a party even after it's been sold out to the public.

The last notable military discount is on **Memory Maker**. It can be purchased by eligible military members (or their spouses) for $98. Obviously, military ID will be needed and you can only purchase this in person at a Guest Relations at Disney. This is subject to the December 19, 2018 expiration date as well.

All Summed Up:

If you or someone in your party qualifies, the military discount will likely be your best move. And with tickets that don't expire after 14 days like civilian tickets, you can book a couple of weekend trips very inexpensively.

Part IV:
Lowering the Price of
Disney World Admission

I bet a day doesn't go by that someone doesn't ask in the Facebook group, "How can I get my Disney trip tickets as inexpensively as possible?" And I sort of want to throw this book at them because there's so much more to that question than they realize. I mean, there're three chapters in this section all about getting your tickets for less, I couldn't fit all that info in a Facebook comment.

We're going to go into lots of ways to lower the costs for your tickets, but before we get into those, I want to underline that everything we learned in the first section— Discounted Gift Cards, can be a huge way of getting your tickets for less. I've been getting my gift cards for over 20% off for years. That's a huge discount on tickets. Sometimes, you can stack that with the options we're going to learn about now, so keep that in mind.

I know you'll find something in here that will make your tickets cost quite a bit less.

The chapters in this section are:

Chapter Nineteen: Annual Passes for Everyone

Chapter Twenty: Authorized Resellers

Chapter Twenty-One: Lesser Known Ticket Savings Tricks

Chapter Nineteen:
Annual Passes for Everyone

(Even if you are only planning to go to Disney once, do **not** skip this chapter.)

It's no secret that Annual Passes (AP) can save you money if you go to Disney a lot. This is one of my biggest savings. I simply could not go to Disney World as often as I do if I had to pay for regular tickets. Platinum Annual Passes for those of us who aren't lucky enough to live in Florida cost $779. They come to $829.64 with tax. Platinum Passes are for the parks only and they do not have blackout dates. Platinum Plus Passes include the water parks and are about $80 more. The price is the same for anyone over 3 years old. My little Asher is turning three tomorrow as I write this and it's a little tough for me to think about paying $830 for his Annual Pass. Discounted gift cards make it a lot easier to swallow. (Writing the Second Edition now and Asher is four and I just renewed his pass.)

Annual Passes are a no brainer for my family, but they might be a saver for yours too. A lot of families like to go to Disney World once a year. I personally don't know how they go that long in between visits, but it seems popular. ☺ If you are going to go to Disney World twice and get four-day hoppers both times, you'll pay more for those eight days of tickets than I pay for 365 days of tickets with my Annual Pass. If you don't get hoppers, the breaking point is two six-day tickets.

How do you save with an Annual Pass? Simple, take two vacations, once per "year", but have them fall in the same 365-day period. So, trip #1 is scheduled for May 30, 2018 for seven days. Your Annual Pass will activate on May 30, 2018 and will expire on May 29, 2019. Plan trip #2 to end any time before May 30, 2019. Your Annual Pass will still be active and you won't need tickets.

Bonus if you figure out a way to add in a long weekend somewhere in between. But be careful, it's a slippery slope. This is how I started: "Babe, it's a savings. We want to go once a year, right? So, we have to get Annual Passes." Fast forward one year and I was figuring out how to get to Disney once a month (sometimes twice.)

Let's get into comparing the savings.

If you are going to go to Disney for a week once per year and you bought Hopper tickets each time, you'd pay $1,033.06. This is $203.42 more than an Annual Pass would be.

And that's just the savings from tickets. You also get a lot of discounts being an Annual Passholder. You get Memory Maker for free. You'll also save on your room, food and merchandise. You'll get free parking at any of the parks as well.

If you'd like to break up your Annual Pass costs into "payments" or if you haven't definitely decided on Annual Passes, you can book your package like normal and upgrade once you get to the parks if you'd like. This is especially good for stacking with the free dining promotion when it's offered. If you upgrade at the beginning of your trip you can use the perks the whole trip.

Another option is to buy passes from home and then be able to book your room at the Passholder rate. Disney almost always has a Passholder Room Only Discount available and it is usually much more attractive than what's available to the public. Even with all the tricks I know for getting rooms less expensively, the Passholder Discount beats them often. I used the Passholder Discount to book rooms over half the times that I went to Disney last year. This should tell you that it's a significant savings.

Read Here If You're Only Going Once

One other little trick to keep in mind before we really dig into the savings: if it's less expensive for your family to get tickets twice instead of passes (or maybe you're **only going once** and tickets are way less than passes), you may still be able to reap some savings with the Annual Pass discounts. You don't have to have passes for every member of your party to get a lot of use out of the discounts.

For example, if you get an Annual Pass, you're eligible for the room discount since you're the one booking the room. If you're in the car and you have an AP, the car still parks for free- even if you're only a passenger. If you're the one checking out with souvenirs you still get your discount, even if the item you're buying is for your son who is not a Passholder. You can still buy Tables in Wonderland (this will be discussed at length later) and use it to discount meals for up to ten people whether they are Passholders or not. You still get Memory Maker included so as long as your MagicBand is scanned OR you're friends on My Disney Experience with the person whose band is scanned, those pictures will show up on your account with no watermark.

As you can see, this can be a huge savings! You can also still plan the trip so that you get to use your Annual Pass (and all the discounts) twice so you don't need to purchase tickets again. Then, if it were me, I'd be planning a long weekend trip with my girls or maybe a one-on-one with one of the kids to make even more of my Annual Pass, but you already knew that I would suggest that, didn't you?

Annual Passholder Room Discounts

We went into the room savings in the resorts section, but I'm going to go over it again here too, because I feel like it will be helpful to have that all together in one place while your deciding if you should get Annual Passes.

Annual Passholder discounts typically range from 20%-35% off. In case you aren't familiar with how the discounts work, when the discounts are listed as a range (like 20%-35% off) the first number is usually for most Values and the second number is usually for most Deluxe Resorts. Moderates will fall somewhere in between (probably around 30% in this example.) Sometimes, some resorts or room classes will not fall into the usual category and those will be noted on the offer. Art of Animation and Fort Wilderness Campground are the two resorts that will usually have some sort of exclusion. You can find the current Passholder Offers here:
https://disneyworld.disney.go.com/special-offers/?type=passholder-offer

Looking at the past to try to predict the future, there were only three nights in 2017 that weren't covered by an Annual Passholder discount at some point. Comparatively, there were nineteen nights that weren't discounted for the general public.

Obviously, for those sixteen days that were covered by an Annual Pass discount, but not discounted for the general public, being a Passholder was a huge benefit. But even for all the other days where there was a discount for both, Passholders had an edge in two ways:

- First, the Passholder discount is 10%-15% HIGHER than the discount offered to the general public. The Passholder discount is usually 5% higher than the discount offered to Florida Residents as well. For example, the discount offered to the general public for stays May 28th-August 31st 2017 was 15%-25%. For Annual Passholders it was 30%-35%.

    o To put this in perspective, if a Value is $120 the general public will save $12 a night with a 10% discount. Over a seven-night stay, that's a savings of $84. A Passholder received 30% off during this time which would be $36 off a night, for a total of $252 on a seven-night stay. $168 more than a member of the general public.

- ○ This gap is somewhat intensified if you stay Deluxe. The general public would save 25% on a room that's around $400 a night. That's $100. $700 over a seven-night stay. Annual Passholders would save 35%: $140 a night or $980 over the same time period. An additional $280 over a member of the general public.

- Second, Passholders receive a lot more flexibility in booking. I believe that this is because Disney counts on being able to fill their rooms at the last minute with Passholders dropping in for a few days. Passholders don't have to plan so far in advance to be able to receive discounts (provided there is availability.) The Passholder and general discount do not usually run exactly on the same timelines so this is a little hard to quantify but look at these examples.

  - ○ Members of the general public had to book by December 21, 2016 for a discount on April 8, 2017 while Passholders could have booked up to April 7, 2017 for a discount on that same date.

  - ○ Members of the general public had to book by July 14, 2017 for a discount on

August 31, 2017 while Passholders could have booked up to August 30, 2017 for a discount on that same date.

○ Members of the general public had to book by October 7, 2017 for a discount on Christmas Eve, 2017 while Passholders could have booked the day of and still would have received the discount.

To wrap up resort savings, let me say that this has been a great benefit for our family. It's one of the things that has enabled us to travel to Disney so often, as the Value rooms are now maybe $84 for us. Then we pay with discounted gift cards at 23.5% off and that room only costs us $64.26 a night. For a four-night stay (which is what we normally do when I take one-on-one trips with the kids), the resort costs us $257.04 while it would cost a member of the general public $480 at full price, $432 if they received the 10% discount. You can see how this easily becomes a core part of my strategy.

Off topic tip: there is a weird situation with MagicBands if you order your passes from home. I can't understand it; it's very un-Disney to me. Here's the problem: you can't order your Annual Passholder MagicBand until your Annual Pass is active. You can't activate it until you get to the park. You can't pick up your Annual Passholder MagicBand in the park. You see the issue here?

You have to go to the park to activate the pass, THEN order the MagicBand to be sent to your home. So... you're at the park and your MagicBand is being sent to your home. If you have no MagicBand from a prior trip AND you're staying off site, you'll have to go without or buy one in the park. If you are staying onsite, you would be able to get your MagicBand from your resort stay with no issues and you can order your Annual Passholder band as an extra.

It's very strange and I can't believe this is Disney's policy, but I called multiple times to ask (because sometimes you get different answers with different Cast Members) and then also spoke to them in City Hall and they confirmed. I guess they assume you have a MagicBand already, which I do, of course, but my mom didn't and I found the whole thing annoying. I was able to add her to my room as a Day Guest (something we'll talk about further in the dining plan section) and use that MagicBand for FastPasses, but it didn't have her tickets or the room key on it. This is really no big deal, but I thought I'd mention it since it frustrated me for days! #typeA

So, that's the resort discounts. But wait there's more! Usually, Passholders save 10% on food and merchandise, but for some undetermined amount of time Disney is celebrating Magic Kingdom's 45th Anniversary and Annual Passholders are saving 20% off merchandise and 15% off some table service dining. You can also use your discounted gift cards to pay. So, if you have a gift card that's discounted by about 25% (like mine usually are) and you show your Annual Passholder card for another 20% off, you're suddenly buying merchandise at 40% off. The math is like this: the item is originally $10, you get $2 off as an Annual Passholder. You pay $8, but with a gift card that you only paid $6 for using our other strategies. So, you only paid $6 for a $10 item. Of course, since Disney is expensive to begin with, this puts it into the realm of reasonable!

Disney has already quietly ended the 45th Anniversary celebration and the 20% has continued so let's hope they'll continue the 20% forever. Regardless, you can go to this website and check out the discounts for Annual Passholders: https://disneyworld.disney.go.com/passholder-program/passholder-benefits-and-discounts

In addition to the discounts listed here, you are also eligible to buy the Tables in Wonderland card if you are a Passholder (or Florida Resident, or DVC member). Since this affects your dining costs, I'll go into a lot more detail about it in the Dining chapters but just so you aren't dying of curiosity, it is a card that costs $150 (it's $175 for Florida Residents, $150 for Annual Passholders and DVC Members) and it gives you 20% off at most Table Service restaurants. You can buy one for your spouse for $50, but one card covers up to 10 people as long as that person is paying the bill. That means that if you and your spouse both had the TiW (this is the common abbreviation for Tables in Wonderland, now you'll know it when you see it) card, you can extend the discount to 18 of your family members or friends and still cover yourselves. The list of participating restaurants will be in the dining chapter. Find out more about Tables in Wonderland here: https://disneyworld.disney.go.com/dining/tables-in-wonderland/

Disney also offers a renewal program on Annual Passes. If you renew 60 days before expiration or 30 days after, you receive 15% off your Annual Pass. This won't be beneficial to you if you are buying the Annual Pass to go twice, once per year. You'll want to let it lapse and then purchase it again for your third trip and time it right to cover your fourth trip as well. But if you turn into the addict that I've become (or maybe you just want to go a couple times a year) that renewal rate is really nice. And sometimes they renew for 13 months instead of 12. Between the extra month and the 15% off, it's kinda hard not to want to renew.

If you have trouble figuring out if Annual Passes would be a savings for you for your own situation, be sure to check out the pages in the workbook for this chapter. There are blanks to fill in that shows you which is a better option for you once you follow the directions. It's easy to follow.

But it's not hard to do it on your own if you don't have your workbook handy. Go here: https://disneyworld.disney.go.com/tickets/, choose the tickets you'd like for this year. If you want Park Hopper, and the Water Parks, make that selection. Then write that cost down.

Guestimate the number of days of tickets/Park Hopper/water parks for next year's trip and write that cost down. Then decide if you want Memory Maker for this year or next or both. If you want it one year, but not the other add $149. If you want it both years add $298.

Now, you need to add parking that you would pay if you aren't a Passholder. If you stay onsite that's $0, but if you stay offsite, take the number of days you'll park at Disney and multiply by $22. Don't forget to do this for both trips.

Lastly, estimate the savings you'll receive as a Passholder. The room (if staying onsite) is hard to quantify, but I'd figure at least 10%. Probably more, but 10% is safe. 10-20% on souvenirs (since we don't know if they'll extend the 20%), 10% on food. Don't make yourself too crazy, just make an estimation. Once you add that all up, compare it to $829.64 multiplied by the number of people in your party.

So, it looks like this. Add all of these:

- Tickets for the family for this trip including park hopper if you want it
- Tickets for the family for next trip including park hopper if you want it
- Memory Maker for this year if you want it
- Memory Maker for next year if you want it
- Parking for both trips
- Money that would be saved by having the Annual Passholder Discounts (room, food, merchandise)

Compare that total to:

$829.64 times number of people for whom
you are buying tickets.

If the first option is lower, buy tickets, but don't forget to look if you might save by buying an Annual Pass for yourself to nab all the discounts. If the second option is lower, buy passes.

All Summed Up:

Buying Annual Passes isn't just for Florida Residents and crazy people like me who go to Disney World as often as possible. It can save you money even if you typically only go once per year and even if you're only planning ONE TRIP EVER! Run the numbers and you may be surprised how much this little piece of magic can save you.

Chapter Twenty:
Authorized Resellers

This chapter is about how to get your tickets just a little bit less expensively. This is a strategy that is quick and easy, and if you aren't interested in playing around with gift cards/gas/checking accounts, etc. and are only looking to put in a minor amount of effort for a minor return, this is your chapter.

And you'll still be ahead of the game. The vast majority of people just go to Disney's website or ask for a quote from a travel agency and then they just pay whatever price is quoted to them. And they pay with a credit card or (heaven forbid!) a debit card with little or no cash back. These are the same people who complain about how expensive Disney is— I have no pity for them. They should have taken a few steps to change their situation. My policy is if you don't try to change your situation, you don't get to whine about it.

Let's talk about authorized resellers. What are they? They are companies who buy up tickets from Disney, and then resell them at a discount with Disney's permission. There are not that many of them out there, and if they don't say "Authorized Reseller" they are not one.

Do not take your chances on buying tickets from someone who is not authorized. You may be one of the lucky ones and it might work out for you, but I wouldn't chance it. It's too little gain for too much risk. And you already know that I'm not the risk averse type. I take lots of calculated risks, but buying tickets from an unauthorized source is not a good risk. Don't do it. Don't buy from eBay or from those places on I-drive that say they sell tickets for $60 a day. Don't buy from Craigslist. **Under no circumstances should you consider buying used tickets. They are attached to the person who has used them and you're likely to have trouble trying to use them.**

The reason that you do not want to buy from these types of places is because if something goes wrong or doesn't work, you have no recourse. The piece of plastic "ticket" someone sells you could be empty. It could be assigned to someone else. There's no way of knowing if the ticket will actually get you in.

Who should you buy from? First choice, Disney directly paying with discounted gift cards. But if you don't want to go that direction, my second choice is Undercover Tourist.

Because the resellers bought tickets at different times and different prices, the deals they offer on different options are different. My best recommendation is to decide what tickets you need as far as how many park days, and if you want hoppers or water parks. Then, compare the resellers on that particular option. Make sure that they all include tax and any shipping to compare apples to apples.

I'm going to compare a five-day base ticket for you here just so you can see the differences.

At this moment, from Disney directly, you will pay $370 plus $24.05 in tax for a total of $394.05. Now, I hope I'm not getting annoying with mentioning this again, but if you did a little work you could pay for these with discounted gift cards. From previous chapters, you learned to get gift cards for between 5% to over 25% off which would make these tickets $374.35-$298.30.

For now, let's ignore that and just say Disney's online price is $394.05. Shipping is not included, but Disney offers an email option so you shouldn't ever have to pay shipping.

If you buy at the gate, Disney's price jumps by $21.30. So, this same five-day ticket at the gate will cost you $415.35. That's what NOT to do!

Undercover Tourist would charge you $380.95 for the same ticket. Shipping is free, tax is included. You can have this ticket shipped to your house and it's refundable that way. If you have it emailed, it's not refundable.

Park Savers would charge you $381 also including shipping and taxes.

Orlando Fun Tickets would charge you $382.75 including shipping, taxes and "fees" whatever that means.

So clearly, Undercover Tourist wins by a hair vs. the other Authorized Resellers. I also looked at several others, but their pricing wasn't even good enough to mention. These are the ones I would advise you to compare. You can also google "Disney authorized resellers" and check more prices if you are so inclined.

I have purchased tickets from Undercover Tourist back in the days before I knew about gift cards and they were excellent. They have great customer service, and their tickets carry the EXACT same benefits as those purchased from Disney directly. I'm going to be a little obnoxious here and restate that because I see it asked again and again: Undercover Tourist's tickets are EXACTLY the same as Disney's.

That said, there is one little thing that you should know about them if you are planning to upgrade your tickets while you're at Disney (for example to add a day or to upgrade to Annual Passes.) When Disney upgrades a ticket, they take the value of the ticket when it was purchased and subtract it from the value of the upgraded ticket. This is true for all tickets.

What you need to know about Undercover Tourist tickets is that they may have been purchased for less than Disney's current prices and are therefore going to be valued less than Disney's current ticket prices.

So, take that five-day base ticket that we were talking about before: it's $394.05 with tax from Disney, but only $380.95 with tax from Undercover Tourist. If you wanted to upgrade to Annual Passes from a ticket you'd bought from Disney, it would cost you about $436 which is the cost of an Annual Pass ($830) minus what you'd paid already ($394.05.) If you wanted to upgrade to an Annual Pass from tickets that you bought from Undercover Tourist, you would pay $830-$380.95.

This means that when you upgrade you basically lose the discount you got from the tickets. Well, you would... if you didn't have this book! Because there is a way to keep it. Two things: make sure you use the tickets at least once before you upgrade. This may cause the value of the tickets to automatically bridge to the Disney price. Be sure you know your numbers going in, do your math and if you find that the price they give you to upgrade is wrong ask them to "bridge the tickets from the Undercover Tourist price to the Disney price." Reports are saying that they are not offering this, but if you ask for it, they have been honoring the request.

One other note on Undercover Tourist before we close out this chapter: they work with Mousesavers.com. Mousesavers has an email newsletter that goes out monthly. There is usually a promotion in there that can save you a few extra dollars. If this is something you think you might want to use, you should sign-up right away because their newsletter only comes out every so often. You can't sign-up and have the discount in your mail right away, so it's good to be proactive. Go here to sign-up: https://www.mousesavers.com/mousesavers-newsletter-signup/

I'm not an affiliate for Mousesavers, but just a note, I have learned a lot from them. They are really great with empirical data. They have lots of numbers on their site. I'm a fan. Check it out if you get a chance.

Once you receive their newsletter, look for this banner in the email:

Undercover Tourist Walt Disney World Hotel & Ticket Discounts

And here is the portion to look for to be able to save a few bucks on each ticket. You'll click through their link to save a little extra. I left in the part where they say their tickets have the EXACT same benefits as Disney so you could see that.

Tickets purchased from Undercover Tourist have the EXACT same benefits as those purchased at the Disney gate. You just log into MyDisneyExperience.com, create an account if you don't already have one, and enter the numbers off your Undercover Tourist tickets to link the tickets to your account. You can then use the tickets with FastPass+ and MagicBand wristbands.

Undercover Tourist's prices include tax and FREE shipping. When comparing prices with Disney, note that Disney does not include the 6.5% tax on its price lists.

- Click here for exclusive savings on Walt Disney World tickets from Undercover Tourist!

All Summed Up:

Authorized Resellers can save you a modest amount of money for very little effort. You should compare Authorized Reseller prices to see which works best for you.

If the Smiths just showed up and paid gate prices they would pay: $1,533.60 for their four-day base tickets (two adults and two kids.)

If they bought these same tickets from Undercover Tourist, they would pay $1,437.80. This is a savings of $95.80

If the Robinsons bought their tickets at the gate, they would pay $2,646.55 for their seven-day park hoppers (three Disney adults, two kids.)
If they bought these same tickets from Undercover Tourist, they would pay $2,385. This is a savings of $261.55

Chapter Twenty-One:
Lesser Known Ticket Savings Tricks

So far in this section, we've learned about two ways to lower the cost of admission to Disney World: Annual Passes and Authorized Resellers. In this chapter, we're going to learn about three more:

- Convention Tickets
- YES Tickets
- Tickets At Work

These strategies only work in certain circumstances and are less likely to work for you than the other items we've learned in this book, but I didn't want to exclude them. Skim this chapter and if nothing here works, no problem. But if it can help one person, I thought it best to include it.

Ok, first (and most likely to work for you, I'd say) are **convention tickets**. What are they? They are tickets that have been purchased in bulk for a big group.

They don't usually have **all** the power of regular Disney tickets, but the savings is so great that it might not matter.

Where can you acquire such a thing? A couple places. If you search for conventions going on at Disney World, you may find one that you'd like to attend that also offers convention tickets that would save your family quite a lot of money. I just went to a convention that cost around $500 for me to attend. I was offered convention tickets. I didn't need them since I have an Annual Pass, but the savings was over $100 per ticket and was even more as you added days. I also booked the hotel (Coronado Springs on Disney property) for quite a bit less than I would have been able to had I been booking on my own.

It seriously would have made sense for me to book the convention, pay the $500 and just do Disney had I not wanted to go to the convention. The discounts more than covered the cost of the ticket. Bonus if you can find a convention you're actually interested in and you hit a couple sessions and learn something! Also, you may be able to find less expensive conventions and lower your costs that way too.

If you are booking a convention that might further your business or income, many of your costs may be tax-deductible as well. We are going to learn a LOT more about this (because I am a total fan of legal tax avoidance), but for now, I'll just say your hotel, travel and some of your meals would likely be deductible if you're traveling for business.

And remember when we talked about Agency Exclusives? Those travel agencies have access to convention tickets when booking through an agency exclusive. No convention needed.

Let's talk about why you might not want to get convention tickets. First, they don't usually have the ability to be upgraded. If you're planning to get Annual Passes or maybe add an extra day to your tickets while you're at Disney, don't get convention tickets. There are rumors that certain Cast Members who know how can upgrade these tickets, but I would not chance it.

There are sometimes rules about them- for instance you might be limited on the number of them you can get. Or there may be rules about getting in after a certain time of day. They might expire sooner than normal tickets. Do not be scared by these things. They will let you know up front if any of them apply to you so you can make a good choice.

You can use Disney gift cards to pay for your tickets and hotel with most conventions. I couldn't do it from home so I just booked with a credit card and then asked at the hotel desk to have that refunded and to pay the whole balance with Disney gift cards. No problem.

Let's move on and talk about **YES Tickets**. This used to be a more useable strategy than it currently is, but it still might work for you.

YES stands for Youth Education Series and it's a program Disney has been putting on for years. It's very cool. I've attended several of Disney's backstage tours (though not a YES class) and they are amazing. You can learn so much in a very fun environment.

If you have kids that are the right ages, they might love to take one of these classes. You can see the classes offered and learn a lot more here: https://www.disneyyouth.com/programs/education/youth-education-series/

You will need to go as a group as these are designed for classroom field trips, but a group is only ten students (various ages welcome) so you may be able to make that happen even if it's not specifically a classroom of children-- a big group of cousins might do the trick.

The rules are not widely published any longer, but I'll tell you what I remember from when they were. The tickets were a STEAL. They were awesomely priced, but couldn't be upgraded. There were rules about when your class was held in relation to your vacation. The rules seemed gracious to me. It was something like you could get the discounted tickets for up to ten days before and ten days after your scheduled class. I believe you could get two discounted adult tickets for every participating child.

I'd speculate you can still use gift cards to pay for your tickets since they are directly through Disney. I have not done this, but I would be very surprised to hear that they wouldn't allow it.

The whole thing is very neat and I wish I could be a part of it. This may not help that many people who read this book, but if even one extra kid gets to go to Disney who wouldn't otherwise have gotten to go, I'll consider it a huge win and worth all our time learning about this.

Ok, finally, **Tickets at Work**. This is a corporate benefits program that offers discounted tickets to just about everywhere, here's the locations they offer:

Their pricing is decent. Better than Undercover Tourist, worse than convention tickets, but they can be upgraded so they have that going for them.

To get tickets from Tickets at Work, your workplace has to partner with them. Lots of big companies work with them and I see many mentions of them in the Facebook group. If your workplace doesn't already partner with Tickets at Work, you might even ask your company if they've considered adding them as a benefit. I got the feeling that it wasn't super expensive for the company.

I have used them before and I seem to remember that they saved me around 12%. You cannot pay with Disney gift cards. This means that if you can get your gift cards for more than 12% off, you should go that route rather than Tickets at Work. That said, I just shared a table with a family at Hollywood Studios and they said that they saved quite a bit more than 12% on their tickets, in conjunction with the education association in their state because the husband is a teacher. So, there may be tiers or some other mechanisms to save even more.

You can find out more here:
https://www.ticketsatwork.com/tickets/

All Summed Up:

These three strategies are less common and will work for fewer people, but they are worth learning just a bit about to see if maybe, just maybe, they can save you a bunch of money.

Part V:
Eating Well on the Cheap
With or Without the Dining Plan

Dining can be a pretty huge cost at Disney World. Depending on your party and your tastes, it's probably your first, second or third biggest cost associated with your trip, and yet it's one that lots of people don't plan for appropriately.

Even if you don't do ANYTHING to save money on dining (I totally know you're going to, but let's just pretend for a sec) even just having a good idea of what your costs are going to be will go a long, long way to improving your trip. You won't have that horrible "I'm not sure how I'm going to afford this" feeling in the pit of your stomach every time your kid says she's hungry.

But beyond that, you can do so much to reduce your costs. And you know my style by now: I'm not about living on bread and water. I want you to have the experience YOU want to have no matter what that looks like; I just want you to do it less expensively (providing that's what you want to achieve.)

Here are some worthy dining goals:

- To eat as inexpensively as humanly possible so that you can save your money for an extra day, an extra nice hotel, souvenirs, or just because your budget is so tight that it's the only way you can GO to Disney World (been there)

- To eat without needing to think about price

- To eat at all the best restaurants and drink all the drinks

- To just come away feeling satisfied, knowing you did your best to reduce costs, and you ate good food and had great experiences

Maybe one of those resonates with you, or maybe it's something else entirely, but I want you to know that your goal is the one that matters and what everyone else thinks is not important. So, as we move through this discussion remember: I don't have a dog in this fight. I don't want you to choose one thing over the other, I just want to give you the tools to make the decision and want you to have the best experience possible.

Here are the chapters in this section:

Chapter Twenty-Two: Intro to the Dining Plans,
Changes to the 2018 Plan

Chapter Twenty-Three: Should I Get the Dining Plan?

Chapter Twenty-Four: Dining Comparisons

Chapter Twenty-Five: Hacking the Disney Dining Plan

Chapter Twenty-Six: Stretching the Dining Plan

Chapter Twenty-Seven: Hacking Disney Dining
Without the Dining Plan

Chapter Twenty-Two:
Intro to the Dining Plans,
Changes to the 2018 Plan

I know that choosing whether or not to add the Dining Plan can be a volatile issue. Some people are dead set against it. Others are just as sure it's perfect for everyone. I don't believe it's near so black and white. It might be good for you and not for me. It's good for me some trips and not others.

But there are ways to maximize it, and I feel that if you do take these maximizing steps it can make any dining plan a much better deal for you.

The dining plan is a huge convenience. It's so nice to know that everything is paid. I'm a very frugal person (as you might be since you're reading this book) and it's hard for me to splurge. The dining plan helps me to know that it's all paid and I've done everything I can do to reduce the cost of our food. It allows me to relax and say yes more. I have to say no a lot. All the time. My three-year-old wants to take a bath by himself. No. My seven-year-old wants to go see what the electrician is doing in the barn. No. And the grocery store... it's a no mine-field. And I try to say yes whenever I can. I let my kids do unconventional things as long as they aren't in danger. I say yes.

The dining plan allows me to say yes more. You want a $5 slushy? Yes. Snack credit. You want a Dole Whip Float? Done. You want cotton candy? Sure. You want popcorn? OK, let's get some. And before we started staying onsite and I learned to hack the dining plan, I always had to say no to those things. Because three $5 slushies are $15 and five Dole Whips Floats? $22.50. So, I'm up to $37.50 and we haven't had a single meal. They still need breakfast, lunch and dinner and I know they'll want popcorn at some point every single day that we're at Disney.

Before the dining plan, I was a "no" mom. No, we can't have popcorn. No, we can't get slushies. The dining plan has changed my life and allowed me to see how nice it is to be able to have (some of) what you want. When I don't have it, the experience is lessened for me. I'm a huge fan and I urge you to think about your costs and make a good choice, but if you wind up on the fence or if it looks like the dining plan would cost just a bit more, my vote is to splurge a little and get a dining plan. I think you'll find that it makes you happier, and that's money well spent in my eyes.

The Plan<u>s</u>

I underlined the letter "s" in the title of this section, because, yes, there actually are three plans. Disney is very good at suggesting that most families chose **The Dining Plan** sometimes called the "regular plan" or the "table service plan."

This plan includes: one table service meal, one quick service meal and two snacks, per person, per night. Also includes one refillable mug per person.

- Per adult (10 years old and over) per night: $75.49
- Per child (3-9 years old) per night: $25.80

A lot of first time Disney go-ers do not even realize there is more than just one dining plan. If you call in to book your trip, you'll likely not even hear mention of the other options. They'll ask you if you want "the dining plan" and then book this one for you. They even named it "THE" Disney Dining Plan as though there was just the one. But you DO have options!

Here are the other two plans:

Quick Service Dining includes: two quick service meals and two snacks, per person, per night. Also includes one refillable mug per person.

- Per adult (10 years old and over) per night: $52.49
- Per child (3-9 years old) per night: $21.75

The **Deluxe Dining Plan** includes: three meals (any combination of quick service or table service that suits you) and two snacks, per person, per night. Table service meals include an appetizer on this plan. This plan also includes one refillable mug per person.

- Per adult (10 years old and over) per night: $116.24
- Per child (3-9 years old) per night: $39.90

Note: All prices in this chapter are from the 2018 dining plan. It goes up every year-- which is really the perfect segue into the next section...almost like I planned it.

2018 Changes

The big news is alcohol. It's included now. Yep, it sure is. Anywhere that serves alcohol and accepts the dining plan will allow you to order an alcoholic beverage as your drink with your quick service and table service meals.

You're also supposed to be able to include slushies, smoothies, premium hot chocolates, milk shakes and other premium drinks that weren't really included before. I say "supposed to" because I've already stayed on property six times with the dining plan in 2018 and I've yet to find a situation where I got more drink-wise than I would have gotten before. That part of it felt like Disney was already giving those to you for the most part, although not advertising it, and nothing changed except the advertising-- just my two cents on that.

To be honest with you, I was a little trepidatious about the whole thing because I thought the price was going to have to go up quite a bit to make it possible for Disney to offer alcohol and still make a profit on the dining plan. And the price did go up as it does every year. But how much was it going up? More than normal? Less than normal? Was there a normal?

Well, to answer that, I went back to 2015 and looked at four years (2015, 2016, 2017, and 2018) of dining plan prices. Here's what I found. (These numbers are rounded and in cases where the various plans changed by a close amount, averaged. Where the difference was significant, I mention it.)

- In 2016, the dining plan increased by 2% for adults and 9% for kids.

- In 2017, the dining plan increased by about 12% for adults and 19% for kids, but the Deluxe plan for adults actually decreased by 5%.

- In 2018, the dining plan increased by 9% for adults and 3% for kids.

I very rarely drink alcohol and would love to see an option to pass on having the dining plan cover alcohol/premium drinks at a lower cost, but I don't think Disney needs to complicate the dining plan any more than it already is.

That said, when I ran the math, I didn't feel like the addition of alcohol added that much cost to the dining plan. The prices went up by less than they had the previous year. It honestly feels more like Disney shifting to find the sweet spot more than the cost of alcohol driving the price up. Although, obviously, I'm sure they accounted for that somewhere.

All Summed Up:

There are actually three dining plans, not just "The Dining Plan" as many first time (and even second and third time) Disney World visitors believe. So, you're actually making a decision between four options:

- The Quick Service Dining Plan

- The Table Service Dining Plan

- The Deluxe Dining Plan

- No dining plan

Price increases and changes for 2018, aren't as concerning as they looked at first glance. They probably wouldn't change whether or not you would pay less on the dining plan or not. If the dining plan was a good choice for you in 2017, it's probably still a good choice for you in 2018. If you don't know whether it would be a good choice, then or now, don't worry, because the next chapter is going to help you sort that out.

Chapter Twenty-Three:
"Should I Get the Dining Plan?"

It's possible that this is the #1 most frequently asked question in my Facebook group. Whenever I ask y'all what you want to hear about, the dining plan has a 100% chance of showing up on the list. I believe it's because there's so many moving parts. Three different options (really four, if you include having no plan as an option... which it clearly is), different costs, different allowances. My brain is a decision-making machine (I mean, obviously, that's what brains do 😊, but mine is especially good at it) and I can even get myself in trouble with all the options.

I noticed though that I was getting pretty good at figuring this out for people with very little information. There were a few questions that I could ask and if I got the answers I could ask a few more and with that info, I could give them an answer that I felt had a high probability of being the right one.

With that in mind I created a quiz and uploaded it to my Facebook Messenger. You can click this link if you're reading the ebook, type it in (case sensitive) if you're reading the hard copy:
http://bit.ly/shouldigetdining You will probably then need to answer in the affirmative to give permission to open the link in your Messenger.

The quiz will ask you the questions that I would ask you if you wanted my opinion about whether you should get the dining plan or not. At the end, it will give you what my answer would be if we chatted about this. I'm not saying it's 100% guaranteed to give you the RIGHT answer, only you can truly arrive at that for yourself, but it will give you my opinion on your situation. Go do it if you're curious. It's fun! And free, obviously, 'cause you are my reader whom I love!

If you're not by your computer or phone (the quiz actually works best on a phone) or if you just aren't in to all that, I've given you a version of the quiz below. Since I can't hear you answer back, it gets a little convoluted and confusing, but I think it has value and if you work through it, it'll get you the tools you need to make the right choice for you. Here we go!

The single most important question that will help you answer whether the dining plan will save you money or not is:

Even with all the sharing that's comfortable for your family, will you use the entire dining plan?

The reason this is the most important question in my opinion is because in general the dining plans sell you a lot of food at a reduced rate. The Sam's Club of Disney food, as it were—buy in bulk and save. For the most part, if you'll eat all the food on the plan, it's a good indicator that you should keep entertaining the idea of the dining plan. If you wouldn't be able to finish everything in the plan, for everyone in your party, the dining plan may not be a good fit.

Also, if you didn't get the plan, would you eat differently? Eat less or less expensive things? And would you still be satisfied with the experience? If so, you need to keep reading because the decision isn't made yet. At least, it's not made from a "which is more cost-effective" standpoint. It's certainly made from the "better experience" standpoint, at least in my mind.

The next question that really makes a big difference in whether you should buy a dining plan is:

Will you want drinks other than tap water?

Drinks are included in the dining plan at every level. If your family would typically just get glasses or cups of water and forego the soda, chocolate milk, coffee, smoothies, and alcohol, you'll see less of a savings than another family who likes beverages and is willing to pay for them whether they are on or off the dining plan. Another way of looking at this would be to ask "Would having drinks included be valuable? Would it elevate your experience?"

If you can answer "yes" to both these questions (will you use the entire dining plan? Do you want drinks other than tap water?), there is a high probability that the dining plan is for you. If you got one "yes" and one "no" it might still be a good value.

Two "nos" makes it a pretty uphill battle for you to save money with the dining plan, except in certain circumstances that we'll get into later.

Let's dig just a little bit further into each plan.

Is the Quick Service Dining Plan Right for You?

Do you have at least one child for every two adults in your party?
Will you use the entire dining plan or close to it?

If you answered yes to both of these questions, the Quick Service Plan will likely save you money. If you want drinks other than tap water, the plan is even more likely to save you money. This doesn't mean it's absolutely the right plan for you, but it's something you should entertain. It is probably a better choice than paying out of pocket. Let's discuss the two questions a little more just to be sure.

Do you have at least one child for every two adults in your party? First, let me give you some examples of parties that would answer "yes" for this statement: One child, one adult. One child, two adults. Two children, one adult. Two children, two adults. Two children, four adults. Parties that would say no to this statement: two adults. One child, three or more adults. Two children, five or more adults. Three children, seven or more adults. Hopefully, you see what I mean. (If not, email me with who's in your party and I'll sort it for you.) Maybe it's just me, but I feel like people have a hard time understanding what I mean when I say this, so I tried to make it clear.

Ok, now that we know if you are a yes or a no, let me tell you why this matters. Done correctly (like you'll learn to do in the coming chapters), children save a lot on the quick service plan, while adults usually do better paying out of pocket. Children save so much that one child actually offsets the cost of two adults, and tips it into favorable territory.

Will you use the entire dining plan or close to it? Two meals, two snacks per day. It's not that much food for an adult who is used to breakfast, lunch and dinner and maybe a snack or two each day. Many adults may even need to supplement. I actually cannot live on just one quick service dining plan per day— I need to eat three times each day. But luckily, my kids don't eat their entire plan so I'm able to eat some of theirs.

Look at your party and think about whether they will eat two meals and two snacks each day. Then think about who would eat their extras if they won't finish it all. For instance, my son, Asher, will not eat two meals and two snacks every day. He's four. He may eat one snack and nibble off someone else's plate the rest of the time. But Mike and I will easily use his quick service credits for breakfast, leaving ours for lunch and dinner. Think about how that would play out in your family.

For me, I only need to get close. If 80%-90% of the plan will be eaten, I feel good about going ahead because I enjoy having the plan and because we can then bring home snacks and a little piece of Disney.

Is the Table Service Dining Plan Right for You?

Are you planning to do expensive one-credit table service meals, like character meals for example?
Will you use the entire dining plan?

If you answered yes to both of these, the Table Service Dining Plan will likely save you money. Bonus points if you want drinks other than tap water at most meals because the dining plan will cover those for you and you'll end up saving even more compared to paying out of pocket.

Let's discuss the two questions so you have all the info.

Are you planning to do expensive one-credit table service meals, like character meals for example? If you compared the out-of-pocket costs with the table service plan cost on inexpensive table service meals (meaning table service meals that cost less than the median for Disney table service meals), you would find that you'd pay less by paying out of pocket. Conversely, if you compare Disney table service meals that are above the median cost of a table service meal, you'll likely find that the plan will be less expensive.

Also, remember how I said this all gets a little confusing? We're there. If you are struggling to get through this, just head over and take the quiz. It's guaranteed to be easier than figuring out that last paragraph. http://bit.ly/shouldigetdining

Basically, it boils down to this: if you're tastes run on the expensive side, the plan is more likely to save you money than if you're happy at The Plaza with a burger and fries.

Will you use the entire dining plan? Just like we discussed before, it will be tough to save money on the plan if you are going to have some of it left over. This is because you are then using these credits that you paid for to buy things that you wouldn't otherwise buy. AND there's even more at stake with the table service plan since you paid more for it than the quick service plan and yet any unused credits still spend the same: a quick service credit can buy three snacks to take home and a table service credit can buy three snacks for the road, regardless that they cost you different amounts of money.

If you are planning to eat at the more expensive one credit table service locations and you'll use the entire plan, it's likely that the Table Service Plan will save you money over having no plan.

Is the Deluxe Dining Plan Right for You?

Are you planning to do expensive one-credit table service meals, like character meals for example?
Will you use the entire dining plan?
Will you use your meal credits for table service rather than quick service?
Do you have more children than adults?

If you answered yes to all of these, the Deluxe Dining Plan will likely save you money. Bonus points if you want drinks other than tap water because the dining plan will cover those for you and you'll end up saving even more compared to paying out of pocket.

Let's discuss the four questions so you have all the info.

Are you planning to do expensive one-credit table service meals, like character meals for example? If you compared the out of pocket costs with the deluxe plan cost on inexpensive table service meals (meaning table service meals that cost less than the median for Disney table service meals), you would find that you'd pay less by paying out of pocket. Conversely, if you compare Disney table service meals that are above the median cost of a table service meal, you'll likely find that the plan will be less expensive.

Also, remember how I said this all gets a little confusing? We're there. If you are struggling to get through this, just head over and take the quiz. It's guaranteed to be easier than figuring out that last paragraph.

Basically, it boils down to this: if you're tastes run on the expensive side, the plan is more likely to save you money than if you're happy at The Plaza with a burger and fries.

Will you use the entire dining plan? Just like we discussed before, it will be tough to save money on the plan if you are going to have some of it left over. This is because you are then using these credits that you paid for to buy things that you wouldn't otherwise buy. AND there's even more at stake with the Deluxe plan since you paid more for it than the quick service or table service plan and yet any unused credits still spend the same: a quick service credit can buy three snacks to take home and a Deluxe credit can buy three snacks for the road, regardless that they cost you different amounts of money.

Using the entire deluxe plan for everyone in your party is a TALL order. Three meals, two snacks per day. It's a lot. And if you share, you are likely to have a lot of food left over. Be very careful with this plan.

To put it in perspective, my family of six covered all our meals for four days with three deluxe meal plans for three nights. My kids are little, so it would likely not be enough for six adults, but still, I'm just saying: it's a lot of food. Another time, we used six deluxe meal plans to feed ten of us, and six of them were adults. The party was six adults, plus my four children. We actually had enough credits left over to take sandwiches from Earl of Sandwich with us to eat on the way home. That's become a tradition now. It's nice to have one last Disney meal on the road and Earl of Sandwich travels well and is delicious.

Will you use your meal credits for table service rather than quick service? The meal credits on the deluxe plan are not differentiated between quick service and table service. You can use them all for anything. So, as we learned before, you'll get more bang for your buck when you're spending them on expensive table service meals, rather than inexpensive quick service meals. If you're planning a lot of expensive table service meals, the deluxe plan could pan out for you.

Do you have children in your party? Just like with the quick service plan, the value for kids is a lot greater than for adults (we're going to talk about why in the Hacking the Dining Plan chapter). This means that if you have kids, it's possible that the deluxe plan might be good for you. Just be careful booking this. I don't want to see you pay too much, only to be bringing lots of seriously expensive snacks home.

All Summed Up:

The biggest factor in whether or not you'll save money on the dining plan is whether you will use the entire plan or not. Second biggest is whether you want drinks other than tap water.

Read through this chapter, but if it gets confusing, just head here: http://bit.ly/shouldigetdining and take the quiz in Messenger. It's fun and free and easier than slogging through this chapter.

Chapter Twenty-Four: Dining Comparisons

Now that you've looked at the three plans and their prices and perhaps taken a stab at either the last chapter with the questions to ask yourself or maybe the quiz, you're probably much better equipped to make a decision than you were coming into this section. And honestly, if you feel really good about your choice, you can skip this chapter completely. You probably have enough information to make an educated choice.

But if you are still on the fence or if you're a hyper-type A like me and you want even more information, I wanted to give you another tool to use to make these comparisons. This chapter is basically all the backstory of the quiz and the questions. It's the math I've done a lot of times that's made me able to tell you with some level of certainty whether the dining plan will be good for you or not after only asking a few questions. Here we go!

Let's look at two scenarios:

First, a family of four (let's call them the Joneses) is eating at the Plaza in Magic Kingdom. Mom and Dad get the two most expensive entrees: The meatloaf is $21 and the cheesesteak sandwich is $17. The two kids also have expensive tastes and they order the two most expensive kid's entrees: the cheeseburger is $11 and the chicken strips are also $11. The kids get their drinks included. Mom and Dad pay $3.49 each for a soda. Their bill comes to $66.98, but $71.33 with tax. The tax rate is 6.5% inside the Disney World restaurants (and at all the restaurants in resorts EXCEPT for the All-Star Resorts. They are in another county and their tax rate is 7%.)

Luckily (or is it?), they are on the Table Service/Regular/THE Dining Plan. They "spent" two adult table service credits and two child table service credits.

Did they really get a good deal?

Let's look at the cost of the Table Service Plan to see. They paid $150.98 (two at $75.49) for the adult plans for that day and $51.60 (two at $25.80) for the child plans for that day. It's tough to really compare here if you don't know a lot about the food at Disney because the cost for all four items (two snacks, one quick service and one table service) is lumped into one. Plus, the resort mug is tossed in there to complicate things further.

You can go crazy doing math if you're looking at menus thinking, "Well, if I got a waffle as a snack credit that would be $5.49, but then later popcorn is only $4.25 so that's $9.74. Our quick service meal might be Friar's Nook at $8.99, plus a drink. I wonder if I'll be too full for a slushy. Hmm, that's $4.69. But, if I only want a soda it's $3.29. But, I might even do water. And I always wanted to try Pinocchio Haus and it is right next door, practically. So, what would a quick service meal cost there..." And on and on and on and this is just one day we're looking at. You might just throw up your hands in confusion and say, "I have no idea how to compare this without going nuts and I don't care anymore. I'm going with whatever Disney (or my travel agent or my friend or LJ at Smart Moms Plan Disney) says I should do!"

But don't despair. You can compare this relatively easily by holding everything constant except for the one thing you're comparing at the moment. We are trying to decide if this particular table service is a good deal on the plan. So, first we are going to find a number that the table service credit cost the Joneses. Then, we can compare that number to their bill.

They paid $75.49 for the adult plan for that day and $25.80 for the child plan for that day. Multiply by two for two adults and two kids and they paid $202.58

((75.49+25.80)*2.) These prices include all taxes (so we'd want to compare the bill with taxes included.) They don't include tips and neither does the bill that we discussed before. This means we can just leave the tips off the calculations and tip the same no matter what. Tips are a non-issue.

So, starting with $202.58, let's back out the value of all the other items that the Joneses get and see what we're left with for the Table Service portion. Then we can easily compare the two and see how they did.

Total Price: $202.58 includes: two adult and two child table service credits, four quick service credits, eight snacks, mugs

Let's first back out the mugs. This takes a little thought. The mugs cost $18.99 if you pay cash for them at Disney, but I don't think that's a great way to value them. Would you pay that much if you weren't on the plan? Maybe, maybe not.

We drink water mostly, so the mugs aren't that valuable to us. We wouldn't buy them if they weren't included. Or maybe we'd buy one and share. So, I think about how much we really use it and decide how much that's worth to me. I probably drink two to three sodas out of the mug in a weeklong trip. My husband would drink about the same, plus he likes hot chocolate or coffee usually every night. I don't let my kids drink soda, but I let them get flavored water and they enjoy that quite a bit. I've decided that the mugs are worth about $1 dollar per night, per person to us. You may be similar or completely different.

How I came to this conclusion is by thinking about what I'd be willing to spend on the experience they give me. I only drink soda every other day or so on vacation, but I'd be willing to spend $2 on that soda so $1 a day makes sense for me. I'd buy my kids a flavored water for $1 every day. Mike gets a little more use out of it, but he would probably skip those drinks without the mug. So, a buck a person per night feels right to me.

If you drink soda out of the mug twice a day, and you'd be willing to buy those sodas at full price if you didn't have the mug, your value per day would be $7. If you get a coffee every morning and that would cost you $3 if you didn't have the mug, it's worth $3 to you. Look at your kids and spouse's usage of it too. Once you calculate it, you know that for every other calculation we're going to do.

If you would like more data as you decide what the mugs are worth you can take a look at this poll I took in the big Facebook group: https://www.facebook.com/groups/SmartMomsPlan Disney/permalink/2172948209595234/ I was actually surprised to find that the vast majority of families are using their mugs twice a day or more than twice a day, with once a day being the next most common response. This means that most families should probably value their mugs in the $6-$8 a day range.

Back to the Joneses. They like the mugs, they use them at one meal per day and they estimate that the mugs save them from needing to buy soda or coffee so they value them at $3/day per person.

Mugs: $3*four people= $12 in value each day. $202.58-12= $190.58 so now:

$190.58 includes: two adult and two child table service credits, four quick service credits, eight snacks

Now, let's attack the snacks because they are the next easiest to predict. Some snacks are $2, some are $6. A few are even $8. But for our purposes, we'd like to find an average value and stick with it. This will allow us to make a good decision without needing to do a bunch of extra decision making (what snacks are we going to want?) and math (adding all those up and finding the average cost.)

I figure the average value of a snack credit to be about $4.75. Sure, I could go nuts trying to only spend credits on the $5 and $6 and $7 snacks, but those aren't as readily available and they aren't the things my kids ask for. My kids want popcorn for $4.25. They want pretzels. They want what they can see. They don't want to go off hunting for the rumored pumpkin elephant ear that is $7.79 but is still counted as a snack credit.

If you know your family's snack preferences, feel free to come up with your own value of a snack credit. If you don't know yet, I feel comfortable telling you to go ahead and use $4.75.

The Joneses get eight snacks per day on their plan. At $4.75 each, they're worth $38 of the total cost. $190.58 is what we still had left to account for so we're going to subtract $38 from $190.58: $190.58-$38= $152.58

$152.58 includes: two adult and two child table service credits, and four quick service credits

Now, let's discuss the quick service credits. If you're observant, you noticed that I separated the adult and child table service credits, but I lumped all the quick service credits in together. This is because Disney does not differentiate between child and adult quick service credits. This is good news for us. We can use our quick service credit for an adult quick service meal. Two kids can share one adult quick service meal. This makes our job of comparing easier because we don't need to back out two separate amounts for child and adult quick service credits.

Now, let's discuss their value. Quick service credits range in value quite a bit. Some quick service meals are $7.99 some are $14.99. But I find that most of them are in the $11-$13 range and by the time you add your drink to it, you're closer to $15. It should be mentioned that you might want to look at what you would choose without the dining plan and think about the true value that way, like we did with the mugs. You can certainly go online and look at a few menus and get a general idea of the costs of things that your family likes to eat.

At this point, I use $15 because of my experience. Some will be higher, some will be lower and they probably don't average out to EXACTLY $15, but I feel good about my estimates. You can use this number too if you don't want to do the research, because this number won't vary as widely as the mugs.

From the "what would I pay in cash" angle, perhaps with scrimping I could eat cheaper than $15 per quick service meal. But, I have done that and don't want to do it again. In fact, I did this once when I stayed at All-Star Sports. I came away feeling like their food court was awful. But I liked the resort otherwise so I stayed there again, this time on the dining plan. Suddenly, their food was excellent! It was a life lesson to me. I'm not so interested in saving money that I'll sacrifice to that extent again. So, that makes $15 a good dollar amount to use looking at it from both perspectives.

The Joneses get four of these per day so the value for them is $60 (4*15=60). Let's subtract that $60 from the running tally: $152.58-60= $92.58

$92.58 includes two adult and two child table service credits

Now, we can easily compare. The Joneses paid $92.58 for the credits that they used for their meal at the Plaza. Their bill would have been $71.33. It's now obvious that they overpaid by about $21 for this meal.

So, should they have skipped the dining plan? Or chose a different one? We'll we don't really know that yet. We've only looked at one meal. Let's look at another.

Scenario number two: the next day, the Joneses have lunch at Garden Grill in Epcot. Garden Grill is a buffet and it costs $42 per adult and $23 per child. The Joneses' bill comes out to:
$138.45 ((42*2) + (23*2))*1.065 (tax).

All the math we did above, doesn't need to be done again. It's still going to come out to be $92.58 for two adult credits and two child credits. So, this time the dining plan SAVED the Joneses $45.87 (138.45-92.58). That MORE THAN makes up for the $21 they overpaid the day before.

Now, we've made this simple to go through and compare each table service and see where it falls when compared to the dining plan.

If the Joneses have enough expensive meals in their plans and those are important to them, The Dining Plan (Regular Plan/Table Service Plan) is right where they want to be. If they aren't all that interested in the expensive places, or they're planning late and can't get into all the "best" places, they can save money by paying out of pocket at the less expensive places or by choosing a different dining plan.

Quick Service Dining Plan

Now, let's move on and discuss when the Quick Service Dining Plan might be right for you. I'm a tiny bit hesitant to write this because I feel a bit like the quick service plan is a well-kept secret. I think it could work for a good many more people than take advantage of it, and I'd hate to see Disney raise the prices on it if more people start choosing it.

But you are my reader and I want good things for you so I'll share my secret!

Let's use the same method to compare the quick service plan. We'll add up what it costs per day and then break all the little costs out and see if we're ahead or behind.

Back at the beginning of the chapter, I told you the costs of the plan:

Per adult (10 years old and over) per night: $52.49
Per child (3-9 years old) per night: $21.75

And it includes two quick service meals and two snacks, per person, per night. Also includes one refillable mug per person.

If we looked again at the Joneses (two adults, two kids), they'd pay $148.48 for the quick service plan. (52.49*2) + (21.75*2) = $148.48

$148.48 includes eight quick service credits and eight snacks, and mugs

Now, let's back out the mugs. They might use it a bit more if they're on the quick service plan. They might choose to eat more of their quick service meals at resorts. But for the sake of comparison, let's just keep it the same. $12 So, $148.48-$12=$136.48

$136.48 includes eight quick service meals and eight snacks

Snacks are also going to be the same. We figured them at $4.75. $4.75*8= 38 So, our new number is $98.48

$98.48 includes eight quick service meals

We valued quick service credits at $15 each, so eight of them would be worth $120. Clearly, we've only paid $98.48 and we're getting $120 in value. This is a good deal. But I also like to look at it from another perspective too. We paid $98.48 and we are getting eight credits. That makes each credit worth $12.31. So, every time I get a quick service meal that costs more than $12.31, I'm saving money. When you factor in an entrée and a drink, almost every single meal that Disney offers will be over this threshold.

This plan is a good deal. If you're like most families and you use it all, it'll save you money. It pretty much doesn't matter where you eat. It's a good plan and I'm sad when I have to stay offsite and can't use it. But, I need to underline that this is a good deal because the Joneses have kids and use the kids' credit to pay for adult quick service meals. If the Joneses were two adults and they both paid $52 for two quick service credits and two snacks, that's no good:

        $52.49
        - 30.00 Value of two quick service credits
        $22.49
        - 9.50 Value of two snacks
        $12.99

$12.99 is a lot of money to make up for with a drink mug (it would have to be worth $12.99 to you EVERY DAY, not for the whole trip), or by choosing more expensive snacks or quick service meals or maybe with alcoholic beverages. To me, the adult quick service plan makes almost no sense. But toss a kid in there, and you're golden. The kid's breakdown would be like this:

$21.75
-30.00 Value of two quick service credits
-$8.25
- 9.50 Value of two snacks
-17.75

This means you're receiving $17.75 MORE value than you're paying for AND you haven't even factored in the mug. With the mug values added in, one kid can actually offset the extra cost of two adult meals plans. If you have a better than 1:2 kid to adult ratio then the plan gets better and better. Note: I have heard of people adding fictitious kids to their reservations. You can if you have the occupancy and aren't buying tickets with your package. Disney doesn't ask, doesn't care. That may break your moral code and if it does, don't do it. I'm luckily not in that situation since I have more than enough kids without adding fictitious ones. 😊 Just be aware that this means you will have quite a bit more food because of the extra people so do your math.

So, should all families with enough kids just get the Quick Service Dining Plan? No. Not at all. It's not going to be beneficial if you want to do a bunch of table service meals. If you want to do a few table service meals out of pocket, but mostly quick service, this is for you!

Deluxe Dining Plan

The last option available is the Deluxe Dining Plan. I've only used this plan in very specific situations. But when it's appropriate, it can save A LOT of money. But you have to use it like a scalpel. Very directed, very purposeful. Otherwise, you'll pay too much for it and then end up with too much food. Two wrongs that don't make a right.

See in theory, you can save quite a bit with the plan. $116.24 per adult and $39.90 per child. So, here's a little comparison to show you how this can save. The Joneses are two adults and two kids. They'd pay $312.28/night for the DxDP (this is a common abbreviation for the Deluxe Dining Plan).

> $312.28 Buys them 12 credits (table service or quick service), eight snacks, mugs
> - 12.00 The mugs are still worth the same to the Joneses so let's back that out first.
> $300.28 For 12 credits (table service or quick service), eight snacks
> - 38.00 8 snacks at $4.75 each are worth $38
> $262.28 For 12 credits (table service or quick service)

$262.28 for 12 credits means that the Joneses own these credits for $21.86 each (262.28/12). It would be tough to get $21.86 of value out of a quick service credit, but you could save quite a lot of money if you used those $21.86 credits to dine at table service restaurants.

To help illustrate this without getting too derailed on pricing for particular meals, I want to show you one meal price. I've chosen Hollywood and Vine's lunch pricing. I chose this because it is pretty much middle of the road in price for character meals. The costs are $41 per adult and $25 per child.

So, if the Joneses dined at Hollywood and Vine for lunch without the dining plan, their bill would be $140.58 with tax. With the Deluxe Dining Plan, credits to cover the meal would only cost $87.44 (21.86*4), an obvious savings of $53.14.

If the Joneses ate most of their meals at table service restaurants they would save a lot of money, especially since deluxe dining plan credits include an appetizer at table service restaurants. When we do this plan, we are usually able to feed the children with the appetizers (nachos, quesadillas, etc.), leaving the entrees for ourselves. If the Joneses ate at quick service restaurants, they would pay more on the dining plan than they would out of pocket.

It should be noted that, again, kids are what makes this work. The adult pricing is so high that it would be very difficult to make the plan worth it.

It's very hard to maximize this plan over any length of time. Do you want to eat three table service meals per day? You might want to one day, but the next you'll be dreading the thought of all that food-- not to mention all that time spent in restaurants. This is where the scalpel techniques I mentioned before come in handy. We are going to learn more about those in the next chapter: Hacking the Disney Dining Plan.

All Summed Up:

Comparing the different dining plans and the option of having no dining plan can be incredibly confusing and overwhelming because there are so many moving parts. We can make this a lot easier by holding everything else constant and just choosing one thing to compare at a time.

Chapter Twenty-Five:
Hacking the Disney Dining Plan

I hear a lot of surprise that I'm SUPER pro-dining plan, especially among the DVC/Annual Passholder set because a lot of the Disney veterans out there have experienced a dining plan fail and feel like they know better now. I just think maybe they haven't gotten creative enough.

I get it. I've done it too; I've had a dining plan fail, way back when I was a newbie. In fact, the first time I ever got the dining plan was a fail for me.

Quick story: The year was 2015. Mike and I and three of our kids (Cy wasn't born yet) were planning a stay at Port Orleans Riverside. Free dining was the discount we were using. I read somewhere that if you had free dining you could buy your children adult tickets and they would also get the adult meal plan. So, I called up Disney and asked and they said, "Sure. Just put them on the reservation as over 10 years old and they can have adult meals." Well, I figured we'd order one adult meal for them and they could share.

We had to pay for Adult tickets which were $20 more than Kids tickets, but we were planning to upgrade to Annual Passes anyway and there are not kids and adults Annual Passes, just one set price for everyone. So, that extra $20 would just go toward their Annual Pass anyway. It basically meant they could eat off the adult menu for free. I'm in.

Then, my mother-in-law asked to come along for part of the trip, but Disney wouldn't let her be on the res for only part of the trip so she had to be on the reservation for the entire time. There was a small fee for having three adults in the room ($15 a night if I remember right), and she paid for that herself. She stayed for four or five days and our trip was nine days. Since she didn't need as many days of tickets as we did, we all booked four-day tickets and then my immediate family upgraded to passes once we were on property.

I was super excited to realize that we could use her credits for the days that she wasn't going to be there. Between the kids sharing and my mother-in-law's extras, I was booking table service meals left and right. I wanted to try everything.

Well, where the fail part comes in is not at the price like so many DVCers' and Annual Passholders' experience. Our prices were super low (free!) and we had oodles of credits. In fact, THAT is where the fail comes in. I didn't realize how supremely frustrating it would be for us to need to be at a reservation at a certain time. And we ended up having two table service meals scheduled for many of the days. We aren't great at being places on time (#kids) and I felt harried most of the trip. It was so frustrating that we ended up cancelling several of the meals and then we had boatloads of snacks to take home.

So many snacks, in fact, that we physically could not take them all and ended up passing out Disney snacks to people at the airport. We had Disney snacks for months. We had so many that we got sort of sick of some of them. So, I learned a valuable lesson. You can have too many dining credits. I also learned that we don't enjoy having reservations. We'd rather fly by the seat of our pants. Now when we do have table service or deluxe dining, we just book a reservation an hour or so before we want to eat. We aren't picky about the restaurants at this point and we enjoy the variety.

In fact, this "fail" helped me make a personal policy: I never book a dining reservation that forces a park hop. I only book reservations where we're going to be because I just don't like feeling like we have to rush somewhere.

On that trip, we may have done better to forgo free dining and get the Annual Passes up front, book the Annual Passholder room discount and buy the quick service plan. I haven't run the numbers, but my gut says that actually would have saved us money because you pay full price for the room when you get free dining. It definitely would have saved us the frustration of running around to different reservations all day. Live and learn, right?

That said, this strategy of adult tickets for kids to get the adult dining plan does still work if you have free dining and it makes sense for you. I guess that was a bonus tip. Just make sure you run the numbers!

But on to some better hacks, because that one is not really that wonderful since you have to be on free dining and have kids to use it. In this chapter, we are going to cover several different ways to make the dining plan work better for you. I truly believe that Disney would want you to take advantage of these. They improve your experience and that is what Disney cares about. In fact, I think that if a significant number of people start doing these things, Disney may make changes to their dining plans—because they really do want you to have a great experience. They aren't trying to make that more difficult.

Why are kids such a good deal?

The first things that I want to remind you about are kids credits on the quick service and the deluxe plan. Remember we talked before about how kids make those plans a better option than they would be without children? Well, the reason for this is their credits are not designated for use on kid's meals alone. Their credits can be used on an adult meal as well. Disney doesn't differentiate them in any way. On the table service plan, kid's credits have to be used on kid's meals, but on the quick service and deluxe plans they do not.

If you're on one of these plans you can use this information to stretch your plan considerably. Let me give you an example: recently, we stayed at Fort Wilderness. We were eating at their quick service location. I ordered three adult meals. Mike and Seth (my oldest, 8) wanted burgers so we ordered two burgers with fries, and I ordered the half chicken with two sides. I got two sides of macaroni and cheese. I took some of Seth's fries and gave him some mac and cheese then gave the rest of that side to Cyrus who proceeded to pick up one noodle at a time in that adorable way babies do. The other mac and cheese was split between Ezra and Asher (6 and 3 at the time.) They actually eat less than the baby usually!

I had a ton of chicken and gave some to all the kids as well, and Seth gave me about a quarter of his burger in trade. Mike had his burger and fries and he even had leftovers. We had plenty of food. We even took some of the leftover chicken in a little box. We had a surplus. We spent three quick service credits.

The next day we were back there and while I was waiting for my number to be called, a mom came up and ordered food for her family. She got three kids meals: one chicken and two mac and cheese. She also ordered two adult meals. She spent five quick service credits. Here's the thing. The adult chicken comes with MORE food than three kids' meals. In this case, they were using the exact same containers for the mac and cheese— so what is a side on the adult plan is an entire meal on the children's plan and yet the credits can be used for either interchangeably.

If you use this hack at every meal, you can save quite a lot of credits and then of course use those to pay for an entire meal later— getting adult meals with those credits too.

For us, this means that we can use three credits instead of five at each meal. It almost doubles the meal coverage for us for the dining plan. We've gotten pretty good at eating on seven or eight credits per day without anyone feeling hungry or unsatisfied. If we were to eat the standard one-credit-per-person-per-meal (not including the baby), we'd use 15 credits per day So, we're saving about half with this technique.

This is also useful on the deluxe plan because none of the credits on the deluxe plan are differentiated by kid or adult. They are all just in one big pot. So, you can order an adult meal for your child at a table service meal with the deluxe plan, and those come with appetizers as well. We can usually eat on only two deluxe credits at table service locations because Mike and I will order what we want and will give the appetizers to the kids. They are often more food than a kid's meal. I usually end up sharing my food with the children too. I like to eat often, but I don't eat a lot at a sitting. And I still don't love booking reservations. We usually don't book and just try to get in somewhere an hour or so beforehand, like I said.

I know that what works for us will not work for everyone, but I share these examples to show you how this works in real life. For you, it might be different, but this at least gives you some tracks to run on and gets your wheels turning.

Now, this may actually create the problem of having TOO MUCH dining plan. Remember how we talked before about the #1 most important thing being that you'll use the entire plan? Well, if you're able to do all this sharing will you still use the entire plan?

For us, if our entire family has the dining plan (quick service or table service), we get ten meal credits per day, but we only use seven. This creates an undesirable surplus because we're paying for credits that we won't use. So, I put my thinking cap on and came up with several different ways to right-size the dining plan for us. I think you may find something that will work for you too.

Right-Sizing the Dining Plan

Before we really get into it, let me say: everything we're discussing here can be used for all the dining plans, but in some instances, I give examples from a specific plan. Don't let that throw you off.

Basically, the problem at hand is that we're getting a good deal on the dining plan, it just happens to be too much food for us (and for many out there), turning a good deal into a bad deal.

So, I thought about ways that we could fix this problem and here's what I came up with. The dining plan would be a better fit for us if:

- We had fewer plans for our family. We are a family of six (kids ages 8, 6, 4 and 1½), so we'd get 5 dining plans, but can eat with no out of pocket on only four quick service or table service plans or three deluxe plans.

  OR

- We had more days to spread the plan out a bit.

After I boiled that down, I got to thinking about how we could accomplish these things. Everyone on the reservation has to have a dining plan, so getting fewer plans was out. Or was it?

And you have to have the dining plan for your entire reservation so "spreading" the plan out over more days was out. Or was it?

Look at me trying to create some drama and suspense. It's probably just coming off as annoying though, so I'll get to the point.

I realized I could engineer those situations to a degree (and don't worry, because I'm going to explain these further):

- I could get fewer plans than people. If you're screaming, "Everyone has to get the dining plan or no one does." You're right, but keep reading because there's a loophole of sorts.

- Dining plans are sold by the night. So, you always get one "extra" day to use the food (four nights of the plan for the five days of your stay), but most of the time that makes sense because you're arriving and departing on your first and last days. That's like two halves making a whole. But I realized I could book a short stay with the dining plan and use it to cover the day before. I'll explain in much greater detail, don't worry.

First, let's get into ways to get fewer plans than people. There are a couple.

1. The Day Guest Method
2. The Two Rooms Method

The Day Guest Method

Everyone on the reservation has to get the dining plan. It's a Law of Disney. Well, one trip a long time ago, my mom came along unexpectedly and she wasn't on the reservation, but we had the occupancy for her. When we checked in, I added her to the reservation. The Cast Member was happy to add her, but he said, "She won't have ALL the privileges of an Onsite Guest. She will be what's called a Day Guest. She can utilize Extra Magic Hours, and I can give her a MagicBand but it can only open the door OR work for FastPasses, not both. Oh, and she can't get the dining plan."

WHAT? There's a way for someone to be on your room when the party has the dining plan and yet not need to have a dining plan????? There sure is. And it doesn't require you to break any rules.

Since that conversation, I have used this method at least ten times...actually, probably more like twenty. I will typically leave my husband off the reservation and then add him as a day guest. This also means we pay for one less adult dining plan. We usually do it that way if we are doing the quick service dining plan. We end up with four plans (one each for me and the three kids who are over three years old) and we have plenty of food at a low cost.

If we are REALLY splurging, we will do the deluxe dining plan for me and only TWO of the children. I'll leave Mike and one of the kids off the reservation to accomplish that, and then add them upon arrival.

Hurdles to making this work (and how to jump over):

- Magical Express: Technically, Mike shouldn't be allowed to ride ME because he's not on a room. When I get there and add him, he can then ride ME. This would leave him waiting for 45 minutes or so while I get to the resort and add him. However, we've just explained that he's a last-minute addition at the Magical Express check-in and they have let him ride with us 100% of the time.

- FastPasses: The person/people who is/are your day guests will not be able to book FPs at 60 days out.

  - This isn't a big concern for us since we have been able to use rider switch. I just book for myself and then rider switch for Mike to ride.

This may not work in the future, and it may not work for you, depending on your family.

○ There's another way to get around this, but it takes a bit of doing and might cost you $50 (probably not though.)

- Book your room as normal, leave the dining plan off

- At 60 days out, book your FastPasses.

- At 29 days out, call and remove your day guest from the reservation. As long as they have separate tickets or an annual pass, their FastPasses will stay in place.

- During that same call, add the dining plan.

- Technically, any change after 30 days should trigger a $50 fee but generally, Disney waives the fee if the change makes the trip cost more. So, adding the dining plan at that point should make them waive the fee. They could change that policy (and any policy) at any time.

- Tickets: If you are buying tickets for the entire party, you might feel like you need to have your day guest on the room at that point so they get tickets, but you can actually just buy their ticket separately. It makes it super easy if you have Annual Passes. Yet another reason to take the annual pass leap!

  o If you are doing the gymnastics above to keep your day guest able to score FastPasses at 60 days out, you should purchase his/her ticket separately first (and remember that tickets bought without a package are non-refundable except in certain circumstances. They can usually be transferred though.)

  o The day guest should then also be on the room with tickets until 29 days out. He'll have two tickets assigned to him at that point.

  o 29 days out, you remove him, remove his tickets that are with the package and add the dining plan. See above for info on the $50 fee.

Since I just listed the problems and made this sound really hard to do (it's not), let me give you a little math so you can be convinced this is worth sorting out.

When we do the quick service plan we get four quick service plans for the six of us by leaving Mike off (and the baby is under three.) We pay $52.50 for my plan and $21.74 for each of the children's plans. For $117.72 per night, we get four mugs, eight quick service meals and eight snacks. If you remember from the comparison chapter, I value quick service meals at $15 each, snacks at $4.75 each and the mugs at $1 per night each. At those prices, we receive $162 worth of food for $117.72.

When we do Deluxe it's even more of a savings. We do one adult plan ($116.25) and two kid's plans ($39.99 each), for a total of $196.23. For that, we get nine table service or quick service meals and eight snacks, plus the mugs.

If we just did quick service, this would not be a good deal. But back out the eight snacks at $4.75 ($38), and then take the $158.23 you have left ($196.23-$38=$158.23) and divide it by nine (the number of meal credits per day.) $158.23/9= $17.58. That's how much a meal credit costs us when we do this.

Chef Mickey's for $17.58 per person, even adults? Yep.
Ohana for $17.58 each? Uh-huh.
1900 Park Fare for $17.58 a person? You betcha.

It suddenly becomes affordable to do some two-credit meals. $35.16 per person for Brown Derby, Critricos, Le Cellier, Hoop-Dee-Doo Revue? This is worth looking into.

We just did Yacht Club with this method. Mike and I both ordered lobster thermidor. Ezra and Asher ate the appetizers and some of my surplus mashed potatoes. We paid out of pocket for a kid's meal for Seth. $12 for a kid's steak and he shared some of his sides with Ezra. We all shared the two desserts (and took a huge piece of cake home because we couldn't finish it.)

So, let's total this up:
Two credits for me: $35.16
Two credits for Mike: $35.16
Kid's meal for Seth: $12
Total cost (before tip): $82.32

That's right. My family of six ate lobster and steak, with appetizers and dessert at the Yachtsman for under $100. Actually, considering I paid for the dining plan with gift cards that were discounted by more than 20%, we ate for WELL under $100. Probably around $65. The check was over $200 before they applied the dining plan.

So, that's the day guest method. It's a good one.

The other strategy I mentioned was the **Two Rooms Method.** I'm thinking of when there's a larger party and you need two rooms. Remember we talked about this in the Resort Hacks chapter? So, a family of five books two Value rooms, instead of going up to a Moderate that sleeps five. Or when two parties travel together and get two rooms-- maybe grandparents or friends. You want to be on vacation together, but you don't want to share a room. This is a time for saving money.

I'm going to use my own family as an example here because this is perfect for us. We are a family of six. Right now, Cyrus is under three so we can stay in a room for five. Disney World offers standard rooms with an occupancy of five at some Moderates and most Deluxe Resorts, but not at any Values. You'd have to go up to a $300/night suite to accommodate five in one room at a Value. We compare the cost of a room for five and two Value rooms. If the Values win, this is a perfect situation for us to save on the dining plan.

The tendency here would be to split the family in two and put half on one reservation and half on the other. But this is not what we do. We are strategic about who we put on each room reservation. Again, I have three kids old enough for the dining plan. If I put those three kids on one room with one adult, I can buy the deluxe or the quick service plan for them and have enough to feed the other adult. That adult would be on their own reservation with no dining plan.

Let me emphasize, because I can hear you rule-followers screaming in my head, that this is not against any of Disney's rules. You are allowed to decide who is on which reservation. You are allowed to get the Dining Plan for one room and not the other. You are allowed to share your dining plan credits with anyone you'd like. I'm not big on rules. I think Dr. House said it best, "Rules are for people who can't think for themselves." But, this does follow the rules. Actually, let me say it this way: Disney does not have any rules preventing this.

Basically, in both these scenarios (the day guest method and the two rooms method) We created one party who has credits, and one who does not and then we shared with them. But I want to go a little more in depth and mention some other situations where this might work.

One idea that comes to mind is grandparents wanting the deluxe plan so that they can treat their kids traveling with them, but staying separately. Or kids wanting to bring Mom and Dad along and cover their food this way. This is still very similar to what I mentioned in the section above.

Where it starts to get a little different and make you think a bit more, is when you think about onsite vs.

offsite. Say you want to stay onsite, but friends or family are offsite. You can work it out with them and have them use some (and pay for some) of your credits.

I'm going to take this one step further into a gray area. This next step doesn't have any rules one way or the other. But, I feel like that's because Disney doesn't really know about it. If they did, they would probably make a rule against it. Just my thought. Still, there is no rule against it at this moment.

So, the scenario is this: you are staying offsite for whatever reason. Maybe it's a big party, and onsite would be too expensive. Maybe onsite is booked, maybe you prefer offsite (?!) You could theoretically (because I've never done this, but I would if it made sense), book a cheap room or campsite and add the dining plan on it and never use it. Just use it to get the dining plan.

You might be thinking, "Yeah, but you have to pay for the room/campsite." Sure, you do. But done right, and in the right situation this would still save you money:

If you had a big group with a bunch of kids, like when my brother-in-law and our family went to Disney two Februarys ago. We had five kids between us. And my in-laws came too so there were five adults as well. We stayed in a vacation home. I wasn't wise to this strategy then, but we could have rented a campsite and put one adult and the five kids on the reservation, booked the deluxe plan and had enough food to take care of all five kids and all five adults at a low price. When the campsites are $49 a night, this would be easy to cover in savings. Even when they are $79, it's possible to save.

You would think that staying offsite where you have a kitchen and can get groceries would challenge this and it really would. You would need to do the math and see what would work if anything. And, you'd have to be comfortable with the idea of renting a campsite and allowing it to sit empty while some other family could be using it. That personally doesn't bother me. I paid for it, it's serving my purpose, if they wanted it, they should have booked it before me. Maybe I should sublet it to them. Kidding, kidding, kidding (that really would be against Disney's rules.)

Now that we've talked about ways to get fewer dining plans than we have people, let's talk about how to get more bang for your dining plan buck when it comes to stretching the plan over more days.

Remember when we talked about **split stays**? Well, you could also do a split stay solely to use the deluxe or really any dining plan to your advantage. You could even stay at the same resort. You may even be able to stay in the same room! But if it's two reservations, you have more flexibility. It should be noted that you no longer need to have a package with tickets to book a dining plan. You do not want to do two ticket packages. Your tickets should be attached to your first reservation. Your second reservation will just be a room and dining plan, no tickets.

The way this would be advantageous is if you booked one or two or three (or really however many you wanted) days in one reservation with the deluxe (or any dining plan). Then the other reservation you would be able to skip the dining plan (or get a different dining plan.) This allows you the flexibility to save money.

My friend, Beth, and I did this not long ago. We did three nights on the quick service plan and three on the deluxe plan. During the deluxe plan time, we ate soooooo much great table service food. During the quick service time, we spent more time at the parks and grabbed food on the go.

You would load your more expensive meals during the time when you have the dining plan. Cinderella's Royal Table, Le Cellier, Brown Derby, and character meals.

Because the credits are good on the day you check-in and on the day you check-out, you can stretch the usage of them out a bit. So, if you checked in on Friday and had that reservation for two nights, checking out on Sunday, you could use the deluxe plan Friday, Saturday and Sunday. This would allow you to use the credits from two nights over three days. Suddenly, six table service credits seem more usable. You could do two table service meals a day for those three days (a character breakfast, light lunch with snack credits and then another table service dinner.) Or you could do Signature Meals that take up two credits.

This book would be a million pages if I went into all the ways you could use the plan to save at this point, but I think you have enough to go on and start doing a bunch of math. Enjoy dreaming about and planning for all those meals that you always wanted to do, but could never find a way to afford. Don't forget, it's also completely possible to combine the two methods.

All Summed Up:

Creativity counts when using the dining plan. It's a good thing many of us love to plan and treat it as though it's a part time job. This chapter has a lot of strategy in it that makes me want to break out a calculator and do some figuring. You can save by right-sizing the dining plan. You can do this by:

- Reducing the number of dining plans you have for your party,

- Strategically booking your stays to be able to use the dining plan for as long as possible.

Chapter Twenty-Six:
Stretching the Dining Plan

No matter what you do, which plan you get, no matter who's on it or who's not on it, optimize your dining plan with these four strategies:

- Share

- Ask

- Swap

- Save

Share

When it comes to food at Disney, if you don't share, you will either waste an alarming amount of food or stuff yourself so full that it will be hard for you to walk around and enjoy the parks. The portions are very large.

My kids are still little so we get away with this more than you probably could if you had teenagers. But we order two or three quick service meals and share them among the six of us.

As discussed before, Disney doesn't keep track of kids quick service credits and adult quick service credits. So, we simply do not buy any kid's quick service meals with our credits. We use them all to buy adult quick service meals and then we share. An adult quick service credit will feed all three of my big kids easily with some leftover for me to share. Then depending on how hungry my husband and I are, we'll get one or two meals. If we opt for only one, we might also use a snack credit for a side and share that too.

To stretch the table service plan, choose your restaurants carefully. Look at the restaurants that are not buffets. At buffets, you must use one credit per person, so there isn't the opportunity to share. That means my four-year-old son is using a table service credit for two chicken nuggets and a chocolate milk. We do like to do one or two buffets each time for the characters, but the food usually isn't the reason for a buffet at Disney. So, we mostly choose places that allow you to choose off the menu. This way we can share and stretch our meals a little further.

We talked about The Plaza in Magic Kingdom (remember the Joneses ate there?) so I'll use it as an example here too. It's not very expensive if you were going to pay cash, so if you aren't on the dining plan, it's a good option for you too.

At the Plaza, my three older children would order two children's table service meals. They don't need two meals, one would probably suit them fine, but I'll share some of their food. I'll also share some of the meal my husband orders. I enjoy this because I get a lot of little bits of food which is what I like. I feel like committing to an entire hamburger is a lot. If you dine with me, I'm going to ask you if we should order two things we both like and share them both. You're warned.

If I'm very hungry, I might order a side or soup as well, and just pay out of pocket for that. I pay with a discounted Disney gift card, not cash. For convenience, I charge it back to my room and then go pay with a gift card the night before check-out.

In this scenario, we've used one adult table service credit and two child table service credits, instead of two adult and three child credits. We can then do this at another restaurant, and use the one adult table service credit and one child table service credit that we saved at The Plaza. I would just pay for one more child table service meal at that time.

To balance this out, I like to sprinkle the buffets in throughout the week so that we don't feel constantly stuffed by too much food.

But all meals are not created equal. Some are better for sharing. I asked in the big Facebook group for the meals that were best for sharing and here's some of the responses:

½ Chicken at Cosmic Ray's, comes with two sides, Magic Kingdom
Hot Dogs anywhere, but especially at Casey's where you can get the chili cheese dog and have the chili on the side if you want, Magic Kingdom
Bounty Platter at breakfast, at most resorts
Turkey Leg, various locals
Combo Meal at Flame Tree BBQ, Animal Kingdom
Rancho Nachos at Pecos Bills, Magic Kingdom
Flat Bread Pizzas at Pinnochio Haus, Magic Kingdom
Fish and Chips, Epcot
Fajitas or tacos at Pecos Bills, Magic Kingdom

And here are some snacks that eat like a meal (or that at least will get you over the hump to the next meal):

Cinnamon Roll at Gaston's, Magic Kingdom
Beignets (six for a snack credit), Port Orleans French Quarter
Biscuits and Gravy in the Food Courts
Funnel Cake, Sleepy Hollow, Magic Kingdom
Egg Rolls from China, Epcot
Sushi from Japan, Epcot
Ham and Cheese from France, Epcot

Pulled Pork Fries from Flame Tree BBQ, Animal Kingdom

Three Different Kinds of BLTs at the Smiling Crocodile, Animal Kingdom

Mr. Kamals Seasoned Fries, Animal Kingdom

Chicken Curry Puffs from China, Epcot

Ask

There are almost always options that are not on the menu. Ask for what you want. Explain to the cashiers what you want to do. One way that this helps me is with snack credits. There are lots of things on the menu that you can buy with a snack credit. But there are even more things OFF the menu that you can buy with a snack credit.

I just ask at the counter, "Is there anything that's not on the menu that I can get for a snack credit?" Or I might be more direct, "I'm running out of meal credits so I'm trying to save them, but that (pasta, chicken, salad, anything not portioned already) looks yummy. Can I do a small serving for a snack credit?" They say yes more than they say no.

And so what if they say no? I'm no worse off than I was before I asked. But they usually say yes, especially if you're ordering other food. It's a good way to use fewer quick service credits. Get two meals instead of three, then use a snack credit for a small portion of something and then share it all between three people.

Swap

Swapping is a perfect way to get a little more out of the dining plan. You trade something in for something else. You can trade lots of things in. When we've had too many fries, we can trade those in for another side. Chips for fries, potatoes for salad. It's a way to get food that fits your situation a little better. This is another place where it can't hurt to ask.

At most resorts (almost all, I believe. Ft. Wilderness you cannot), you can also trade your drink in for a snack. You can only use this technique at your resort. You used to be able to swap everywhere, but the plan changed in 2017. You might still find some locations in the parks that will allow swapping, so I ask frequently, "What do I get with the dining plan?" and "Am I allowed to exchange my drink for anything?" Some Cast Members will allow it.

But this is very useful at the resort. We drink water most of the time anyway, but at the resort the mugs are great for coffee for my husband, flavored water for the kids and maybe one or two sodas a week for me. So, when we get our meals, we trade the drink in for something.

My kids love those three-to-a-pack oranges so they are a favorite. Or packs of grapes, or celery and carrots with ranch, yogurt, dessert. I'll try to grab something to supplement the meal since we're sharing credits. But we often don't even need it and we end up taking it with us to the park or back to the hotel room for a midnight snack. I like the fruit and celery for that purpose. My kids will eat them more readily when they are actually hungry. So, when they say they need a snack, I pull out the carrots and they get eaten. Magic.

Don't feel like you have to get a drink with every meal. Always ask. It's a great way to make the dining plan go a little further.

Using these strategies, we've not needed to buy any additional food for several trips now. We can feed all five (really six) of us with four meal plans this way. And we usually have extra credits to bring snacks home. We've gotten quite used to having Disney candy around the house for when a sweet craving hits. We almost always bring some of Goofy's Candy home with us.

Save

I had a really good friend who never took food home from restaurants. I asked him about it once and he told me he'd never really had enough food at home growing up and every bit of food had to be saved.

Getting a to-go box to take home made him think of the times when he would steal left-overs out of his neighbor's refrigerator. In short, it made him feel like he was poor and didn't have enough.

I felt bad for ribbing him and grateful that my own childhood was not riddled with such memories. To me, that to-go box just means bonus food. It means something that was tasty gets to be enjoyed again. And that no one is going to have to cook later.

Portions are large at Disney and you will have food leftover and if you don't have any hang-ups about it, taking your bonus food with you can be a great way to save some money. Just be prepared with sandwich bags or containers of your own because Disney is not that great about to-go containers. I grab a box of Ziplocs to take to Disney and throw a few in one of the stroller pockets to go into the parks with us.

Also, be smart about food and heat. If it's something with a bunch of mayonnaise (or anything that spoils easily), probably best to just toss it because of the mess and the spoilage factor. You don't want to take any chance of getting sick on your vacation.

For me though, my kids are going to eat three bites at lunch and say they're done. I can throw that away or I can put it in a plastic bag. Twenty minutes later, when they are hungry again, guess what's for snack? (Also, they eat more this way, knowing that they will get this chicken again as snack if they don't finish it. There's not going to be the option of a tastier treat down the road.) As I'm typing this, I'm sitting in the lobby at Bay Lake Tower at the Contemporary and we have the following leftovers in the bottom of or stroller: a piece of a cupcake (to yummy to trash), a taco from Pecos Bills (two of us shared one order and still had one left) and a half a container of bacon macaroni and cheese (ordered a side instead of a kid's meal and saved $3 and he couldn't finish.) It's a way of life.

All Summed Up:

Disney truly wants to make you happy so asking for what you want is a great way to get it—good advice for Disney and at home as well. Getting creative with how you order, sharing among family members, saving your leftovers for later and planning what you'll order can help you stretch whichever plan is right for you even further.

Chapter Twenty-Seven:
Hacking Disney Dining Without the Dining Plan

In this chapter, I am going to give you tracks to run on if you don't have the dining plan. There are many times that the dining plan doesn't make sense and there are still some things out there that can make dining at Disney a lot more affordable. In fact, I'm typing this from the bar at Port Orleans French Quarter and I don't have the dining plan this trip. So, I understand about not choosing the dining plan and I know the strategies to keep your costs low even without it.

Let's start by talking about the **discounts** that are available on dining. And I can't forget to remind you that you can pay for your dining at Disney with discounted gift cards, so your costs can be even lower than face value. You can either pay directly with a Disney gift card or, if you're staying onsite, charge it back to your room and then go pay your room charges with a Disney gift card the night before check-out. I actually prefer to charge to my room, because it's quicker and I get a printout of all my charges. It really helps since I hate keeping receipts, but like to keep track of my expenses, so I can make good decisions.

Ok, discounts:

- Annual Passholder- typically 10%

- Tables in Wonderland- 20%

- DVC Member- 10% usually, though it's not offered at many restaurants and at some Epcot restaurants it's up to 20% off

- Disney Chase Visa- 10% but only offered at a handful of restaurants

The Annual Pass, DVC Member and Disney Chase Visa discounts are self-explanatory, but Tables is Wonderland (TIW) needs a little explanation. If you remember, we mentioned TIW in the annual pass chapter because Annual Passholders are eligible to purchase it, as are DVC Members and FL Residents. It's not available to the general public.

So, what is it? Well, basically it's a discount card. It costs $150 for the first card and $50 for your spouse to have one too. But one card covers up to ten guests, so you can save your money on the second for your spouse unless you will split up or have parties of over ten. Otherwise, just one will do the job.

If you show the card at one of the 100 participating locations, you'll receive 20% off your bill. You also received complimentary valet parking when dining with your Tables in Wonderland card.

Good to know about the Tables in Wonderland card:

- All Tables in Wonderland locations are blocked out for Mother's Day, Easter Sunday, Independence Day, Thanksgiving Day, Christmas Eve, Christmas Day, New Year's Eve and New Year's Day.
- An 18% gratuity is added to your check regardless of party size
- You can get all the details straight from Disney here: https://disneyworld.disney.go.com/dining/tables-in-wonderland/

My Two Cents on Tables in Wonderland

I actually get this question a lot so I'll just tell you, I'm not a huge fan. I did do TIW once and found it to be quite a hassle for little return. Here's why it wasn't good for my family:

- We don't drink.

- Our checks are relatively low so 20% off doesn't amount to a lot.

- We already get 10% off at most locations because of the Passholder discount so the extra 10% isn't enough to get me excited.

- To break even on the $150 upfront cost, we'd have to spend $1,500 in food at the participating restaurants, without being on the dining plan. Even coming one week every month, we don't even come close. Here's the math on that: ($150/10%=$1500, the 10% is the difference between the AP discount and the Tables in Wonderland discount: it's the discount actually reaped by the TIW card.)

- When we had it, the locations that accepted it took forever to ring us out when using Tables in Wonderland. I think only a manager can do it or something. It was seriously crazy.

- I don't love being forced to tip. I'm a generous tipper unless you make me, then my rebellious spirit kicks in and I'm a grouch about it. I probably need to schedule a trip to a psychologist about it.

That all said, I don't think it's bad for everyone. If you have a large party, you ring up big tabs, you drink and have costs associated with your drinks, you go to Disney often and eat at Table Service restaurants without the dining plan, or do some combination of these things, Tables in Wonderland could be very good for you.

Here are the in-park restaurants that offer at least one of the four discounts:

Magic Kingdom:
Be Our Guest (Dinner Only): 10% for AP, 20% TIW
Cinderella's Royal Table: 10% for AP, 20% TIW
Crystal Palace: 10% for AP, 20% TIW
Liberty Tree Tavern: 10% for AP, 20% TIW
Plaza Restaurant: 10% for AP, 20% TIW
Tony's Town Square: 10% for AP, 20% TIW
Diamond Horseshoe: 10% for AP
Skipper Canteen: 10% for AP, 20% TIW

Epcot
Akershus Royal Banquet Hall: 10% for AP, 20% TIW
Biergarten: 10% for AP, 20% TIW, 10% Visa (Visa discount is Lunch Only)
Coral Reef: 10% for AP, 20% TIW, 10% Visa (Visa discount is Lunch Only)
Rose & Crown Dining Room: 10% for AP, 20% TIW, 10% Visa (Visa discount is Lunch Only)
Garden Grill: 10% for AP, 20% TIW
La Hacienda de San Angel: 10% DVC, Dinner Only

Le Cellier Steakhouse: 10% for AP, 20% TIW, 10% Visa (Visa discount is Lunch Only)
Les Chefs de France: 20% TIW Lunch Only
San Angel Inn: 10% for AP, 20% TIW, 10% Visa (Visa discount is Lunch Only)
Restaurant Marrakesh: 20% DVC, 10% AP, 20% TIW
Nine Dragons: 20% DVC Lunch, 10% DVC Dinner, 10% AP, 20% TIW
Spice Road Table: 20% DVC, 10% AP, 20% TIW
Teppan Edo: 10% DVC Lunch, 10% AP Lunch (AP discount is Monday through Friday only)
Tokyo Dining: 20% DVC Lunch, 10% AP, 20% TIW
Tutto Gusto Wine Cellar: 15% DVC, 10% AP
Tutto Italia Ristorante: 15% DVC, 10% AP, 20% TIW
Via Napoli Ristorante: 15% DVC, 10% AP, 20% TIW

Hollywood Studios
Hollywood & Vine: 10% DVC, 10% AP, 20% TIW, 10% Visa
Hollywood Brown Derby: 10% DVC, 10% AP, 20% TIW, 10% Visa
50's Prime Time Café Mama Melrose: 10% DVC, 10% AP, 20% TIW
Sci-Fi Dine-In: 10% DVC, 10% AP, 20% TIW
Tune-In Lounge 20% TIW

Animal Kingdom
Flame Tree Barbecue: 20% TIW
Pizzafari: 20% TIW
Restaurantosaurus: 20% TIW
Nomad Lounge: 20% TIW

Rainforest Cafe: 10% DVC, 10% AP
Yak & Yeti: 10% DVC, 10% AP
Tiffins: 10% DVC, 10% AP, 20% TIW
Tusker House: 10% DVC, 10% AP, 20% TIW

Ok, now that we've talked about discounts, let's get into some other strategies for making Disney Dining less expensive, even if you're not on the dining plan.

One strategy is to **eat at restaurants that are less expensive**. There are lots of locations that aren't really that bad in price in comparison to non-Disney restaurants. Some of these that come to mind are: The Plaza, Grand Floridian Café, Sanaa, 50's Prime Time, Beaches and Cream, Be Our Guest for lunch, Chef Art Smith's Homecoming, Coral Reef, Kona Café, Rainforest Café, The Wave. Among many others.

And you can always choose the less expensive items on any given menu. That can be a big savings. I'm thinking of a particular menu where the most expensive entree is over $60, but the least expensive is around $25. That's a big difference. Of course, if you have the cash and plan to splurge, ignore these tips and just get what you want. I'll show you how to search by price range soon.

Another strategy is to **eat breakfast or lunch at restaurants instead of dinner**. I actually like to eat a light breakfast in the room or grab a snack when we first arrive at the park and then eat "second breakfast" at around 10:30am or whenever the last breakfast reservation is for that restaurant. This way you get to pay the breakfast prices, but if it's a buffet they'll bring out the lunch offerings too. Plus, it's a really good time to take a break if you've been running around since rope drop.

For meals that have per person prices, you can't just order something small and save that way. But you can choose where you want to eat more carefully. When we were off the dining plan, but still desiring a couple of character meals, we **chose the less expensive restaurants, and the less expensive time of day**. Same experience (usually, maybe a different character or something, but nothing too crazy) and much less effect on our wallets.

Below are the prices for the meals that charge per person. Please note that the prices typically rise and fall based on demand, so they will likely be a few dollars different than listed if you go in a particularly slow or particularly busy time.

Set Prices for Meals:

First number is the estimated price per adult, second is estimated price per child.

*Cinderella's Royal Table Breakfast $60, $38
*Cinderella's Royal Table Lunch or Dinner $79, $46
1900 Park Fare Breakfast: $32, $20

1900 Park Fare Dinner: $45, $27
Akershus Lunch: $45, $27
Akershus Dinner: $50, $30
Chef Mickey Breakfast: $41, $25
Chef Mickey Dinner: $50, $30
Crystal Palace Breakfast: $34, $29
Crystal Palace Lunch or Dinner: $45, $27
Garden Grill Breakfast: $34, $20
Garden Grill Lunch or Dinner: $ 47, $28
Hollywood & Vine Dinner: $50, $30
Ohana Breakfast/Lunch: $34, $20
Ohana Dinner: $46, $26
Tusker House Breakfast: $30, $18
Cape May Café Breakfast: $36, $21
Be Our Guest Breakfast: $25, $14
**Be Our Guest Dinner: $55, $35

Dinner shows

Prices include tax and gratuity.

*Mickey's Backyard BBQ
        Category 1: $72 adults, $47 children ages 3–9.
        Category 2: $62 adults, $37 children. Prices

*Spirit of Aloha
        Category 1: $78 adults, $46 children ages 3–9.;
        Category 2: $74 adults, $44 children;
        Category 3: $66 adults, $39 children.

*Hoop-Dee-Doo Revue:

Category 1: $72 adults, $43 children ages 3–9.;
Category 2: $69 adults, $39 children;
Category 3: $64 adults, $34 children.

*Two Tables Service Credits
**Newly changed to Two Table Service Credits

To help plan for the meals that aren't price-fixed, here's how to **search by price range** on the Disney Reservation site:
(https://disneyworld.disney.go.com/dining/)

Just choose the type of dining you're looking for ("reservations accepted" will get you all the Table Service restaurants) and then check the two boxes for "$14.99 and under" and "$15 to $34.99".

Another strategy to help you pay less for dining while you're at Disney is to **supplement your meals with some groceries** in your room. You can have them ordered in from Instacart (https://www.smartmomsplandisney.com/instacart-explained) and it'll save you a lot of money. I like to have breakfast-y foods like yogurt, fruit, cereal, Larabars, etc. and then also things that make a good bedtime snack. Then, I don't have to leave the room to eat which is very important because my four-year-old son and I are both blood sugar babies. We need to eat or life is basically not worth living.

Sodas and beer, as well as milk are also much less expensive from Instacart than from Disney. If you want to get really crazy about saving, you can order stuff to make sandwiches, and take them to the park with you too. I do order soda to take into the park. It's easy to put a few cans under the stroller or in a backpack and then get a cup with ice at the parks. Like $0.30 a can instead of $3.79 for a fountain drink.

My final go-to strategy for saving on dining at Disney is to **order from the kid's menu**. No one cares if you do. And lots of times they have unique tasty items on the menu that sound better to me than the adult meals. I don't eat a lot, but I eat often so the portions are perfect for me. To be honest, I often can't finish a kid's meal.

Let me give you two examples: a couple hours ago, I arrived at French Quarter and I was pretty hungry. I had Bell Services take my bags and I went right to get some food. They have a choose-your-own pasta dish that is so amazing I come to French Quarter for it even when I'm not staying there. It was right around $14 with no drink. I was able to eat about a third of it. I put the rest in my fridge for a midnight snack.

A few hours later, I was hanging out in the courtyard doing some work and was hungry again. I thought about going to my room to finish my pasta, but I didn't want to drag everything back and forth so I went to check out what else they had.

I ended up ordering the kid's fish and rice bowl which came with one side (I picked carrots.) Picture below. It was a HUGE amount of delicious fish (they said catfish; I've never seen it prepared like that! But it was SO good) rice, beans, super yummy carrots AND kid's meals come with a drink. The cashier rang me up for milk, but I actually got apple juice. You can get soda too, or any of the other bottled drinks. I took a picture of my receipt for you too. It was $7.77 with tax, about half of what I paid for the adult meal. And I couldn't finish it all!

Now, I would advise caution with this technique because some kid's meals leave something to be desired and it's just not worth the savings in my opinion. At the nicer restaurants or places where there is a lot of theming, the kid's meals are likely to be delicious. At the Value food courts and restaurants with plain menus, you're more likely to get something bland. You can usually tell by the menu. Chicken fingers, hamburgers, pizza, and mac and cheese are going to show up regularly and generally not be fit for an adult's pallet. But I've ordered the kid's steak at Be Our Guest, Le Cellier, and The Yachtsman and it was every bit as amazing as the adult menu.

Before we finish this chapter, I want to mention something that is NOT a saver, because people sometimes think that it is and I don't want you to fall for it: leaving property to eat. This is not cost effective. We are going to talk more about the value of our time while we're on vacation in a later chapter, but let me explain briefly.

If a trip costs $2,500 for seven days, you're paying $357 per day to be on vacation. If you sleep for eight hours a day, you're paying $22 per waking hour. If you leave property to go to Burger King, it will take you at least an hour to get there between walking to the exit, catching the monorail, waiting for the tram, getting to your car, and driving to International Drive. Then you eat, drive back, wait to show your parking receipt, park again, wait for a tram, take the tram to the monorail, get through back check. It's at least an hour back, probably more.

So, you just wasted at least two hours of your vacation. That's $44 on the low end, probably more like $66 to save $10-$20 on a meal. It's a bad decision. Don't do it. Just use discounted gift cards to take the sting out of Disney's premium and stay in the park. Enjoy that two to three hours, and your lunch and know that you're doing the right thing.

All Summed Up:

There are lots of different ways that you can save on food at Disney even without the dining plan.

- Discounts: Annual Passholder, DVC Member, Disney Visa Cardholder and Tables in Wonderland.
- You can also pay for all your food with discounted gift cards.
- Eat at less expensive restaurants.
- Satisfy your Table Service desires at breakfast and lunch rather than dinner and you'll pay less.
- Supplement your Disney dining with some groceries ordered in. This is less expensive and very convenient.
- When appropriate, order from the kid's menu. Save about 50% and still enjoy delicious food.

In Conclusion:

I started this section on dining by telling you why I enjoy the dining plan. Here's a story to elaborate and close out these six chapters:

A few days ago, we were at Magic Kingdom for our last night in the parks. We were heading home the next day. We got some food and with one of the meals, I chose a slushy for the drink. That slushy was perfection. We were at Cosmic Ray's and it was the strawberry-lemonade one. Highly recommend.

Well, it was a perfect night for a slushy and we were all sharing it and really enjoying it. When we ran out, we decided to go back and get some more. We had extra snack credits anyway so I let the kids each have their own and I got one for myself too. The total on the cash register was $18.76 for 4 slushies. I'd never pay that in cash, but knowing that it was snack credits that were already a good deal, AND I paid with discounted gift cards... it just made the experience sweeter than it already was. We sipped our slushies and said goodbye to Disney World. Well, not goodbye, but "until next time."

Part VI:
Travel and Staying Off-Site

Let me start by saying I'm not the expert on traveling cheaply. Friends email me and ask for tips and I have to tell them, "If you're traveling to Disney, I can help you. But anywhere else, and your guess is as good as mine." Well, almost. I mean I do know some things. But I know A LOT about getting to Orlando on the cheap. And that's what you care about if you're reading this book.

And I have stayed off-site quite often over the years. And my brain just always searches for the least expensive way to do anything, so obviously, I'm good at staying off-site frugally.

This section contains four chapters:

Chapter Twenty-Eight: Flights
Chapter Twenty-Nine: Rental Cars
Chapter Thirty: Driving, Food, Hotels and Gas
Chapter Thirty-One: Staying Offsite

Chapter Twenty-Eight: Flights

In my mind, there are five big ways to save money on flights: **budget airlines, flying Southwest, using points, flying into and out of different airports and booking at the right time**. Let's discuss these individually.

Budget Airlines

I fly with budget airlines a lot. Enough that I'm pretty close to earning their frequent flyer designation for the year-- in March. This is by far my preferred way to save. But it may not work out as well for you. You'll see why.

The three budget airlines that I'm aware of are Frontier, Spirit and Allegiant. My favorite is Frontier. I love them. I've gotten flights for $19 each way from Cincinnati to MCO. For $19 each direction, they could throw cow manure at me as I boarded and I would still fly with them, but they have always been very kind and courteous. I sometimes feel like I have to pay more for good service, but not with them.

I used to fly Allegiant a lot, but they fly into Sanford (SFB). This is a big problem for tight budgets because you can't take Magical Express from SFB to Disney. You need to either rent a car or take a taxi or Uber/Lyft. This can add quite a bit of cost to the situation. And now with parking fees at Disney resorts, renting a car looks even less attractive. Uber is less expensive, but still up there. We Ubered from Beach Club to SFB and it was right around $80, but we needed Uber Family. The four seaters would be much less.

I have not flown Spirit, but I hear good things. They fly into MCO which is good.

On all of these airlines, you'll pay extra fees for things that are free with other airlines. I always hear the naysayers, "Watch out, you have to pay for bags and seats and your Coke. It's just not worth it." Apparently, naysayers are bad at math. If you pay $350 round trip and get 2 free bags, and I pay $100 round trip and pay for two bags at $50 round trip each, who is ahead? And a coke is $3. Come on. Don't be so lazy that you pay extra for the same thing to avoid math. How much harder is it to earn $100 verses doing some math and saving $100. Do it! I'm saying that to the naysayers. Not to you. You are probably not a naysayer if you made it this far into this book.

Another thing: I don't pay for those extras. You get a free personal item, pack your clothes in that. I do. My kids do. We *might* check one bag if we all go, but even then, we probably won't. We never pay for seats, we never pay for the flight to be refundable. We just pay the basic rate and take our chances. We have always been seated together, even when we've had a party of eight.

Go directly to their websites to compare:
Flyfrontier.com
Allegiantair.com
Spirit.com

The reason that you should go directly to their website is because their fares are less expensive there. I've seen them marked up by 50% on Expedia. I don't know who is getting that money, but I'm not falling for it.

It's not always that crazy, but it's always more. On the flight I just checked, it was about $10 more.

Expedia:

	3:15p - 5:32p	2h 17m	Nonstop	$157.40
	Frontier Airlines	CVG - MCO		roundtrip
				Select

Flight details and baggage fees ⋮   Satisfactory Flight (6.9 out of 10)

Flyfrontier.com:

CVG ✈ MCO   EDIT

1 👤 TRAVELING   12 MAY 2017 DEPARTING   18 MAY 2017 RETURNING

$147.40
BALANCE DUE

Another thing about Frontier, you should see if their Den Deals Program is worth it to you. You pay $50 to be a member and then you get cheaper rates. I have been doing it for years and it saves me quite a bit. But like I said, I fly with them almost every month. You should do the math and see if it would be worth it for you.

Just on this one flight it saved $16 per person. Across the five of us (baby is still free), that would save $80- paying for the price of being in the Den and still saving $30.

But these airlines don't fly out of everywhere you wish they did. I myself have to drive almost two hours to get to an airport where Frontier flies. I'm a-ok with the drive because it saves me a lot of money. I see a lot of people saying they can't fly Frontier because they don't fly out of their local airport, but they don't fly out of mine either. Search around and see if there might be somewhere they do fly from that might be worth it. Even if you have to drive five or six hours, if you save $200 a person across several family members, the drive might be worth it. You can add an extra day on your trip with that kind of savings!

I know that they are some extenuating circumstances, like maybe you have a job to get back to and you just don't want to "waste" a half a day driving, I get it. If you can't fly Frontier, Spirit or Allegiant, you have some other options.

Let's talk about Southwest. They are not a budget carrier per se, but their flights are always among the more reasonable. You definitely need to go to their website to search. They do not allow third party companies like Expedia to pull their prices.

You get more perks with Southwest:

- You can change flights without losing money.

- They offer more flight options than budget airlines.

- You get TWO free checked bags (what are these people taking with them? That would be ten bags for my family... we could fit nearly all our possessions in ten bags.)

- They don't assign seats.

- They sell priority access for $12.50 each way which gets you nearer the front of the line to choose seats.

- And they have famously good staff/customer service.

Another reason to choose them? Their credit card program. I already explained that I don't mind opening credit cards if there's a good enough reason. Well, this is a pretty good reason: getting almost free flights/massive discounted flights for my family for a year (or almost 2 years if we time it right). What? Yes. Let me explain.

Southwest has a credit card program through Chase. When you open a credit card with them, you can earn 50,000 Rapid Rewards points. You can use those points to fly Southwest. To give you an idea of how much points are worth, remember those dates I was looking at with Frontier above? Well, for similar flights Southwest would charge just under 15,000 points, plus the government would charge $11.20 for the September 11th security fee. This means that for opening a credit card, I'd get 3 free (almost free, stupid government) flights. That's not the same as basically free flights for a year, but we're not done yet.

		Subtotal	$11.20
			Fare Breakdown
		Total Points	14,835 pts
You can't find this great fare on any other website. Southwest fares are only on southwest.com®.	1st and 2nd Checked Bags Fly Free®* *Weight and size limits apply.	Bag Charge	$0.00
		Air Total:	$11.20

The 50,000 points count toward something called a Companion Pass. A Companion Pass gives your companion a free flight every time you fly. You can change your companion up to three times a year. So, in my family, I could earn the Companion Pass and choose my oldest son to be my companion. My husband could earn it and choose our daughter. The baby flies free, but we'd have to pay for our four-year-old son.

So, how would we earn it? You earn the Companion Pass by earning 110,000 Rapid Rewards points in a calendar year. The easiest way to do this is to open two credit cards each. Southwest has four different cards. Open two of them each, hit the minimum spend requirements for the bonuses and you should be at or right near 110,000 Rapids Rewards points each. Ding, ding, ding!

You don't have to spend the points on the Companion Pass; you aren't buying it with points. You just have to earn them to get the pass. This means, that between you and your spouse, you now have 220,000 points and two companion passes. For my family, this would buy us around 14 round trip tickets to Disney World, but with the companion passes, we only need three tickets per trip (Me, hubby, and four-year-old, the two big kids will be our companions and the baby is free.) This means we can go to Disney almost free (just government fees $11.20/person) four times, with points left over to cover two more tickets on the fifth trip. This would probably cover our travel for an entire year. I go to Disney more often, but my husband only likes to go once a quarter. I usually only bring one or two of my kids when I go without Mike.

Be aware that there is an annual fee for all the cards. And you'll get charged $5.60 by the government for each direction. The Annual fees vary from $69-$99 so the most you could pay is $400. The government's fees add up to $280 for the five trips. $680 for my family of six to fly to Disney five times? I just shake my head when I hear people say they can't afford to travel.

A few more things:

- You get the Companion Pass for the Calendar Year in which you earn it and in the next year as well. So, if you earn it in January 2019, you would have it for 2019 and 2020. So, time it right and you can have it for almost two years.

- You can use the Companion Pass even when you aren't redeeming points. Those flights we looked at before? We could pay for those and EARN points toward our next flights. They would cost $246.40, but remember that would cover your companion too! $123.20 per person? That beats Frontier, you still get all the perks we discussed from Southwest (like bags) AND you'd earn almost 10% of the points you'd need for another free flight. Those points would be worth around $20. That's *almost* like getting the flights for $113.20 each.

Enroll in Rapid Rewards and earn at least 1238 Points for this trip.
Already a Member? Log in to ensure you are getting the points you deserve.

You can't find this great fare on any other website.
Southwest fares are only on **southwest.com**®.

1st and 2nd Checked Bags Fly Free®*
*Weight and size limits apply.

Subtotal	$246.40
Fare Breakdown	
Bag Charge	$0.00
Air Total:	**$246.40**

- You can easily buy discounted Southwest gift cards. Sam's Club has them for about 5% off all the time. No shipping on them either. Remember, stack with Discover or Chase Freedom for 5-10% cash back. eBay, Raise, and Cardpool, often have sales as well and you can also get them at grocery stores—meaning you can use the strategies from the grocery chapter to get them for over 25% off.

- BUT, you can only use four forms of payment for each Southwest transaction. In our case above, we could easily break up the flights from a round trip into two one-ways and cover them with gift cards. If there are more people in your party you can break those up too. Check out for each person, or each leg separately.

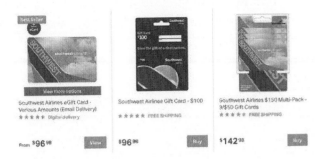

If we got these gift cards for 15% off and used the companion pass, we're looking at $96.22 flights to Orlando. Round Trip. $113.20*.85= $96.22 And remember this would be AFTER the five free flights my family would get from the sign-up points. I can't believe people say they can't afford to travel-- like it's expensive or something. ☺

Before you do this four-credit-card (or two credit card, if your family is smaller) maneuver, do your research. The Points Guy is very well informed about the Companion Pass. You can find his article on it: https://thepointsguy.com/2014/11/southwest-companion-pass-16-things-every-flyer-should-know/

While we're on the subject, **points** in general are a good way to save on airfare. I opened the Chase Sapphire Reserve card and got 100,000 points— $1000 for opening one card. These can be turned into Southwest Points. That was a special deal, but they are offering $750 in travel at the time of this writing:

http://bit.ly/ChaseLJ (case-sensitive) They have a $450 annual fee, but you get a $300 travel credit so that basically brings the fee to $150 and my favorite thing about this card is that it gets me into the airport lounges. This. Is. An. Amazing. Benefit. Open bars, free snacks, nice bathrooms, comfy chairs, showers at most international airports, it's worth the $150 for sure.

Also, you earn points by spending on a card. If your goal is to reduce your flight cost, you can choose a card that will benefit that end. Almost any of the Chase cards can help because you can save when you book through their portal, or you can transfer your points to Southwest. Make sure the card you're considering pays points in Ultimate Rewards points. The ones I have that do not are: Chase Amazon and Chase Disney.

Make sure you're paying for everything possible with your points card. Groceries, gas, dining, cell phone, utility bills, everything. If you're paying for it, pay for it with your points card. Go through your checking account and switch everything possible to your points credit card. Pay it off every month to avoid interest charges. If you can't do that, don't use a credit card. It's not worth going into debt over.

Next up, **using surrounding airports**. It's no secret that it's more expensive to fly out of some airports. If you have a few within a few hours of you, make sure that you're checking flights from them all. There are four near me that I routinely check. Cincinnati is the cheapest usually, but not always. You can set up your search for the carrier of your choosing and just change the "From" airport. This can be tedious, but it might turn out to be worth it.

Also, be mindful about where you're flying into. Most people choose MCO because that's where Magical Express picks up and drops off, but it's worth checking. If you have Allegiant in your area and they only fly into SFB, you might save more than the cost of a car rental by flying into SFB. I enjoy having a car. Magical Express takes a long time by comparison. So, if you can end up with a rental car and flights to SFB for less than the cost of flights to MCO, that's a no brainer to me.

Be sure to check Tampa. It's about an hour and fifteen-minute drive from Disney and you can usually get a fairly cheap rental car out of there. If you're staying on site, you could fly into Tampa, rent a car for one day and return it in Orlando. This is easy with National or Alamo (which are owned by the same company. They also own Enterprise as well.) The Car Care center on Disney property offers Alamo. National and Alamo are available at the Swan and Dolphin. You can return to those locations and take Disney transportation from that point on.

As a former rental car employee, I suspect that they actually need cars moved from Tampa to MCO and renting them one-way is a way for them to make money while getting the cars back to where they need them. This means that they are willing to rent cheaply, and you might even be able to negotiate for an even better deal.

You can then book a car back to Tampa OR fly home out of MCO. Just check around. It doesn't have to be as expensive as it first appears.

My last point on saving on airfare is **when to book.** It matters more than you think. Popular wisdom says to book 54 days before your flight and on a Tuesday or Wednesday if you can. That might be the lowest your flight ever costs. But then again, it might not. The only way to really get good at getting good deals is to practice.

How do you practice? Pretend you're booking flights for a few months out. Watch them. Decide that moment when you'd lock in the price and then watch and see how you did. Did you save yourself a bunch of money or did flights go down again after you "bought"?

Try again. Try again. Try again. It's not that time consuming and it gives you a really good sense of how you're doing. It gives you a level of confidence when you're ready to actually book. Getting good at this has saved me a lot of money over the years. I remember sitting next to a woman who had paid over $300 for the flight. I had paid $39.

People have written entire books about saving money in connection with flights, but this is a really good jumping-off point for flights to Orlando. There are other strategies out there—if you find something really great, send it to me and I'll add it to the next edition. Happy searching!

All Summed Up:

Flights are one of those beautiful things that really give me something to sink my obsessive money-saving brain into. There are many different strategies to think about and lots of math to do.

If you're not down for all that, start by seeing if Frontier flies to any airports near you. If they do, they're likely your best bet. If not, go to Southwest and check them out.

So much savings to be had with these five strategies:

- Budget Airlines
- Flying Southwest
- Using points
- Flying into and out of different airports
- Booking at the right time

Chapter Twenty-Nine:
Rental Cars

I'm not even sure if there's enough information here to justify a whole chapter, but I'll tell you what I know. I mentioned that I worked for a rental car company. I worked for them for almost a decade so I know how it works. Most "free upgrades" and coupons are smoke and mirrors.

Most rental car companies pay their employees some form of commission or otherwise incentivize them to sell you more stuff. That's why you need to tell them three times that you don't want the extra insurance. If you, in fact, do not want the extra insurance. I find more and more as I mature and so do my finances, that I'm willing to pay small amounts of money for peace of mind.

Your best bet is straight up negotiating with the salesperson. The person who is writing your contract is the only one who has skin in the game. Actually, the branch manager may have some, but not much. The young guy dressed too nicely to be renting cars? His paycheck and promotion is riding on what you decide.

A couple ways to work this: buy a coupon for $0.99 on eBay. Do not tell anyone that you have it when you make your reservation. Make the reservation for the vehicle size that you want. At that time, get a quote for the price for the next car size down. Write it down, date it. Get the person's name who gave it to you.

When you go in let them get most of the way done writing your contract. Ask if they have any cars that are nicer. Ask if they have any that are less expensive. If they quote you a lower price for the immediate car class below the one you have booked, you can say, "Oh, so that's the price I'm being charged? I have a free upgrade coupon here." If they only have more expensive cars, say "So, I can be upgraded to that for free with this coupon?" If you start the conversation with, "I have a free upgrade coupon" you have very little chance of actually getting an upgrade for free.

You can also negotiate if you're willing to pay for a bigger car or for their insurance products. Give them an amount you could spend. "If I had $10 more per day, what would that buy me?" Or "I'm interested in your insurance products, but they are too expensive. Can you give me a break on the car?"

I don't enjoy these conversations. I think it's because I was on the other side of it for too long so it feels like work to me. I feel slimy just thinking about how some of these companies conduct business. I generally don't try and save anything off what I'm quoted. To me, this is one strategy that just doesn't sit well with me. I just pick the lowest onsite car rental company and use them. I NEVER go offsite. Made that mistake once and I will never do that again. The car rental location was very shady AND it took me about 30 minutes to even get over there. I ended up Uber-ing and didn't even rent from them. I wish I could remember their name and tell you who to definitely avoid, but honestly, just stick with those onsite. They have rules to follow in order to stay there and they want to make you happy.

At MCO, the low-price winner is usually Advantage. I have rented from them many times and they are good. No trouble. No pressure.

You can also book your rental car early and continue checking for the rates to go lower. They usually do. You can **cancel and rebook** as often as needed to get the lowest rate possible. I have ended up paying less than half of what I was originally booked at.

The only other "trick" I know to getting rental cars cheaper is by using Discover Cards rewards. They will give you a $40 certificate for $20 in rewards points for any of the Enterprise Holdings car agencies:

Enterprise, National and Alamo. These can be used like cash at these locations. Unlike most other coupons, these will really save you $40. Discover is paying the rental car company the $40. I know because I use to process these receivables on the regular.

This is a stretch, but a huge saver on a rental car- have you thought about not getting one? The parking fees at Disney make it pretty unattractive to drive. Just hop on Magical Express and then use the internal bus system. Uber when you want.

If you're staying offsite, Ubering might be less expensive than a rental car. Say you're going back and forth to the parks every day. $15 each way? Could even be less. $30 a day and you will save on parking too. That can be quite a saver and it's super convenient too. Much more convenient than driving and parking for sure. One tip on Ubering to Magic Kingdom- they don't pick up or drop off at MK, just the Transportation and Ticket Center then you ride the monorail to MK. Instead, you can have them drop you at The Contemporary and you can walk to MK. When leaving at night, walk to The Contemporary and then summon an Uber.

I definitely Uber any time there is more than one step in Disney transportation because of the time it takes. I figure I'm on an expensive vacation—time is costing me; I'm paying a lot to be there. Let's just say the average (inexpensive) vacation costs $2,500 and lasts seven days. We're being very conservative here. If that's the case, you're paying $15 an hour to be on vacation—including hours you're asleep! If you only count waking hours, those are $22. So, if it's going to take a half hour longer to use Disney transportation, that's $11 of your time. That should usually be plenty to go ahead and get an Uber.

I would like to encourage you to figure out your cost per hour on vacation and use it as a benchmark when deciding what to splurge on and what to save on. If you are frugal to a fault, like I can sometimes be, this can really help you relax and spend the money to enjoy your time because it's logical.

All Summed Up:

Rental cars are no longer a necessity to a fun Disney World vacation, even if you're staying offsite. Uber and Lyft have made it pretty easy to get around without strings attached and without paying a boatload for parking.

If you do need a rental, use a coupon, book and rebook, always book the onsite rental companies and if you have Discover Rewards, you can sometimes double them as rental credits.

Chapter Thirty:
Driving, Food, Hotels and Gas

Driving is deceiving. It seems to cost very little, but it costs more than you see at first glance. Gas is all people think about, but there is a lot more to it than just gas. There are costs to your car— the wear and tear on your tires and brakes, the mileage, the depreciation. Your car will be worth less money at the end of the trip than it was at the beginning. Since you aren't planning on selling it soon (probably) you won't think about that stuff, but it is worth considering. There's other costs to consider as well—your time is valuable and it will probably take longer to drive; you might have extra food or lodging costs to consider as well.

The IRS says you can write off 54.5 cents when you drive business miles. That's interesting to us for this chapter because we can use that figure to approximate how much a mile might actually cost us. 54.5 cents per mile includes all costs, but it turns out I was going to have insurance that month anyway, so I don't think it's fair to consider my insurance cost. Same with my driver's license, my license plates and the tax on my vehicle. I was going to incur that anyway so 54.5 cents just feels too high to me.

I should say that this is what I did for a living for a long time. Almost a decade. I was employed by a company that small businesses paid to evaluate their vehicle usage and help them put a plan in place to lower their vehicle costs. I've run more numbers on this topic than I care to remember, so when I have a feeling it means more than the average Joe's feeling.

So, I figure my costs at 40 cents a mile. That's how I decide if we want to drive or not. Other factors play a part as well, but cost is always a big one. We drove last month. It was because I would have needed four plane tickets at over $200 a pop. Not expensive to most people for sure, but I didn't want to spend $850 on flights.

Compare that to the 1,700 miles we needed to drive (850 miles each way) and you see that driving was a little less. 1,700*.40= $680 ($680 vs $850.) This left me $170 to cover hotels and food on the way there, and back. I was able to stay in that budget.

So, why would I choose to drive vs fly when it cost virtually the same thing? A few reasons.

- I am good at buying gas, food, and hotels so I knew I would actually pay less for those things.

- $800 in cash today for flights is a lot different than around $370 in cash (gas, hotels, food) plus $400 in wear and tear on my car. Cash is king as they say.

- Also, I'm in no hurry. We didn't have a limited amount of time to be on vacation. We could go when we wanted and return when we wanted.

- The airport with four kids in tow—do I need to say more?

That's a basic "how to" on making the decision to drive vs. fly. It can really help to think about the true costs to drive, not just the cash costs.

Ok, now on to saving money. We've got three moving parts here: gas, food and hotels. Maybe you can drive straight through and not need hotels. If that's the case, I'm happy for you. And jealous. I thought I was moving close enough to be able to drive straight through. It's 12.5 hours for me, but it expands to about 18 hours with four kids. I've given up trying to drive it straight for the time being and I figure it'll be easier when they're older.

My best advice for saving on gas, food and hotels is the same: discounted gift cards. Some of the same strategies from previous chapters will work here too:

- **Raise/Cardpool/CardCash/eBay**: buy gift cards at a straight discount. Be sure to stack a cash back card in. You can get all kinds of restaurants at a deep discount this way. Hotels.com is occasionally on sale through eBay too, so set up a search for that. There is an app called Swytch that also offers gift cards at a discount occasionally (especially on Hotels.com)

- **Grocery stores**: my Kroger has all kinds of restaurant cards and gas cards. I like to stock up before we travel. I try to buy different ones that I know my kids like. Wendy's and Panera Bread are always favorites. They also have gas cards and Hotels.com gift cards. Using my fuel points tricks, that means I can get at least 23.5% off hotels, gas and food. Go check out the grocery chapter if you need a refresher.

Hotels.com has become my go-to to book hotels. The prices are decent when compared to other sites and they have a program where after you book and stay ten nights with them you earn a night for free. That's basically 9% off. And I do very well getting discounted Hotels.com gift cards from many different sources: Kroger, eBay, Amazon (Lightning Deals), Raise, Cardpool, Swytch.

One other trick- especially for those who don't have a Kroger or Giant Eagle near them. Kroger is in the following states: Alabama, Arkansas, Delaware, Georgia, Indiana, Illinois, Kentucky, Louisiana, Maryland, Michigan, Mississippi, Missouri, North Carolina, Ohio, Oklahoma, South Carolina, Tennessee, Texas, Virginia, West Virginia. But the main one we care about right now is Georgia.

If you're driving to Disney World, chances are good that you're going to be in Georgia at some point and you're going to need gas while you're there. Well, if you plan it out right, you can stop at Kroger, open up a Kroger card, and buy some gift cards. You probably won't get them at 4X Fuel Points, but you'll at least get them at 2X. That's 7% off if you get the max of 35 gallons. You may even get lucky and get them at 4X.

You could buy Disney or Hotels.com, or restaurant gift cards. Go back out to the parking lot, fill up your tank and get the savings right there.

I've heard rumors that Kroger is piloting a program that would allow the cost of gas to be depleted all the way to 1 cent instead of limited just to $1.00 in Fuel Points. I ran into this in Tennessee on the way down once and we were able to use $2 at one time. Let's all say a prayer that they roll this out to the entire country!

All Summed Up:

Food and gas are some of the easiest categories to save on. It does take a little thought and a little planning, but it's not difficult.

Look at each time you pay for something as an opportunity to save. But don't take it so far that it isn't fun anymore. Don't stay somewhere gross to save $20. You will know when you go too far with saving money because it'll be uncomfortable. Just back off a little from that line and enjoy the savings and the experience.

Chapter Thirty-One:
Staying Offsite

This chapter wasn't in the original book. Honestly, it was a situation where I felt like what I knew was pretty common knowledge, but I've realized after years in the Disney space that many people do not know how to balance saving money with still having a great experience. I can help with that.

First, you'll remember that I'm pretty hard-core about staying onsite. I find the experience to be so much better and more enjoyable. But I do still stay offsite sometimes. Here are the situations that I find make staying offsite make sense:

- If you have a large party and want to stay all together- you aren't interested in booking a couple or a few rooms at Disney.

- You have serious food issues (like allergies or want to eat all organic, etc.) and you need a kitchen. Kitchens at Disney are expensive.

- Lots of private space is important to you or maybe you want a private pool.

- Disney is sold out or super-expensive for your dates.

I go to Disney at least once a month, and a few times a year I run into one of these reasons to stay offsite. I travel with many people so sometimes we have a large party. My hubby really likes organic food so we sometimes like a kitchen. Sometimes, I book last minute and Disney is sold out (or like only Yacht Club is open for the bargain price of $7,383,373 per night.)

Where do I head to check for good deals?

Five main places:

- eBay
- VRBO.com
- Airbnb
- Hotels.com
- Credit Card Points

eBay? Yes, eBay. I seriously save so much money on places to stay on eBay. There are lots of private vacation home owners who list their properties on eBay and remember you can grab discounted eBay gift cards from the grocery store and save even more.

I usually start by searching in Lodging with a search term for the month that I'm hoping to travel. If I have a specific arrival or departure date I look for that too, but most of these places will have some flexibility with dates.

The homes I have booked last minute on eBay for pennies on the dollar are amazing, but even if you can't do last minute, you can probably still save quite a bit of money.

Next, **VRBO.com**. This is a site that brings vacation home owners together with people who want to rent them. The site takes a portion of the income, but I find the pricing to still be good. You can search pretty effectively on the site too- you can select the bedrooms, bathroom, pool, hot tub, etc. and it's nice to not need to sift through all of their properties for what you really want.

If you are new to the idea of a vacation home, it's no big deal to rent one. You'll pay, sign a contract and fax it back. No big thing. They might take a security deposit in case you trash the place, but just don't trash it and you should have no trouble getting it back.

I always look for Disney themed bedrooms for the kids and they also really love bunk beds. It's nice to mix it up a little bit too. We also really like having our own pool and hot tub just out the back. It doesn't quite make up for it not being Disney, but it's better than not being on vacation.

Another little saver that I've found over the years, is using VRBO to find a good vacation home and then looking for that home elsewhere on the internet. I can sometimes find the owner advertising in another way and because they aren't paying VRBO the booking fee, they can offer the home less expensively.

Airbnb is very similar to VRBO.com, but I find them to be a bit more expensive. You can usually get discounted gift cards for Airbnb so that evens it back up for me. There are more unique situations on Airbnb in my opinion. More space sharing, which isn't really my thing what with the four crazy children. Also, I found a nudist home on there once. #tempting #not #dotheywashallthechairs

I just talked a bit about **Hotels.com** in the last chapter because I use them all the time for my hotels on the way to and from Disney, but they have hotels everywhere. From the previous chapter: Hotels.com has become my go-to to book hotels. The prices are decent when compared to other sites and they have a program where after you book and stay ten nights with them you earn a night for free. That's basically

9% off. And I do very well getting discounted Hotels.com gift cards from many different sources: Kroger, eBay, Amazon (Lightning Deals), Raise, Cardpool, Swytch.

Finally, **credit card points**. This isn't one that I thought of immediately for offsite, but many of my credit cards that give me points for spending allow me to turn in those points for travel at a discounted rate. Chase is one of the best. My PayPal card is decent too. We talked about this at length in the Chase Sapphire chapter.

They basically offer travel as one of the reward options and they list the points values that are needed. Cash in your points for hotels, flights, sometimes gift cards. They even have Disney hotels, but not at great rates.

I have booked the small cheap hotels on I-drive with points and had a good experience. Just make sure you don't go too cheap because some of those hotels are not so comfortable. Been there.

All Summed Up:

Staying offsite can make sense occasionally, and when it does there are things you can do to make it less expensive and a better experience. These are my go-tos:

- eBay
- VRBO.com
- Airbnb
- Hotels.com
- Credit Card Points

Part VI:
Saving via Mindset Change

Let me start by saying that this section is sort of my baby. This information has without a doubt changed my entire life. It's the piece of the puzzle that I needed to live a much better life. And it's the thing I didn't completely say in the first edition. I felt like I needed to focus and stay on the topic at hand: Disney. But now I'm more confident that you'll get to this section and give me the benefit of the doubt. Hopefully, I've provided enough value so far that you'll read on even knowing that some of this won't directly impact your Disney trip- except for that if you spend a lot less overall, you'll have a lot more to spend on Disney!

Here are the chapters in this section:

Chapter Thirty-Two: Lower Taxes, Please
Chapter Thirty-Three: Tax Savings via Disney

Chapter Thirty-Four: Saving on Life and Applying it to Disney
Bonus Chapter Thirty-Five: Planning for All the Hidden Expenses
Afterword: Learning to Find These Strategies Yourself

The second tax chapter, Chapter Thirty-Three, will get into how Disney can help you apply this info. You may be tempted to skip Chapter Thirty-Two, but please don't. If I had to pick what part of the book is most valuable in dollars saved, it would be Chapter Thirty-Two. Taxes are most people's (almost everyone's) highest expense. If you can find a way to lower that amount, it's a huge mountain to chip away at. Most of this book can save several thousand on a trip that was going to cost you maybe ten grand. But this part can save you thousands upon thousands over your lifetime.

Chapter Thirty-Four will address lots of other places in your life where you can save money. Every cent you save in your life can go to Disney. Or you know, retirement, financial freedom, whatever it is you want. Mostly Disney.

The bonus chapter is something that helps me enjoy Disney a little more in connection with money, so I thought I'd include it for you, even though it's not strictly about saving money—more about internal financial peace while at Disney. Good stuff.

Chapter Thirty-Two:
Lower Taxes, Please

Most people give the government too much of their money. This is fact. Most people pay more in tax than they legally have to for a variety of reasons:

1. They don't know any better.
2. They are scared to take their allowable deductions.
3. They don't do a good job keeping track of their expenses.
4. They don't want to think about it.
5. But the biggest reason is: they don't set up their life to pay less tax.

I'm going to put a thread I recently saw on Facebook in one of my business owners' groups. Three reasons to include this:

- Because I get excited when I see Facebook screenshots in my reading material (and I'm hoping you do too.) It's like a break from thinking or something.

- Because this thread is so extremely right on.

- Because social-proof. Smart people out there are saving money on their taxes and it's not tax-evasion, it's not crazy, it's not hard.

 Carlotta Thompson is 😟 feeling concerned. ⋯
February 4 at 10:54pm

Tax Strategy is FREE MONEY! Why do people not care more about it??? I stay baffled at people just going to get their returns prepared and never wondering how to pay less. Most preparers don't provide this service. Get your head out of the sand and keep more of your dang money! It is too hard to earn to give it all to the government.

I am not talking about TAX EVASION or anything crazy! I am talking about making use of the freaking rules that are in place to help you save money so you can in turn put more of it into your business in order to grow the economy!

The government wants businesses to pay less tax because it means you can create jobs and grow!

14 Reactions 53 Comments

 Amy Van Ollefen I know a lot of people who like getting ripped off by the government. Seriously.

One, they love getting a giant tax refund every year, and two they think saving money on taxes somehow equals tax evasion and scamming the government and money laundering. Maybe you can find a way to address some of these things, because I can't believe the mindset I have run into when talking to people about ways to pay less tax. I'm somehow ripping off poor people because I want to keep what is legally mine. Huh? How about this, I do your tax returns, and I keep all the money you save instead of giving it to the inefficient government that wastes money and supports things I don't want my money going to. Sheesh.

Like · Reply · 1w 👍 2

Carlotta Thompson I am trying to educate as an Ex IRS agent. I feel like they may trust me. People have a crazy mindset.

Like · Reply · 1w

Michele Riffe The same way they think by going to one tax prep company over another will get you more money back. HUH? You should get the same money back (or owe) regardless of who prepares your return unless the returns are being falsified. No matter who prepares them (assuming qualified) you should get the same results.

Like · Reply · 1w

Amy Van Ollefen Carlotta Thompson that's part of what people have a problem with. I don't get it at all. Rich people and corporations with legal tax strategies that are not available to poor people so they are unfair and they need to pay! Not really true. I don't get it. People don't even know how the tax system in America works, or where their taxes are actually going or being spent on. Maybe you can start there, that might be the root of the problem.

Like · Reply · 1w

Carlotta Thompson People will fight to double their income to have more after tax income when they could do some tax strategy and have the same after tax income making a lot less.

Like · Reply · 1w

I just happened to see that and thought it was the perfect segue, because honestly for decades, I was one of the people that the original poster was concerned about. I didn't want to think about taxes at all. It hurt my head. It was like this big black cloud of the unknown and I didn't want to take the time to go dig around in that cloud. And honestly, how much money could it be? I did not want to get involved. But, boy, am I glad that I did!

437

I first heard about "bringing down your tax burden" or "paying less in taxes" a few years ago and the concept frustrated me. I often listen to books on my radio as I drive. I remember a particular day, an author I love and respect (Robert Kiyosaki) on the radio talking about lowering your tax liabilities, and I responded out loud (because that's how curious and frustrated I was), "How do you do that? Don't you just owe what you owe?"

Later that day, I found myself with an odd amount of time between meetings and ducked into a Christian book store to kill a little time. Inside, they were playing Christian radio and I heard Dave Ramsey doing his podcast. Wouldn't you know that he mentioned paying less in taxes as a way to get out of debt? Now I was really intrigued. Dave Ramsey and I share the same faith and he definitely has my respect (even if I don't love all his teachings.) I felt like if he said there is a way to lower your tax burden, then I believed it— and believed that it wasn't morally wrong.

I walked over to his section in the Christian book store and started paging through some of his books. I did find some good basic information about tax credits and making sure that you take all of your tax deductions, but his books aren't exclusively about taxes and I knew I needed more information. Next morning, I headed to the library.

Over the next few months, I read several books centering on taxes and I started to get the picture. One of the most helpful ways for me to understand what works to build wealth is to learn about what wealthy people do. I feel like this is truly a rubber-meets-the-road situation. It's not theory. Wealthy people are, almost by definition, good with money. Sure, there are some who inherited their money, or married into it, won it in the lottery maybe. But most of those won't be able to keep it and again the money will find its way into the hands of someone who knows what to do with it and how to keep it. I want to end up as one of those people someday.

One of the books that I read discussed how the wealthy deal with taxes. Let me quote directly from this book. It's titled <u>Millionaire Next Door</u> and it's written by Thomas J. Stanley. "To build wealth, minimize your realized (taxable) income and maximize your unrealized income (wealth/capital appreciation without a cash flow)." The first time I read that, it made very little sense to me, but I stuck with it and came to understand that the recommendation was to increase your money without being taxed on it. Is that even legal? If so, wow, and how the heck do I do it?

The answers to those questions are:

1. Yes, it's legal, if you follow the rules.

2. You do it with unrealized income.

What is unrealized income? Simple answer: it's income that you can't spend, so it's not taxed. It's increasing the value of your wealth, without triggering any modes of taxation. You know about modes of taxation already, even if you don't realize you do: when do you get taxed? When you earn, spend, or die. So, if you can increase the value of your wealth without earning, spending or dying, you won't pay taxes. Let me explain further with an example.

Let's look at my real estate business. If I earn $200 in rent, and spend it on a new television set for my home, I'm going to owe income tax (and sales tax) on that $200. But if I accept that rent check and then spend it on supplies to fix up another home, the business expense will offset the income and it won't trigger taxation. It gets really very interesting to think about this further. Did I add $200 worth of value to my home by purchasing the supplies? Generally, no. Generally, I add far more value to the home than the actual dollar amount invested. This means that my wealth grew significantly more than if I'd bought the television set.

Let's compare: LJ #1 earns $200 in rent and uses it to buy a television set. Come tax time, she owes 25% of her income in taxes. The TV has also depreciated- it's worth far less than it cost. So, LJ #1 owes $50 in taxes and her TV is only worth $100 now. Take the $50 in taxes from the $100 value of the TV and LJ #1 is only $50 wealthier than before she accepted her rent check. Even if she just SAVED the $200, she'd still pay income tax on it so she'd only have $150 after taxes.

LJ #2 is a little bit wiser (she should be, she's like 10 years older than that idiot LJ #1). She accepts the same $200, but she doesn't want to pay taxes on it. She noticed that one of her homes has a breakfast bar that makes it a little nicer than most and with the right set-up a family might be willing to pay $25 more per month for that home. So, LJ #2 goes and buys stools for the breakfast bar and spends the money making the home a little more appealing for a family. She raises the rent for that home by $25/month.

The $200 spent on improving the home is a business expense so she pays no income tax on it. Another way to say this is that though LJ #2 accepted the $200, it doesn't trigger taxation because she offsets it with a business expense.

In addition, she collects $25/month extra for the investment, which is a total of $300/year in increased income. If you measure an asset's value as how much it earns in 60 months (a standard way of measuring), LJ #2's wealth has increased by $1,500 ($25*60=$1,500). Not bad for starting with $200. Then LJ #2 can reinvest her $300/year ($1,500 for 5 years) and continue the cycle. It is much easier to become wealthy (though neither LJ is there yet) when you aren't being taxed on every cent that you earn, as is the case of most W2 income earners.

Real estate is not the only place you can do this. Real estate does lend itself well to it because there are many ways to invest money and improve the value of your property. But there are many other situations that you can do this in as well. And this is how the wealthy shelter their money so that they can continue to use it to grow their wealth.

Let's look at another example so that you can see real estate isn't the only place this works. I buy paper goods (bookmarks, cards, envelopes etc.) from a lady on Etsy. She's a grandma and she has a job, but she does this little business on the side. I occasionally place large orders with her when I run contests and offer her items as a prize. One time, my order was around $300 and she sent me a thank you note and said that she was using the income from the job to purchase a better cutting machine. She'd had her eye on it for a while, and now she had the money.

So, she could have taken the $300 as profit (minus whatever her expenses were), and she would have paid $75 in taxes if she was in the 25% tax bracket (as is common.) She's $225 richer. But she was smarter than that— she used the profit to reinvest in her business. If she reinvests all of the $300, she'll pay no taxes on it. She also makes her business more valuable because she can charge more for the better product that she can produce. I don't have her numbers to be able to say that she ended up making $1,000 more or $2,000 more, but I think you can easily see that she's in a better place than just $225 richer.

Ok, so back to my journey of learning this. Now that I understood the concept of unrealized income, my next thought was that you can't put off the reaper. Death and taxes, the two things you can't avoid, right? I thought that you're just making it worse when you eventually do pay your taxes. Back to the two LJs, LJ #1 had to pay the taxes on $200, while LJ #2 needed to pay the taxes on $300 that year. But then I realized that LJ #2 could just reinvest the $300 and not owe taxes on that either. And the $300 would maybe grow into $600 the following year if invested correctly. And if LJ #2 drew that out of the business, she'd owe tax on the $600. But if she reinvested it, she'd again avoid owing tax on it. This could grow and grow forever.

And even if I don't do that, LJ #1 has $200 and owes $50 in taxes so she's $150 richer. LJ #2 invests the $200, grows it into $300 and then will pay taxes on that: $75. She's $225 richer overall and she beats LJ #1 by $75.

Now, before you get upset that you aren't in the real estate business (though if you can be, you should be. It's so forgiving. I screw stuff up all the time and still make a profit) let's talk about places that you have this ability to shelter your income already. There are some ways that are open to almost everyone, and there are other ways that we'll talk about that you can make possible.

Think about your 401K or your IRA. You are using not-yet-taxed money to buy stocks, bonds and mutual funds (unless you're like me-- 100% of my IRA is in real estate or cash) and letting them grow. You earn 2% or 10% or whatever % and you don't pay tax on that either. It's allowed to sit there and build up and grow and grow. You don't pay tax on it until it becomes realized income- when you pull it out of the account, whether that is next week or in your retirement years. And you pay whatever tax rate you're in at the time when you pull it out, not when you earned it.

And while we're on the subject of stocks, bonds and mutual funds, their growth is another form of unrealized income. Say you invest $100 in a stock and over the year the stock grows in value to $110. You don't owe the government tax on that $10 provided you leave the stock alone and continue to allow it to grow. Only when you sell it will your income be realized and you'll owe tax on the income (but not on the original $100 as you were already taxed on that.)

If there are other ways of sheltering your income from taxes as an individual, I'm not aware of them. You are taxed on your W2 income before you even see it. This makes it very difficult to take excess income and turn it into even more excess income and on and on.

These truths began to make a lot more sense to me, and to be a lot more relevant:

Individuals earn their income, are taxed on it and then they have whatever is left over to live on.

Business owners take their gross revenues, spend everything they can to increase the value of their business and then are taxed on whatever is left over (that's their true earnings.)

This made me think. Remember, I wasn't a business owner when I first started learning all this. I started thinking about the wealthy people I knew and calculating whether or not they were business owners. By and large, they were. In fact, I couldn't think of a single wealthy person from my own life who didn't own his or her own business, even if it was just something on the side while they worked full time. Woah. Really? This got my wheels turning.

Take a minute in your own life and think about the people who you consider to be well-to-do. Do they own a business? The people I thought of immediately were:

- An uncle whose home seemed massive to me as a child. He owned a sand and gravel company.

- A former boss who mentioned to me once that he paid cash for his home. It had to have been over $300K. He had a real estate company on the side.

- A friend of mine growing up always seemed to have the finer things like new shoes and the entire Girl Scout uniform, not just the sash. Yes, those were the finer things where I was raised. And her dad owned his own business.

After lots of thought, I still couldn't think of a single person that I considered wealthy who didn't have a business. There were people with a little money, sure. But no one who seemed to truly break that barrier from the have-nots to the haves without owning their own business. I even thought of someone I knew who had an older relative die and leave her a million dollars. Within a few years, that person was struggling in debt again. Is it impossible to get ahead in life without a business?

Maybe I wouldn't go that far, but it's certainly a lot easier to have the money needed for a comfortable life if you aren't giving a huge chunk of it to the government before you even see it.

I dug further into how the wealthy handle their taxes and how the poor and middle class handle theirs and found one major difference: mindset. **The wealthy**

know that there will be a tax burden and they plan their lives to minimize it. They look into the future and set their lives up to legally lower their tax burden. They read over the rules and follow them carefully to their advantage.

That resonates with me. You're talking to the kid who studied the rules of Parcheesi and used them to kick her brothers' butts every time. So, to be honest, I felt like I'd missed out when I first learned this concept. Why have I been acting like the poor and middle class do about their taxes? I'm smarter than that! I bet you'll feel the same way. I hope it doesn't bother you too much. Let it go and do better in the future. Know better, do better, right?

The poor and middle classes think about taxes as something that's already happened and as something outside their control. When is the last time you seriously thought about your taxes? If you're like the LJ of a few years ago, I'm betting it was sometime between January 1st and April 15th and what you were thinking about was the year-before's taxes. You weren't thinking, "what steps can I take to owe less taxes next year?" You were probably thinking more along the lines of, "I wonder what deductions I qualified for last year?" or "I hope enough money came out of my check that I get a good refund." I know that was me not long ago.

At this point, I realized that there was a way to plan your life to owe less taxes. I knew that a big part of that had to do with owning a business, but I really didn't understand how the two fit together. Enter the hero. Go check out the book: Lower Your Taxes Big Time. http://amzn.to/2mZKxUR

The premise of this book is to use the laws to pay less in taxes. There are many books out there that are similar and I've read through several of them. I like this one the best because he sites everything he says (tells you where to find the exact tax code or case that established the law), he's not boring to read and he used to work for the IRS. I also really enjoy that he takes on the discussion about being audited and gave me a lot of confidence to handle an audit should that ever happen to me (and he also talks about how truly unlikely that is statistically.) He is all about following the law to the letter and not taking risks. I can't recommend the book enough.

Emotional Upheaval

People get upset when they hear about rich people who didn't pay any taxes or didn't pay much in taxes. I used to be one of those people. Once I understood why they didn't pay much or any taxes, I felt very differently. They are following the law. They are just being very smart about it. I started to look up to them, to want to emulate them. Figuring out how to use the tax laws to your financial advantage is the grown-up version of reading the rules of Parcheesi and following them to win. Count me in.

If you are where I was and this whole idea of strategically, legally paying less in taxes bothers you and makes you feel a little dirty, I urge you to take some time and deal with this emotion. Why do you feel like you should contribute more than is legally required? Do you feel like the government needs your money? Do you feel like they are using it wisely to help others? Do you feel that if you followed the laws and legally kept your money that you would spend it unwisely? Would you help others with it or hurt others? Think this through logically, even writing it down and deal with this emotion.

Putting It into Action

Remember how I said business owners take their gross revenues, spend all they can and then pay taxes on the rest? This is where you're lucky to not have your business set up yet. You can choose what you want to do.

What is that thing that you'd enjoy investing your time, energy and money into? I suggest you start with what you love. What can you do 24/7 and not get sick of? What do you wish you could spend more of your own money doing? For me, it's Disney World.

So, there was a moment where I said to myself, "How can I get paid to go to Disney World?" and the answer was to start a business. And guess what? If you're reading this, you bought something from my business. I likely took your money and re-invested it back into the business- maybe by buying a camera for my filming or software I need to support the business infrastructure, or paying my virtual assistants. Or maybe I paid for my hotel stay when I came down to film (we'll learn a lot more about business travel in the next section).

Re-investing in my business is a maneuver that simultaneously:

- makes my life better and easier by getting me better tools

- makes my life more enjoyable: for instance, I just invested $275 to take the Back-Stage Magic Tour so I can create content for my readers from the experience. Super fun, and a business investment. After I was finished, I did a live video about it and used messenger to convert my watchers into followers. I'll be selling them my new product soon.

- makes my business grow by helping me reach more people and eventually sell more things.

- increases the value of my business (and therefore my wealth)

- AND it shelters the income from taxes.

I'm struggling just a bit to help you understand how this can work for you, so I want to share a few more examples here that I think may help you.

My husband is a rambling man at heart and his job right now is our kids. He does almost all the kids' care and the house cleaning, etc. and I earn the money. But I think a part of him always thinks about what he's going to do when the kids are older and he has more time. And since we think about businesses differently than most people, he's always kicking around ideas for a business.

Here are a few of his ideas and how they would improve our lives and shelter us from taxes.

- Fishing Boat Captain: Mike loves being out on the water and he thought starting a charter fishing service would be up his alley. Obviously, this would be when we move away from Kentucky. Some perks to this business:
  - It would allow him to spend time on the water.
  - Other people (his clients) would be paying for the expenses of operations.

- His costs would be tax write-offs. Boat, fuel, all the little things too.
- He'd make money from his business. This profit would be taxed... unless he invested it back into the business (better equipment, etc.)

• Hunting Expedition Leader: Mike enjoys hunting, especially the strategy of it and the feeling of helping some of the younger guys in his circle get a deer. Some perks to this business:

- It would allow him to do what he enjoys- the strategy and the coaching and seeing others reap the rewards.
- Other people (his clients) would be paying for the expenses of operations.
- His costs would be tax write-offs. In this case, the costs could be quite large- travel, owning a property to hunt, bringing in deer, raising deer, etc.
- He'd make money from his business. This profit would be taxed... unless he invested it back into the business (better equipment, guns etc.)

• Breeding, training and delivering dogs: Mike has always been interested in big (expensive) well-trained guard dogs. We have a well-trained 170lb Cane Corso ourselves, but he's always wanted a Fila Brazalero. He talks about someday breeding them. Some perks to this business:

- o He enjoys big dogs and we'd have plenty around.
- o The dogs command a high price tag and even more if they are trained, so profit margins are high.
- o There aren't a lot of breeders in the US and none of them deliver so you have to travel to pick up your puppy. Mike was thinking of offering a delivery service. Sounds like an excellent way to see the country while making money and legally writing off your travel.

Are you starting to see how this works? Start a business doing what you want to do anyway, then you get to do it (at no expense to yourself if your business is profitable), get to make money, get to write-off your costs. It's a no-brainer.

If I'm belaboring the point, please skip ahead, but this is important and probably the thing that can change your life the most out of anything in this book. So, indulge me a little longer as I share two more things on this subject: I want to give you two more examples of how this might look for a mom (since Mike's examples may not speak to you.)

Ok, these are based on real people, but I did make the numbers up because I don't want to use people's real business numbers (other than my own), but I did base them on real life, not just making things up at random.

- Jenn is a mom to two and she's very interested in homeopathy- natural medicines. She starts learning about them and decides to put together a little business. She begins selling some of the items she's making for her family anyway.

o Jenn's business makes a small profit. Enough to contribute to the Disney fund, but not much else. But there are other benefits.

o Jenn can buy in bulk now, lowering her costs for her own supplies.

o Jenn can write-off her costs of goods sold, her supplies, some of her equipment, any business travel she has, and in some circumstances, her home office.

  ▪ A travel example: Jenn goes to the grocery store and picks up her business supplies along with her groceries for her family. The trip for supplies is business mileage. If it's 20 miles round trip, that's a little more than $10 that she won't pay tax on. One trip like this per week would mean $520 that she won't pay tax on. Jenn's customers are her family and friends. She delivers products to her mom. Of course, the mileage for product delivery is a write-off. She gives a catalog to a friend at church. Mileage to a marketing opportunity is a write-off as well. If each of these happen once a week with a 20-mile round trip, that's another $1,040 Jenn's family will not pay taxes on. These travel items result in $1,560 in non-taxed income.

- Home office example: Jenn uses what used to be a spare bedroom as her office. In her office, she works on recipes, takes product photos, keeps her books, and does all her marketing, and product fulfillment in there. Her office qualifies for the home office deduction. She can now write-off a percentage of her utilities as a business expense. Of course, all her business supplies/office supplies are write-offs as well. If Jenn's home office is 10% of her home, she can write-off 10% of her utilities. Probably at least $200 in write-offs.

o Jenn can reinvest her profits into her business in ways she enjoys.

- She can buy a course on home remedies or on digital marketing, anything relevant. Business education is a write-off. Jenn gets better as a result of this reinvestment and she makes more money. She learns how to run Facebook Ads and begins making even more.

- She can buy that new Kitchen Aid Mixer she's had her eye on. It will make her life so much easier when she's mixing up recipes for her products. And as long as she keeps record of sufficient business use, she can use it personally too, and still legally deduct it.

- Jenn can attend a conference about homeopathy. Depending on the structure of the conference, she can write this off as education or maybe marketing/networking.

- Jenn can try different supplies to find what works best. All the supplies tried, success or failure are a business write-off.

  ○ Jenn only makes around $50 a month after expenses. It adds $600 to her Disney fund each year. But it also pays for itself, for Jenn to do all the things she enjoys doing and learning anyway AND Jenn writes off around $3,000 in expenses each year. If Jenn was in the 25% tax bracket, that's an additional $750 in her pocket each year that she's

DISNEY WORLD WITHIN REACH

not paying in taxes. Not too bad at all for something Jenn enjoys. Jenn is at least $1,350 richer, not counting how her life is enriched.

Before we move on to the next example, let me make sure that I explain how write-offs work, because lots of people have this wrong. In fact, someone once got mad at me for writing something off because they thought that it meant that the government was paying for that item. They were mad because they thought that my write-off came from their tax money. Not the case.

A write-off is simply money that doesn't count toward your taxable income. It's money you don't get taxed on. Remember individuals earn, are taxed and then spend so they have very few write-offs. But businesses take their sales, spend everything they need to, write those expenditures off, and then are taxed on what's left over.

So, in the example above where Jenn ended up with $3000 in tax write-offs in addition to her profit of $50 a month, her actual business might look something like this:

Jenn sold $1,600 of her products last year. She reinvested $1,000 of that into her business (she went to a homeopathy convention and also bought an amazing new Kitchen Aid Mixer.) She also had about $2,000 in write-offs from her home office and her mileage. This brings her to her total write-offs of $3,000 ($1,000+$2,000).

This doesn't mean that the government will pay her $3,000, or that she'll get $3,000 back come tax time. It means that she won't pay tax on $3,000 that she otherwise would have had to pay. If Jenn has a job or if her husband works, this $3,000 write-off can go against their other income. If there is no other income to be written-off, the write-off can be carried over to the next year, so if Jenn shows a larger profit as a result of the new mixer and skills she learned at the convention, she can use her write-off from the prior year to avoid paying more in taxes.

More commonly, the write-off can be used to offset a spouse's income. If Jenn's husband made $50,000 last year, her $3,000 write-off can bring his income down to $47,000. They will not pay taxes on that $3,000.

- If they are in the 10% tax bracket, that saves them $300
- If they are in the 15% tax bracket, that saves them $450
- If they are in the 25% tax bracket, that saves them $750.

All in all, Jenn earns $600, gets to keep another $750 in her pocket instead of giving it to Uncle Sam, gets to invest $1,000 into a field that she enjoys, and gets the enjoyment of all the experiences that would otherwise be a hobby. She's at least $2,350 wealthier than she would be if this was just a hobby, but probably even more as she'll turn her business expenses into more sales next year.

- Another friend of mine, Nicole, is the mom of two little girls and the aunt of two more little girls. She found herself spending tons of time and money shopping for adorable matching outfits for them. She realized that she was very good at shopping and the four girls were always being complimented, so obviously, she was good at the style portion too.

  People were always asking her where she got the girls' outfits. After referring tons of business to the boutique she frequented, she thought, "Why couldn't I sell these outfits instead of sending this potential business away?"

  She began her business via Facebook. She set up a group and began inviting people into it. She set up relationships with suppliers and began placing orders. She continued to attract customers based on her style and the quality of the clothes. Soon, Nicole was selling several hundred dollars a month of kids' clothes.

  o Nicole makes a profit from her business. It's not much, but enough to cover the electric bill every month.

○ Nicole enjoys economies of scale in her business now. This means that she buys more outfits than she used to for just her daughters and nieces and gets better pricing on her own purchases.

○ Nicole can write off her cost of goods sold, her supplies, her equipment, any business travel she has and in some circumstances, her home office and space for her inventory.

▪ A travel example: Nicole goes to the grocery store and puts up a flyer on the bulletin board advertising her Facebook group. While she's there, she shops for groceries for her family. The trip is business mileage. If it's 20 miles round trip, that's a little more than $10 that she won't pay tax on. One trip like this per week would mean $520 that she won't pay tax on. Nicole's customers are her family and friends. She delivers products to her mom. Of course, the mileage for product delivery is a write-off. The other mothers at story time occasionally shop her group. She hands out marketing material while the kids listen to the librarian read about the pigeon and the bus driver. Mileage to a marketing opportunity is a write-off as well. If each of these happen once a week with a 20-mile round trip, that's another $1,040

Nicole's family will not pay taxes on. These travel items result in $1,560 in non-taxed income.

- Home office example: Nicole uses what used to be a spare bedroom as her office. In her office, she places her orders, takes product photos, keeps her books, and does all her marketing, and product fulfillment in there. Her office qualifies for the home office deduction. She can now write-off a percentage of her utilities as a business expense. Of course, all her business supplies and office supplies are write-offs as well. If Nicole's home office is 10% of her home, she can write-off 10% of her utilities. Probably at least $200 in write-offs.

o Nicole can reinvest her profits into her business in ways she enjoys.

- She can buy a course on digital marketing, or on fashion trends for the under ten set, anything relevant. Business education is a write-off. Nicole gets better as a result of this reinvestment and she makes more money. She learns how to run ads and begins making even more.

- She can buy that new digital camera she's had her eye on. It will make her life so much easier when she's taking product photos. And as long as she keeps record of sufficient business use, she can use it personally too, and still legally deduct it.

- Nicole can attend a conference about boutique fashion. Depending on the structure of the conference, she can write this off as education or maybe marketing/networking.

- Nicole can try different suppliers to find who works best. Success or failure, all are a business write-off.

  o Nicole only makes around $100 a month with her business. It adds $1,200 to her family each year. But it also pays for itself, for Nicole to do all the things she enjoys doing and learning anyway AND Nicole writes off around $3,000 in expenses each year. If Nicole was in the 25% tax bracket, that's an additional $750 in her pocket each year that she's not paying in taxes. Not too bad at all for something Nicole enjoys doing.

So, hopefully with Mike, Jenn and Nicole's examples you can start to see how beneficial a home-based business can be. If this intrigues you, there is so much information out there, and I strongly recommend starting with these: *Rich Dad, Poor Dad* by Robert Kiyosaki and *Lower Your Taxes Big Time* by Sandy Botkin.

All Summed Up:

The rich think about and pay their taxes incredibly differently than the middle class and poor. They invest in businesses because individuals earn, pay tax and then spend while businesses make sales, spend everything they can to grow and then pay tax on what's leftover.

Starting a home-based business can drastically reduce your tax burden and can give you the opportunity to invest in something you love at the same time.

Chapter Thirty-Three:
Tax Savings via Disney

Yep, it sure can, in three easy steps:

Step 1: Take a trip to Orlando.
Step 2: Conduct enough business while there to qualify the trip as a business trip.
Step 3: Go to Disney World while you're not busy for your business.

This will allow you to deduct a portion of your travel, food and hotel costs. For me, this is easy with both my businesses. The Disney one is obvious, and as far as my real estate company goes I am very interested in someday owning a home in the Orlando area. It only makes sense. I'm down there every month as it is, I could easily manage a vacation home. One thousand a week in almost passive income sounds pretty good to me. So, all I need to do to deduct my travel is to be sure to work toward this business purpose in the right way while I'm traveling.

There are many rules that govern what you can write-off. The book I suggested before (Lower Your Taxes Big Time) will help you there. It's not too dry of a read either. The gentleman who wrote it used to work for the IRS so it has the feel of being insider information.

An example of a rule that can be followed to save more/write more off is working days. Every day that you work or travel for business is a working day. If Friday is a working day and Monday is a working day, then Saturday and Sunday also count as working days. If you have more working days than non-working days on a trip the trip is designated as "primarily for business." If your trip can earn that designation, then you can deduct all your travel. Here is a list of deductions that you can take when traveling primarily for business.

Table 1-1. Travel Expenses You Can Deduct
This chart summarizes expenses you can deduct when you travel away from home for business purposes.

IF you have expenses for...	THEN you can deduct the cost of...
transportation	travel by airplane, train, bus, or car between your home and your business destination. If you were provided with a free ticket or you are riding free as a result of a frequent traveler or similar program, your cost is zero. If you travel by ship, see *Luxury Water Travel* and *Cruise Ships* (under *Conventions*) for additional rules and limits.

taxi, commuter bus, and airport limousine	fares for these and other types of transportation that take you between: • The airport or station and your hotel, and • The hotel and the work location of your customers or clients, your business meeting place, or your temporary work location.
baggage and shipping	sending baggage and sample or display material between your regular and temporary work locations.
car	operating and maintaining your car when traveling away from home on business. You can deduct actual expenses or the standard mileage rate, as well as business-related tolls and parking. If you rent a car while away from home on business, you can deduct only the business-use portion of the expenses.
lodging and meals	your lodging and meals if your business trip is overnight or long enough that you need to stop for sleep or rest to properly perform your duties. Meals include amounts spent for food, beverages, taxes, and related tips. See *Meals* for additional rules and limits.

cleaning	dry cleaning and laundry.
telephone	business calls while on your business trip. This includes business communication by fax machine or other communication devices.
tips	tips you pay for any expenses in this chart.
other	other similar ordinary and necessary expenses related to your business travel. These expenses might include transportation to or from a business meal, public stenographer's fees, computer rental fees, and operating and maintaining a house trailer.

(Citation:https://www.irs.gov/publications/p463/ch01. html#en_US_2016_publink100033812)

I'm going to insert something else here directly from the IRS' website. I'm doing this because I've explained this in person to many people, and they simply don't believe me. You don't have to take my word for it this way. You can click the link or type in the URL and go read it word for word on the IRS's website. This is 100% following the law.

The following are the rules in place for counting whether or not a day is a travel day (emphasis mine):

Counting business days. Your business days include transportation days, days your presence was required, days you spent on business, and certain weekends and holidays.

Transportation day. Count as a business day any day you spend traveling to or from a business destination. However, if because of a nonbusiness activity you don't travel by a direct route, your business days are the days it would take you to travel a reasonably direct route to your business destination. Extra days for side trips or nonbusiness activities can't be counted as business days.

Presence required. Count as a business day any day your presence is required at a particular place for a specific business purpose. Count it as a business day even if you spend most of the day on nonbusiness activities.

Day spent on business. If your principal activity during working hours is the pursuit of your trade or business, count the day as a business day. Also, count as a business day any day you are prevented from working because of circumstances beyond your control.

Certain weekends and holidays. Count weekends, holidays, and other necessary standby days as business days if they fall between business days. But if they follow your business meetings or activity and you remain at your business destination for nonbusiness or personal reasons, don't count them as business days.

Citation:
https://www.irs.gov/publications/p463/ch01.html   -en_US_2016_publink100033812

Ok, so remember how we very purposely and thoughtfully decided who was going to be on which room reservation and we were within the rules to do so? This is a similar situation. There is no rule that you can't plan business activity to give you the greatest deductions possible.

Let's walk through this in my situation and then I'll give you a little more to go on for yours. I'm in real estate. I want to buy a house in Orlando. My business activities in Orlando would be things like: scouring neighborhoods to find the right place where I'd like to own a home, meeting with real estate agents to find one I'd like to work with, viewing properties that I might be interested in, interviewing property management companies, etc. You can see that there are many opportunities to move my business forward each time I'm in Orlando.

To maximize deductions, we can purposely plan our travel and our business. Travel days are business days, and weekends between business days are business days. So, if we fly in on a Friday (or conduct business on a Friday), and we conduct business on a Monday, we have four business days: Friday, Saturday, Sunday and Monday. If we stay for a week, four business days is enough to give us the "primarily for business" designation. But we still have to fly out and that's a business day too. So, by conducting ONE meeting (on Monday) we can earn the designation for eight days. You can fly out on Saturday and still meet the requirements. If you're staying longer than Saturday, you could attend to more business that requires your presence on Friday and then fly out Monday. That would make the second weekend business days too.

Here's how this works for me: I fly in Friday. Travel days are business days (Business Day #1). I enjoy Friday, Saturday and Sunday all to myself. Weekends between business days are business days (Business Days #2 and #3). On Monday, I conduct the business I went there to conduct. I look at a home, or meet with an agent, etc. It takes very little time usually. An hour or two. Some agents are even willing to pick me up or meet me in a place that's convenient for me if I mention that I don't have a rental car available. That makes Monday a business day (Business Day #4).

After the meeting, I'm free to do whatever else I'd like with the day and still consider it a business day. My presence was required to conduct business. Tuesday, Wednesday, and Thursday are not business days. I usually fly home on Friday. Travel days are business days (Business Day #5). This gives me five business days vs. three non-business days. This means that I pass the "primarily for business" test and can deduct all my travel. My meals will be deductible on business days.

Family Expenses

A couple of things to be careful about: your family's expenses are not deductible unless they are employees and needed for the business. You could easily hire your spouse as an employee and then his/her travel and meals would be deductible. I'm not likely to purchase a vacation home without my husband seeing it so he is needed for business purposes when I view real estate.

Hiring your spouse may or may not be worth your time to establish. You can usually write-off your entire lodging anyway since most hotels don't charge extra for two adults. If they do, and your spouse isn't an employee, that additional amount wouldn't be deductible. But in most instances, the additional deductible amount is your spouse's plane ticket, and your spouse's meals on business days. Depending on your plane tickets, this might be worth it. Even the meals could add up over time. We'll discuss that next.

You can also hire your children if they are at least seven years old. That is, case law sets a precedent for being allowed to hire your child if they are at least seven. You can't just pay them for chores, it needs to be actual business-related work (like shredding papers or being a model or test subject. My oldest son blogs with me. And his page views are higher than mine!) This means that when Seth comes along on a business trip and we do Mickey's Not So Scary Halloween Party and then Seth blogs about it and that contributes to the business, I can not only write-off his travel, food and lodging on business days, but I can actually also pay him for his work, and write off the expense. He will not be above the standard deduction amount, so he won't pay taxes on his income.

Mark J. Kohler (Author, Attorney and CPA) says it well in his article for Entrepreneur: Why You Should Hire Your Kids This Summer https://www.entrepreneur.com/article/223968 "Pay your children for services they perform for your business, and you'll actually generate an expense for your income taxes by pushing income to your children. Another exciting aspect to this strategy, is that all of us, including our children don't pay federal income taxes on the first $6,300 of income this year."

Did you catch that? No one pays any tax on the first several thousand of their income. If your children have income from their work for you, they will not be taxed on it at all until they reach the $6,300 threshold. This means that you can shift your money from a place where you are taxed on it to a place where your children are not taxed on it. And it's not difficult to do.

If you want more information about hiring your spouse and children, a simple google search will produce lots of information, but the book I recommended, Lower Your Taxes Big Time gives you all the current laws and ways to audit-proof yourself.

Meals

You can deduct your actual meals on business days. This involves keeping receipts and keeping track of what you eat. I'm not about that inconvenient life, so I just take the per diem meal allowance. For me, it's usually a better deduction, as I'm not a big eater. The Meals and Incidental Expenses (M&IE) rate for Orlando is $59 per day. This is similar to the "standard deduction" that you are probably familiar with. With the standard deduction, you are allowed to deduct that amount even if you wouldn't have deducted that amount had you added up your actual deductions. The M&IE is the same way. If my receipts would add up to $30 for the day, I am still allowed to take the $59 deduction.

This means that for my trip, I can deduct $295 for food (5 business days*59). If my husband is an employee and needed for the business, he can deduct the same.

Here is what the IRS has to say about the M&IE because honestly, doesn't it seem a little too good to be true? You don't even need to keep receipts?

This is copied directly from the IRS' site:

Question:
For business travel, are there limits on the amounts deductible for meals?

Answer:

- Meal expenses are deductible if your business trip is overnight or long enough that you need to stop for substantial sleep or rest to properly perform your duties. Meal expenses are also deductible if the meal is business-related entertainment. You can figure all your travel meal expenses using either of the following methods:
  - Actual cost. If you use this method, you must keep records of your actual cost.
  - The standard meal allowance, which is the federal meals and incidental expense (M&IE) per diem rate. The GSA website lists these rates by location. Note that lower rates apply for the first and last days of travel.

Citation: https://www.irs.gov/faqs/small-business-self-employed-other-business/income-expenses/income-expenses-2

Did you catch that, though? You can deduct **actual** expenses with **no limit,** _or_ the **M&IE**. Seriously, why are there no emojis in Word? I really need that little guy with the blue on his head, making the "WHAT? WOW!!!" face.

Do you realize that this means if on a business day I eat at Pop Century Food Court for breakfast for $7.99, Casey's for lunch at $9.99, and Cosmic Ray's for $11.99 for dinner, plus two snacks at $5 each, I spent $39.97, but can legally deduct $59 (the current M&IE rate for Orlando?)

AND if on a business day, I eat at Crystal Palace for $43, Chef Mickeys for lunch for $50 and Victoria and Albert's for dinner for $185, I spent $278 and can deduct $278. I'm not bound by the M&IE.

Seriously. This stuff is amazing.

Results

Let me now add up all the deductions we can take from one trip. This will help you decide if taking a few hours away from your family to further your business is a good choice or not.

Travel: I usually get very inexpensive fares so maybe $150 for my flights

Parking at the airport: $64 ($8 for 8 days)

Lodging: if I stay at a Value, probably around $100 a day so $500 (business days), but there isn't a limit on this so if I stay at the Grand Floridian, this could be quite a deduction. We'll stay within the realm of reality though and assume I'm at All-Star Sports.

Meals: $295 ($59 for 5 days)

Altogether, I'm able to write-off $1,009.

But what does this mean? I said this in the last part, but I'll explain again in case you skipped it or are still confused. A lot of people are confused about what write-offs are. I've talked to people who think that it means that the government pays for it. No, this isn't the case. What a write-off actually does is lower the amount of income that you need to pay taxes on. If you earned $50,000, you'd need to pay tax on that amount. But if you earned $50,000 and then took a $1,009 deduction, you'd pay less tax. You would only be taxed on $48,991 instead of $50,000.

Still, this is a hard concept. My brain does not understand what paying tax on $48,991 might be compared to paying tax on $50,000 so let's take this further. Most people are in the 15% tax bracket. If you and your spouse make more than $70,000 together, you might be in the 25% tax bracket. If you make less than $17,000, you might be in the 10% bracket. Let's look at all three.

- o If you are in the 10% bracket, not paying tax on $1,009 would save you $100.90
- o If you are in the 15% bracket, not paying tax on $1,009 would save you $151.35
- o If you are in the 25% bracket, not paying tax on $1,009 would save you $252.25

I used a pretty low-key example here, low airfare and staying at All-Star Sports. But if your airfare is expensive and if you are staying at a more expensive resort (or you hired your husband and children), you could easily write-off thousands. Most people would save $150 in this example. Not bad for an hour or two worth of work that will also move your business, life and mindset forward.

Just for fun, let's look at our old friends the Robinsons. They could write-off roughly $5,200 for their room alone, plus $400ish for food and some unknown amount for flights. Paying taxes on $5,600 less income is no joke. In the 15% bracket, it's $840 more cash in your pocket. In the 25% bracket, it's $1,400. You could look at that money as your seed money to start your business. You can do it!

Practically

When you do your taxes, have all your expenses together for the business trip. You don't need to mention Disney World on your documents (though it's not a problem if you do.) I just create a spreadsheet with the deductible expenses and notate at the top "Business trip to see (address of rental property)". The IRS doesn't even see that though because these get totaled up and then the number gets inserted onto a tax form. All the IRS sees is the number. They don't see the pictures of my kids at Disney World. But even if they did, I'm following the law.

Now I can hear you saying, "This works very nicely for you. You have a business. I don't. This won't work for me." Well you're right, but you're also wrong. You do need a business to take advantage of this strategy, but there's no reason why you can't start one. Haven't you always wanted to invest in real estate? There's no law that says you have to already own real estate to start shopping for a property. But honestly, you could choose a more convenient business.

It could be anything. It would be very convenient to start a business that was Disney related. Maybe you could buy and resell an item that people might like to buy for their Disney trips like: cute outfits for kids, toys, shirts, stuffed animals, MagicBand decals, trading pins, lanyards, photo boards for signatures... I could go on and on and on. Just hop on over to Etsy and type in Disney World for ideas. It would cost next to nothing to set up an Etsy shop and start reselling a product. Then, if you need to photograph your product while at Disney World for your business: deduction.

Open your mind. You can do this. You may even find that you're making lots of money from your business on the side. And travel is just one deduction you have with a business. You can deduct a lot more like a home office, your internet connection, part of your utilities, and so much more. Start a business, if only for tax reasons. I'm not saying to start a phony business that you only operate on paper to avoid taxes. That's against the law. I'm saying, start a business to shelter your income from taxes, legally. That is probably the most valuable piece of advice in this entire book.

Think about what you enjoyed most about planning your trip. That might be a good place to start a business. I always loved gathering magic for my kids-little toys to keep them busy in line or while waiting for dinner, light-ups, souvenirs. I just liked shopping for that stuff, trying to get it inexpensively, finding things I knew would delight them. I turned this into my MousekaToy Kits. They were a product that I used to sell when I first started my blog. I loved being able to turn it into a business because I enjoyed it and had a reason to do it even more. Maybe for you, you enjoyed putting together outfits for your kids for every day at Disney. That could be your thing.

I do want to advise caution on the type of business activity that you complete while in Orlando. If you complete business that could be done elsewhere, it's not good enough to qualify. You can't take your laptop and write some emails and call it a business trip.

You need some reason to have traveled to where you are conducting the business. The "presence required rule". If my presence is required there to complete the business, it will qualify. If I could phone it in, it won't. Seeing a home would obviously require my presence. Interviewing potential staff (real estate agents or property management companies) requires my presence. Your business needs to require your presence. An example would be taking photographs of your product in Disney World. If you sell shirts, a photo of the shirt with the Castle in the background would certainly be preferable to a plain stock photo. Presence Required. Tax Deductible.

Here are the rules right from the IRS' site:

"Trip Primarily for Business

You can deduct all of your travel expenses if your trip was entirely business related. If your trip was primarily for business and, while at your business destination, you extended your stay for a vacation, made a personal side trip, or had other personal activities, you can deduct only your business-related travel expenses. These expenses include the travel costs of getting to and from your business destination and any business-related expenses at your business destination.

Trip Primarily for Personal Reasons

If your trip was primarily for personal reasons, such as a vacation, the entire cost of the trip is a nondeductible personal expense. However, you can deduct any expenses you have while at your destination that are directly related to your business.

A trip to a resort or on a cruise ship may be a vacation even if the promoter advertises that it is primarily for business. The scheduling of incidental business activities during a trip, such as viewing videotapes or attending lectures dealing with general subjects, won't change what is really a vacation into a business trip."

(Citation:https://www.irs.gov/publications/p463/ch0
1.html#en_US_2016_publink100033800)

Do not let that last section from the IRS deter you. If I was a conspiracy theorist, I'd say that the wording is *designed* to make you think that your internal reasons for the trip are on trial here, when that is not the case.

There is a legal meaning and definition to the words, "Trip Primarily for Business" and "Trip Primarily for Personal Reasons." Do you remember when we learned about which days count as business and which count as personal? That is how you define whether your trip is primarily for business or personal reasons.

Here they are again if you need a reminder:

Counting business days. Your business days include transportation days, days your presence was required, days you spent on business, and certain weekends and holidays.

Transportation day. Count as a business day any day you spend traveling to or from a business destination. However, if because of a nonbusiness activity you don't travel by a direct route, your business days are the days it would take you to travel a reasonably direct route to your business destination. Extra days for side trips or nonbusiness activities can't be counted as business days.

Presence required. Count as a business day any day your presence is required at a particular place for a specific business purpose. Count it as a business day even if you spend most of the day on nonbusiness activities.

Day spent on business. If your principal activity during working hours is the pursuit of your trade or business, count the day as a business day. Also, count as a business day any day you are prevented from working because of circumstances beyond your control.

Certain weekends and holidays. Count weekends, holidays, and other necessary standby days as business days if they fall between business days. But if they follow your business meetings or activity and you remain at your business destination for nonbusiness or personal reasons, don't count them as business days.

We are conducting actual business and carefully conforming to the IRS' rules. Reading the book I suggested, (<u>Lower Your Taxes Big Time</u>), will help give you confidence to take the deductions for which you qualify. It will also show you other deductions you can take in your regular life. It's worth your time. Last I looked, it was $12. That $12 might save you thousands.

Just so you know, I didn't make this concept up. I'm not the only one taking advantage of it. Like most of this book, I've learned helpful concepts and put them together for you.

If you'd like to do your own research to confirm I'm steering you right, just google "deducting your vacation" and you'll see around 3 million hits for it.

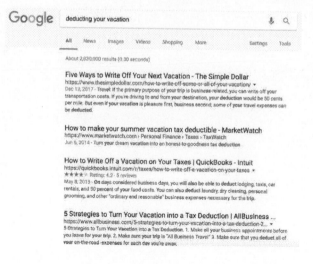

Here are a few of the better articles that explain this so you can get the confidence you need to guard your money from the IRS. They are from Forbes, QuickBooks (same company as TurboTax) and Entrepreneur: all good trustworthy companies you can count on.

https://quickbooks.intuit.com/r/taxes/how-to-write-off-a-vacation-on-your-taxes/

https://www.forbes.com/sites/allbusiness/2014/03/03/how-to-write-off-your-next-vacation/ -2af2a9a27fce

https://www.entrepreneur.com/article/280781

All Summed Up:

Taking a business trip to Orlando and carefully following the IRS rules about business travel can result in a substantial deduction. You may be able to spend only a few hours on business while enjoying the majority of your trip and still net a large deduction.

Take the time to become literate about taxes.

Chapter Thirty-Four:
Saving on Life and
Applying It to Disney

If you're going to get really serious about saving money in every aspect of your life, there is quite a lot of savings to be had. Your motivation has to be strong. I wasn't ever going to just do it on a whim. It's hard. I mentioned before that not too long ago I found myself in almost a quarter million dollars' worth of debt. I don't know if I would have ever found the motivation to work my way out of that (we're almost out now) without Disney World.

I was working very hard trying to climb the corporate ladder and doing well. I was one of the youngest people at my level and I was making close to six figures at 25 years old. I thought I enjoyed my job. I liked the pace of it. Sure, I was tired a lot. I didn't do anything other than work during the week. I worked and then I came home dead and watched a show and went to bed. I only really saw my kids on the weekend. By the time my oldest son was three, I remember him asking when I was going to stay home and we'd count the days until the weekend. We called them "sleeps". I remember very clearly him asking all the time, "How many more sleeps until I get to see you?"

You couldn't really take your vacation time at my job either, but I decided I was going to. I needed to. Seth was only going to be three for so long and I wanted to take him to Disney World. I was a little wiser after our first (basically failed) Disney trip as adults which had been about two years before that. This time, I planned everything out.

I enjoyed the planning. I couldn't believe how much. Something about it just satisfied me. My husband says it's the hunter-gatherer instinct. When I found something that would help us, I felt so good.

We had an amazing time. I mean AMAZING. I'm a little teary eyed writing this because it means so much to me. It was on that trip that I realized I hated my job. I saw my kids clearly for the first time in ages. I saw my husband. The veil of stress lifted from me. I let my phone go to voicemail and my email go unchecked.

My heart soared. I didn't know that joy like that existed in everyday life. Sure, having my babies and getting married topped Disney, but those are once in a lifetime events. I had no idea that you could be this happy without having just pushed a human being out of your body.

The next few months were a blur of changing my life. I needed to get out of debt. I needed to get out of my job. We decided to move and start a farm so we knew where our food came from. We put an offer on a farm two months after the Disney trip. While we were waiting to close, I took another trip. Disneyland.

I went by myself and enjoyed seeing California and spent one day at Disneyland. It renewed my vigor to get free of my work and the stress of it. While I was at Disneyland, I took a pregnancy test and found out that we'd be welcoming baby # 3 the following spring. Joy.

We closed on our farm in Kentucky four weeks after Disneyland, and I walked out of my job shortly after. Literally, walked out: in the middle of the day, with no notice. So, unlike me, the picture of responsibility. But I'd had enough. Nothing big happened that day. No blow up. No fight, no yelling. I realized that I wanted a different life and my job was a hindrance to what I wanted to become.

I called Mike and he was supportive, but hesitant. "How are we going to pay our bills?" "We have a few weeks until we have to worry about that. Let's make tracks to Kentucky and we'll figure it out down there."

I called my dad and told him. He was happy for me and proud. He always wanted more for me than to work building someone else's company.

We had two mortgages, two kids, $248,000 of debt, and no income, or insurance. I was four months pregnant. My job was our only income as my husband has been a stay-at-home dad since we've had kids. My employer owned my car and phone too, so I had to leave those behind as well. We were starting over—only we weren't at zero. We were <u>well</u> into the negative.

That was the bravest I've ever been. I faced the dragon; I took on the tiger. I looked fear in the eye and chose faith. God was telling me to go to Kentucky, and He would not only meet me there, but He'd ride down in the moving van with me. He's never left my side.

I got a job here and worked hard, but it too felt wrong. It turns out it wasn't just my job in Ohio. I was bucking against employment in general. God told me again to have faith. He told me to get some freaking financial acumen already. I began to read. *Rich Dad, Poor Dad* (http://amzn.to/2p48Vmc) *The Richest Man in Babylon* (http://amzn.to/2p7YDDu) *The Millionaire Next Door* (http://amzn.to/2poMivF). My mind started to open.

Soon, I realized the secret to never working for anyone again: get your expenses down and your passive income up. Once your passive income covers your expenses, you're free. I set about it. Expenses were easier to lower compared to raising passive income, so I started there.

We had been spending more than $8,000 a month when we lived in Ohio. We sold Mike's expensive truck, the four-wheeler, anything that wasn't nailed down. We got very serious about every penny that left the checking account. That was a penny that I had to figure out how to earn passively. We called our insurance companies and various others, got new quotes and switched to save. We cancelled our home phone and our TV service. We took a hard look at our cell phone service and made adjustments. We started hanging out at a local diner that had wifi. Convenience items had no place on the grocery list. Bare bones. We even looked at our meals and ate foods that weren't as expensive. We are committed to eating organic whenever possible, and we stuck to that even while cutting our costs.

I made a giant chart of all our consumer debt and we started knocking it out. We'd sell something, and put the money on the credit cards. I'd take a colored sharpie and mark that money off our chart. I had it figured that if things went well, we'd have it paid off in 3 years.

Things didn't go well. We needed an alarming amount of equipment for the farm. Some of it was planned for and some of it was not. It was hard to agree to buy a $20K backhoe when I was so focused on paying off our debt. But we needed it. Things were at a standstill without it. So, we sucked it up and bought it, thinking it would extend our consumer-debt-free day by another year.

But throughout all this, I began investing in real estate. Inexpensive, low income properties: mobile homes. I built up an infrastructure to fix them up. I took on investors. Almost before I knew it, I had more than thirty of them. I had six guys on staff full-time, fixing them up. My payroll was over twelve-thousand a month.

The credit card debt was gone. Then, we were able to pay off the backhoe faster than we expected. Then my student loans were history. In two years and four months, we'd paid down $149,000 in debt. Now only our mortgage on our primary residence remains, and we're chipping away at it. It's slower going because I left my job over two years ago.

We are both stay-at-home parents now. We live on my passive income from my properties. And now a small amount of income from Smart Moms Plan Disney (though most of it is re-invested in the company.) Our expenses are kept very low. We live in a small home—we live modestly. This is so that we can pull as little as possible from the business and keep investing so it can continue to grow. We only have two part-time employees now, we're growing at a slow burn.

I could never have found the motivation to do the work if I hadn't so desperately wanted to leave my job and raise my own babies. I would never have wanted to leave my job so desperately, if I hadn't gone to Disney World and seen what life could be like without the stress of my job.

I just spent three pages telling you my story so that you could trust me when I say: I know it's hard. I've been there. You can do this.

I've already given you some ideas: car insurance, homeowner's insurance, phone, cell phone, internet, cable or tv services. And here are some more: coupons, cash back apps, cash earning apps, discounted gift cards.

Coupons aren't as annoying as they once were. They are digital now. You can download them on to your phone and show it at checkout. It's a lot easier and you don't need to find scissors.

Points Sites: I mentioned SwagBucks (http://www.swagbucks.com/refer/Lauralynj) in the beginning of this book, and MyPoints (https://www.mypoints.com?rb=43756998) is another similar (though not as robust) site. The premise of these is that you do "stuff" online and they give you points for them. SwagBucks has been earning me at least $50 a month since the summer when I really learned to use it. You can shorten your learning curve by reading my blog post about it here: http://bit.ly/SwagbucksPost (case sensitive). There's a best practices video on there too.

Some **cash back apps** you can use are: Ibotta (https://ibotta.com/r/ffpkcno) (we have an iBotta team in the private Facebook group: https://www.facebook.com/groups/18841493351653 19), Checkout 51 (https://www.checkout51.com/) and Shopkick (http://get.shopkick.com/iodine57322). With these apps, you buy something they offer cash back for, then you upload your receipt and they credit your account. I've earned over $250 this year on things I was buying anyway. Shopkick has that same capability, but also offers you Kicks for just scanning things in the grocery store.

And did you know that there are **apps that pay you to use them**? They just want users so that they can sell advertising. It's not a good return on your time investment, but if you're not doing anything else, you might as well earn a little money. Maybe while you're watching TV and relaxing. The ones that I used are the M+ family of apps (no longer available) and Perk. But full disclosure, I'm not that into the cash earning apps scene so do your research and I'm sure you'll find out more than I know.

Here are some others that I've heard of: EarningStation, CoSign, Fronto, Swagbucks, Lucktastic, Pact, Receipt Hog, Mobee, and Surveys on the Go, Fetch. Search them and look into how to maximize them. You can earn from Perk many ways, but I've heard that a good option is to find 10 or 20 second videos and let them play over and over earning points every time. I talked to a woman online who made hundreds per month doing this. She had several devices and she'd set them all up to play over and over and she'd just monitor them. It's not the best use of your time, but it's something if you aren't able to earn another way.

Lastly, I've mentioned this before, but not explained it. I almost never buy anything directly with my credit card. If you see my statement its: Raise, Raise, Raise, Raise, Raise, Cardpool, Raise, Raise, Raise. Because if **I need to buy something, I buy a discounted gift card first**. Why not? Why not save a little money every time I buy something? And just looking at one of my Raise accounts, I've saved $2,000 in 18 months doing this. It takes only a minute and saves serious money. $2,000... I can go to Disney World three or four times on that. I often buy restaurant gift cards that I know I'll use: Wendy's and Panera Bread and Starbucks. And gas cards for when there's no Kroger: Speedway and Shell and BP. It's like free money laying on the sidewalk. Reach down and pick it up.

All Summed Up:

There are lots of opportunities for savings in everyday life. If you can find your motivation to take the steps to save, it can actually change your live. Your cost of living can likely be far less than it is today and that could grant you a lot more freedom. That could mean more trips to Disney, more travel in general, being able to go part time...quitting your job. The sky is the limit.

Bonus
Chapter Thirty-Five:
Planning for All the Hidden Expenses

This chapter doesn't really "fit" anywhere in this book because it's not about saving money, so I made it a bonus. I think it's valuable for decreasing the stress around money at Disney. The only time I've ever stressed about money at Disney World is when I don't know that I need to pay for something and I haven't planned and budgeted accordingly. This chapter is just a list of items that have the potential to surprise you. Plan for them and they won't affect your joy at Disney World.

Parking:

- at the airport ($8/day for me and I think that's normal, but you can check yours online)

- at the hotel (Disney hotels are now beginning to charge for parking at resorts $13 to $27 at the time of this writing, offsite might too)

- at the parks ($22 a day, $45 for preferred. If you're an Annual Passholder or staying onsite, standard is free for you.)

Tolls: Florida is just filthy with toll roads. And you need quarters to pay some of them. If you bring $5 and a roll of quarters you should be fine to get from the airport to Disney and back again. If you're driving, it might be worth it to stop at the Florida Welcome Center and grab a SunPass. The mini SunPasses are only about $5 (plus whatever you add to your account to pay with.) They can save you a lot of time in line.

Resort fees: Disney doesn't charge a resort fee, but many hotels do. This can be hard to ascertain online. I feel it's best to call and ask. And don't just say resort fee. Say, "I'm looking at your price online, are there any fees in addition to this price?" And some of the shadier places won't disclose their fees or will outright lie. 1. Try not to stay in these places. Two Stars or less and you'll start seeing this behavior. 2. If you have to stay there (I've been there!) have a little extra set aside above what they say they charge. That way it's not as stressful. And if it turns out they're honest, bonus!

Dinoland at Animal Kingdom: This is a kid's area that is set up like an old-school carnival. You need to buy tickets if you want to play the games. Your kids are going to want to and honestly, it's fun and fairly easy to win a prize there. That could actually save you money if you spend $5 for a ticket and win a stuffed animal and so forego the $20 stuffed animal from the gift shop. The tickets are $5 each, but when you buy certain amounts you get some for free. I think we got seven for $20. No discount accepted, but you can pay with a discounted gift card. Decide beforehand if you want to do it and plan accordingly. (And Primeval Whirl and TriceraTop Spin are inside the carnival so don't skip it completely even if you don't play the games. There's also an amazing place to get nachos in the corner, almost under the giant yellow brontosaurus, just to the right if you're looking at the dinosaur.)

Souvenirs: This is more obvious. You probably want to buy a few things yourself and a few things for your kids. I save money by taking souvenirs with me for the kids. They cost a fraction of the price. I buy at ShopDisney.com. Plan for souvenirs so they aren't a surprise. You can go online and do a little research to look at prices so there's no sticker shock.

Tips: When you're on the dining plan you don't have to budget much for food, but if you're planning sit down meals, tips aren't included in the dining plan. If you have a party of six or more, there will be an automatic gratuity of 18% added to your bill. Even if you aren't a large party, you should plan for your tips because it can add up to a surprising amount over a few meals. Budget between $3-$5 per person per table service meal and you should be fine.

Extra food: You might want some extra food that's not on the dining plan. With my strategies from the dining chapters, I rarely NEED to spend any extra money when I'm on the dining plan, but sometimes I want to do so. There are some excellent things that aren't covered by the dining plan.

A few that get me are: chocolate covered apples from the bakery or Big Top in Magic Kingdom or the bakery in Hollywood Studios. They have them at Animal Kingdom too- in the gift shop near the safari. I don't think they have them at Epcot. They are amazing. $10. That's $10 I need to plan to spend, because it's happening. #Protip: take a picture and then have them cut it for you. So much easier.

Also, Joffrey's. Their donuts aren't on the dining plan. They are outside of Animal Kingdom and Epcot so you can grab a coffee and a donut the size of your head before you go into the park. They are also inside Epcot (between America and Italy and another one near what used to be Ellen's Energy Adventure) and Hollywood Studios (near Toy Story.) These donuts are superb. I think about them when I'm not at Disney. Good stuff. Share with a friend if you don't want a stomach ache. (Second edition note: I've been able to get the donuts on the dining plan now. I'm not sure if it's all over or select locations. I'm making it my mission to find out. I WILL get donuts at every Joffrey's location or die trying. My job is hard, but someone has to do it.)

Another one that comes to mind is the light up drinks at certain locations. It's a regular drink, or slushy or whatever you order, but it comes with this little light up toy. The kids want one every time. So far, I haven't caved. They're $5. If you want to treat your child, have at it! I might spring for them the next time we're not on a tight budget. There are other souvenir drinks where you get to keep the cup, but I don't find those as tempting. Gaston's Tavern has two options and I know there are a couple Star Wars ones at Hollywood Studios. I have also seen Groot recently.

And if your kids find the popcorn as absolutely craving-inducing as mine do, you might want to plan to buy a refillable bucket. They are $10 and then you only pay $1.50ish to refill it for your length of stay. My kids LOVE Disney's popcorn so depending on how long we're staying, it's usually a good investment to get the bucket. Snack credits cover the normal popcorn, but not the bucket. I figure if we refill it three times we're saving money and can use our snack credits elsewhere. Sometimes my kids want popcorn twice a day. Mongrels. It is nice to be able to say yes because it's only a dollar-fifty. Do they sprinkle that popcorn with crack? Or maybe pixie dust?

All Summed Up:

There aren't that many costs over and above what you'd naturally plan for but it's nice to be able to plan for them all. It's a lot easier to relax when you know that you've budgeted enough for everything.

Afterword:
Learning to Find these
Strategies Yourself

This is an ever-changing area of study. Retailers change their policies; credit cards change their bonuses; Disney changes their rules. I'm planning to update the book annually, but you won't need me if you learn to find these strategies yourself. That way, you won't have to wait to save until the next edition comes out.

The best place to start is with how to think about this. Train your brain to always look for the better deal, the way to save the most. Ask yourself, "how can I save more?" When I first started thinking this way, my brain was lazy about this. I wasn't in debt up to my eyeballs because I was good at thinking about money, that's for sure.

I would hear about something that saved a small amount of money and I would think something to the effect of, "that's not worth my time." I didn't realize that all those little things could add up to the point where I would be able to quit my job. When I was working, I was tired from working. My brain power was used up on selling things and maintaining good relationships with customers and co-workers. I didn't have the stamina at first to force myself to think this way. And I didn't have the motivation because I didn't understand how much better my life could be if I made the effort.

What fundamentally changed this for me was understanding that saving money is how people live better, not by spending it. It's a shift in perception, subtle to anyone watching. It's the difference between the thought, "I need to earn more, so I can spend more" and the thought "I don't need anything else, I have enough." It's telling your money where to go instead of asking it where it went.

There's a book I highly, highly recommend. I mentioned it before. It's called The Richest Man in Babylon (http://amzn.to/2pxAzI4). The title put me off originally. I hated history in school and thought the book sounded historical and boring. But it's not. It's chapter after chapter of secrets about money and the way it works. They shouldn't be secrets. They should be taught in our schools, but they aren't. This book changed how I think. I went from never having enough to always having an abundance.

In the book, there's a story I'll paraphrase here. When the richest man in Babylon tells a poor man to watch his spending, the poor man replies that doing so would make him no more than a beast of burden slaving and tiring under the spending plan. The richest man in Babylon replies with a question: "Who would make the plan?" and the poor man replies, "I would make it myself." With that established, the richest man in Babylon explains that if a donkey got to choose his own burden, he would choose light things, not heavy things. He would choose food for him to eat later and water for when he got thirsty.

The meaning was immediately clear to me: if you carefully choose your burden, you can select the things that are valuable to you. I had things in my life that I was spending lots of money on without really choosing them over other things. As an example, take our Chevy Tahoe. It was decked out, black on black, leather, the whole nine yards. It was probably $60,000 new. We bought it two years old for $29,000. Great deal? Of course, we didn't have $29K so we had a loan on it and paid for it every month. I didn't realize what else I could be doing with that money. I never thought about it. Were there things that I wanted more than a Chevy Tahoe? Yes. Lots. But I never considered that until I read the book. My mind cracked open. I realized that I should be being deliberate about what I was spending. I could improve my life simply by carefully considering what I was spending money on.

That understanding was enough for me to start questioning everything. I turned a critical eye on every expense. Did I want that bag of Doritos more than I wanted financial freedom? No. Did I want pretty shoes more than I wanted to own my own time? No. Did I want to spoil my kids with things, or did I want to be home with them?

Viewed through that lens, it was incredibly easy to make good decisions. Does this get me closer to or further from my goal? And with the clear goal of paying off our debt, quitting my job and earning money with my money and not with my time (a principal clearly outlined in the book), I suddenly had the willpower to cut down anything standing in the way of that goal.

Maybe your Disney trip is that motivator for you. You want to make this happen for your kids, for your family. Is it enough to make you want to say no to dinners out and to Chevy Tahoes? Maybe, maybe not. Maybe your life is already pretty great and you aren't looking to change it. I'm happy for you.

But if it's not, if you're feeling trapped, I urge you to read the book. To change your mindset and to take the steps you need to take to find yourself on a better path- one consistent with where you want to arrive someday.

The practical steps of finding these deals weren't hard. Once I wanted to find them, they were apparent. Here's how I found them, and how I keep finding things that work to get me to Disney:

Hang out in places where people care about good deals. I don't mean physically. I mean on the internet:

- o Search for money saving groups on Facebook and join. Disney Within Reach (the private FB group that comes along with this book) will be a good start. Make friends in there. Friends with the same goals will help you. https://www.facebook.com/groups/188414933 5165319

- o Pinterest: search for articles about saving money and about doing Disney frugally

- o Join the DISBoards and follow threads about saving. This one has been a huge help to me for years: https://www.disboards.com/threads/disney-gift-card-deals.2941964/page-1562 – post-59058307

- o Find people who care about what you care about and get to know them. I've have a lot of great ideas come to me from friends I've met on the internet who heard something they thought was up my alley and sent it on over to me. I return the favor.

○ Set up alerts for deals. These are my favorite deal alert sites: Slick Deals, Doctor of Credit, Brads Deals. These are also available, but not among my faves: Deal News, Ben's Bargains, Offers, Gotta Deal. There are other sites out there that can help you too- things that are niched down in such a way that you might find helpful. When I was couponing, I was able to find couponing sites that sent alerts.
  ▪ My alerts are:
  • Gift cards
  • Disney
  • Raise
  • Cardpool
  • CardCash

  I'm also set up to get emails from all the sites I use to get good deals. I want to know if they are having a sale. I post these in the Disney Within Reach community as well- and I tell you how to use them for Disney.

When you hear about a good deal, don't stop there. Listen to what people are doing already and then try to take it a step further:

○ Is there any way to build a little more savings in?

- o Is there something you know that they don't, that can make it more valuable?

- o Search around on the internet for more information about the idea. Look for ways to save more.

- o Let your mind pick apart the different facets of a deal. Look at each step and see what else could go there. Every step of the process is an opportunity to save more money.

I wish there was a step by step plan I could give you; wish the answer was not, think and think and think. But it is. And if you learn to do it well, you'll be so much better off for it. Put in the time. I wish you all the best as you learn. Hope to see you at Disney World.

Part VIII: Appendices

This book is not a work of fiction; it's not a story. It's as entertaining as I can make it, but it's a work that's designed to impart the reader with the information needed in as clear a manner as I was capable of providing. And with that in mind, I realized that there were readers in common situations and I was the best person to save them time by directing them to the areas of this book that will be helpful in those common situations.

Here are the situations that came to mind:

- Some people want to save THE MOST MONEY POSSIBLE. These are my Type A, sisters of the heart.

- Some are SO busy with life and kids and work—they want to save, but they don't have a lot of time on their hands and they'd like to use the strategies that they can easily work into their lives, even if those aren't the biggest savers. I'm envious that they are so capable of recognizing and accepting their limitations. I'm more likely to try and do it all and mess it all up incrementally.

- Some people are heading to Disney shortly and they don't have time to jump through a lot of hoops or wait on anything because they're boarding that magical plane soon. #jealous Ask in the Facebook group when my trip is—you pretty much have a one-in-four chance of being there the same time as me! #meetup

- Some people don't want to or can't open credit cards and some don't use credit cards at all. I am proud of you for sticking to your convictions.

- Some people want to go to Disney over and over and over again. I totally get it.

I wrote an appendix for each of these situations and I very much hope that they help you:

Appendix A: Strategies to Save the Most

Appendix B: Strategies to Use if You're Super Busy

Appendix C: Strategies to Use if Your Trip is Soon

Appendix D: Strategies Without Credit Cards

Appendix E: Strategies to Use Time and Time Again

Appendix A:
Strategies to Save the Most

In this appendix, I'm going to list the strategies in order of most savings to least. This way, as you're beginning to see which strategies you should try, you can flip back here and try them in order of best return to least.

Percentages:

- Chapter Five: **Kroger 4x Fuel Points, with American Express BlueCash, Gas with the Kroger Visa, Swagbucks/Best Buy**- 25.5%

- Chapter Five: **Kroger 4x Fuel Points, with the American Express BlueCash, Gas with the Kroger Visa**- 23.5%

- Chapter Five: **Kroger 4x Fuel Points, with the American Express BlueCash card**- 20%

- Chapter Nineteen: **Annual Passholder merchandise discount**- 20%

- Chapter Five: **Meijer mPerks with the American Express BlueCash**- 16%

- Chapter Five: **Giant Eagle, with the American Express BlueCash**- 12%

- Chapter Three: **Discover doubled buying from BJ's**- 14%

- Chapter Three: **Discover doubled buying from Sam's**- 14%

- Chapter Five: **Kroger 4x Fuel Points**- 14%

- Chapter Five: **Meijer mPerks**- 10%

- Chapter Nineteen: **Annual Passholder table service restaurants discount**- 10%

- Chapter Three: **Chase Freedom buying from BJ's**- 9%

- Chapter Three: **Chase Freedom buying from Sam's**- 9%

- Chapter Five: **Kroger 2x Fuel Points**- 7%

- Chapter Five: **Giant Eagle FuelPerks**- 6%

- Chapter Five: **American Express BlueCash Preferred**- 6%

- Chapter Four: **Target RedCard**- 5%

- Chapter Seven: **ShopDisney cash back from Top Cash Back**- 5% (Use a cash back form of payment for even more.)

- Chapter Three: **Sam's Club**- 4%

- Chapter Three: **BJ's**- 3%-4% depending on the denominational. This fluctuates.

- Chapter Five: **American Express BlueCash Everyday**- 3%

- Chapter Three: **Citibank DoubleCash**- 2%

- Chapter Three: **Disney Visa**- 1%

Estimates:

- Chapter Thirty-Four: **Life** 0%-100%

- Chapter Twenty-Eight: **Flights**- 0%-100%

- Chapter Nineteen: **Annual pass savings over regular tickets**- 0%-90% depending on usage. They save me over 90% compared to tickets.

- Chapter Seventeen: **Renting DVC from individuals**- 40%-80%

- Chapter Fifteen: **Agency Exclusives**- easily over 50% off rack rate during specials. 0%-5% off normally.

- Chapter Eighteen: **Military discount on tickets**- 40%-50%

- Chapter Thirty-Two: **Lower taxes**- 0%-50%

- Chapter Sixteen: **Renting DVC from agencies**- 30%-40%

- Chapter Eighteen: **Military discount on resorts**- 30%-40%

- Chapter Twenty-Nine: **Rental cars**- 0%-40%

- Chapter Thirty-One: **Savings on staying offsite**- 0%-40%

- Chapter Fourteen: **Bounce Back**- 20%-30%

- Chapter Fourteen: **Pin codes**- 10-30%

- Chapter Nineteen: **Annual Passholder discount on rooms**- 10%-30%

- Chapter Twenty-Six: **Stretching the dining plan**- 0%-30%

- Chapter Thirty: **Food, Hotels and gas**- 0%-30%

- Chapter Thirteen: **Florida Resident discount on rooms**- 15%-25%

- Chapter Twenty-One: **Tickets at Work**- 10%-25%

- Chapter Thirteen: **General Public discount on rooms**- 5%-25%

- Chapter Twenty-Five: **Hacking the dining plan**- 0%-25%

- Chapter Twenty-Seven: **Hacking dining without the dining plan**- 0%-20% (stack with discounted gift cards to save another 5%-25%)

- Chapter Thirty-Three: **Business trip deduction**- 0%-20%

- Chapter Six: **Sears/Kmart from eBay**-5-15%

- Chapter Twenty: **Authorized resellers**- 0%-10%

- Chapter Seven: **Bed, Bath and Beyond or Walgreens**- 6%-8% (or more)

- Chapter Three: **Walmart gift cards from Raise or Cardpool/Sam's**- 5%-7% (or more if you're careful)

- Chapter Six: **Sears/Kmart from Cardpool**-6%-7%

- Chapter Six: **Sears/Kmart from Raise**-5%

- Chapter Eight: **Interest-Bearing Savings or Checking** .25%-2% annually

Flat Amounts:

I'll indicate cash where applicable, realize that you can then run that cash through your discounted gift card machine and end up with even more.

- Chapter Eleven: **Chase Sapphire Preferred**- for both spouses, adding authorized users and spending through Chase's portal- $1500

- Chapter Eleven: **Chase Sapphire Preferred**- for both spouses, adding authorized users- $1200 cash

- Chapter Eleven: **Chase Sapphire Preferred**- Sign-Up Bonus 50,000 points used through Chase's Portal- $625 in travel (flights, rental cars)

- Chapter Nine: **Opening checking or savings accounts** $50-$750 (potential for spouse as well)

- Chapter Ten: **Disney Chase Visa** for both spouses, $500 cash

- Chapter Eleven: **Chase Sapphire Preferred-**Sign Up Bonus 50,000 points ($500 cash)

- Chapter Ten: **Chase Disney-** $200 cash

- Chapter Five: **American Express BlueCash sign-up-** $250 cash

- Chapter Three: **Chase Freedom sign-up-** $150 cash (this can be combined into Chase's Ultimate Rewards if you have an Ultimate Rewards card, making it worth more than cash)

- Chapter Nineteen: **Annual Passholder Discount on Memory Maker-** $150 (free, included with pass)

- Chapter Five: **American Express BlueCash Everyday Sign-Up-** $100 cash

- Chapter Five: **American Express BlueCash Referral-** $100 cash

- Chapter Eleven: **Chase Sapphire Preferred Referral-** $100 cash or 10,000 rewards points (which are worth more than cash)

- Chapter Three: **Discover Referral**- $100 cash (can be doubled)

- Chapter Two: **Eight Website Bonuses**- $51 cash

- Chapter Ten: **Chase Disney Visa Referral**- $50 Disney Rewards

- Chapter Three: **Discover sign-up**- $50 (doubled to $100) cash (or rewards, which can be helpful with a rental car)

- Chapter Eleven: **Chase Authorized User**- $50 cash

- Chapter Two: **Eight Website Referral Bonuses**- $48 cash

- Chapter Two: **eBates Referral**-$25 cash

- Chapter Two: **Coupon Cabin sign-up**- $23 cash

- Chapter Two: **Cardpool Referral**- $5 cash

- Chapter Two: **Raise Referral**- $5 cash

- Chapter Two: **Top Cash Back Referral**- $10 cash

- Chapter Two: **eBates sign-up**- $10 cash

- Chapter Two: **Cardpool sign-up**- $5 cash

- Chapter Two: **Raise sign-up**- $5 cash

- Chapter Two: **Mr. Rebates sign-up**- $5 cash

- Chapter Two: **Swagbucks sign-up**- $3 cash

- Chapter Two: **Swagbucks Referral**- $3 cash

Appendix B:
Strategies to Use if You're Super Busy

I get it. There are things in your life that you'd choose to do rather than spend time on saving money. Life is a constant trade off of what you want to accomplish and what you have time to accomplish (even if the thing you're hoping to accomplish is just taking a bath and then binge-watching Grey's Anatomy. I respect that.)

In this appendix, you'll find about how long these things take. You can then cross reference with the last appendix and see which will give you the most savings in the amount of time you can carve out of your life.

Low Time Investment:

- Chapter Twenty: **Buying tickets from an Authorized Reseller—** no time investment compared to buying online from Disney—these will even save you time.

- Chapter Seven: **Buying tickets from Tickets at Work—** no time investment compared to buying online from Disney— these will even save you time.

- Chapter Nineteen: **Annual Passholder Discount on Memory Maker-** no time investment, this will save you time since you don't have to order Memory Maker.

- Chapter Nineteen: **Annual Passholder discount on rooms-** no time investment over booking rooms regularly.

- No time investment for any of these compared to using any credit card:
  - Chapter Ten: **Using the Disney Visa**

  - Chapter Five: **American Express BlueCash Preferred**

  - Chapter Five: **American Express BlueCash Everyday**

  - Chapter Five: **Citibank DoubleCash**

  - Chapter Four: **Target RedCard**

- Chapter Eighteen: **Military Discounts**- no time investment compared to booking normally.

- Chapter Nineteen: **Annual Passholder discount**- food/merchandise: 30 seconds per transaction to show your Annual Passholder card.

- These will all take about 5-10 minutes. The buying takes very little time, but read below about gift cards. And I find that I'm more likely to have to wait or argue at Bed, Bath and Beyond so that could take longer in those instances.
    - Chapter Three:
        **BJ's,
        Discover doubled buying from BJ's,
        Chase Freedom buying from BJ's,**

    - Chapter Five:
        **Meijer with mPerks
        Meijer with mPerks with a cash back card, i.e. American Express BlueCash**

    - Chapter Seven:
        ShopDisney

    - Chapter Twenty-One:

Bed, Bath and Beyond

- ○ Chapter Twenty-Nine:
  Rental Cars

- ○ Chapter Thirty:
  Gas, Food, Hotel gift cards

- Chapter Two: **eBates/Cardpool/Raise/Top Cash Back/Mr. Rebates, etc. Referral-** 10 minutes or less.

- Chapter Five: **American Express BlueCash Referral**

- Chapter Eleven: **Chase Sapphire Preferred Referral**

- Chapter Three: **Discover Referral**

- Chapter Ten: **Chase Disney Visa Referral**
  These will all take 10 minutes or less.

- Chapter Eleven: **Chase Authorized User-** 15 minutes or less.

- Chapter Ten: **Chase Disney sign-up:** 20 minutes or less.

- Chapter Five: **American Express BlueCash sign-up:** 20 minutes or less.

- Chapter Three: **Chase Freedom sign-up:** 20 minutes or less.

- Chapter Five: **American Express BlueCash Everyday sign-up:** 20 minutes or less.

- Chapter Seven: **Chase Sapphire Preferred Sign-Up:** 20 minutes or less.

- Chapter Four: **Discover sign-up:** 20 minutes or less.

- Chapter Seven: **Chase Sapphire Preferred Sign-Up Bonus:** 20 minutes or less.

- These will all take very little time. The only time investment is to get a quote, learn the process, see if it works for you. Probably 20 minutes or less, unless you go crazy doing math scenarios and comparing (which could happen.)
  - Chapter Thirteen: **Disney discounts**

  - Chapter Fourteen: **Resort hacks**

  - Chapter Fifteen: **Agency exclusives**

- These will take no time other than possibly doing some planning and trying to order food that can be stretched. Less than 20 minutes.

- Chapter Twenty-Six: **Stretching the dining plan**

- Chapter Twenty-Seven: **Hacking dining without the dining plan**

Medium Time Investment:

Any strategy that involves **gift cards** is going to take up some of your time. The way that you buy them will differ, but once you've turned them into Disney gift cards, you will still need to combine them, move them to your "pay Disney" card, and then pay with them. This takes approximately 2 minutes per gift card. So, if you buy ten $100 from BJ's ($1000), it'll take you 20 minutes to enter them. If you buy ten three-packs of $50 ($500), it'll take you an hour to enter them.

- Chapter Six: **Walmart/Sears/Kmart from eBay**: Very little time for Buy It Now, 10-15 minutes per auction over the life of the auction (monitoring it, bidding, paying, leaving feedback). You will also need to wait for them to come in the mail, track them, enter them in to pay, physically go to Kmart (if you get Sears or Kmart cards), or order from Sam's (if you get Walmart cards). It's not a quick process. But it can be very worth it.

- Chapter Three:
  ### Sam's Club
  ### Discover from Sam's Club
  ### Discover doubled from Sam's Club
  ### Chase Freedom from Sam's

  20 minutes to get a membership, 10 minutes to order each time. You have to order in multiples of $500 or less, then you'd have to deal with entering them. And remember, Sam's sometimes only sells three packs of $50 so you could potentially have a lot of cards. Obviously, buy the $100s or $500s whenever possible and this vastly reduces the time spent.

- Chapter Twenty-One: **Convention Tickets**- This could be a small amount of time or larger depending on your preference—researching conventions, signing-up, dealing with checking in there if you need to, potentially attending some of the convention. 30 minutes to days (if you attend the convention.)

- Chapter Sixteen: **Renting DVC points from agencies—** If they have your first, second or third choices available, it shouldn't take long. 15 minutes to fill out the form. If you need to go back and forth a few times it could add 10 minutes or so. You will also need to make your payment and list your occupants. Altogether, this should take less than 30 minutes.

- Chapter Twenty-Eight:
  Comparing flights
  Tracking ticket costs
  Researching and opening the
  Southwest cards
  Any of these could easily take up quite a lot of time if you have it to invest, but you could also hold it to a minimum if needed. I'd say 30 minutes to hours.

- Chapter Thirty-Three: **Tax deductible vacations**- this won't take long pre-vacation. A little planning is all. Less than 30 minutes for sure.

- Chapter Eleven: **Chase Sapphire Preferred- for both spouses, adding authorized users**- 40 minutes or less.

- Chapter Ten: **Disney Chase Visa for both spouses, adding authorized users**- 40 minutes or less.

- Chapter Eleven: **Chase Sapphire Preferred- for both spouses, adding authorized users and spending through Chase's portal**- 50 minutes or less.

- Chapter Two: **Eight Website Bonuses**- Altogether, less than an hour.

- Chapter Nine: **Opening Checking/Savings Accounts**- opening an account can usually take about 30 minutes, but you'll also need to find the offer you want to use (possibly spending time monitoring available offers) and managing your eligibility for the bonus. Then you will also need to cancel the account. Should be less than 60 minutes total for each account.

- Chapter Seventeen: **Renting DVC Points from individuals**- this is more of a start and stop process—more time is spent searching around and haggling than with the renter. I might think I found something good and then have it rented from under me and have to start over. All in all, you should be able to complete the process in under 60 minutes of actual time spent.

- Chapter Twenty-Five: **Hacking the dining plan**- if you are not an Annual Passholder, or are trying to keep the ability for everyone to book FastPasses at sixty days, it can take some time to use the Day Guest Method. Calling Disney twice or emailing your agent, doing all the planning. I would say this is a 60 minute investment.

High Time Investment:

- Chapter Six: **Sears/Kmart from Raise, Cardpool, or Card Cash buying from Kmart**
  Chapter Three: **Walmart from Raise, Cardpool or Card Cash, buying from Sam's Club**:

  All of these can be as little or as much time as you'd like to make them. You can take the low percentages and move along with your day, or you can carefully stalk them and spend more time to get the higher percentages. No matter what, it's a more time consuming strategy because you will have to buy the gift cards, track them as they are shipped to make sure you receive them, enter them in to pay, physically go to Kmart or Sam's or you can order from Sam's. It's not a quick process, but it's still a great savings if you can dedicate the time.

- Chapter Ten:
  - **Kroger 4x Fuel Points, with the American Express BlueCash, Gas with the Kroger Visa**
  - **Kroger 4x Fuel Points, with the American Express BlueCash card**
  - **Giant Eagle, with the American Express BlueCash card**
  - **Giant Eagle FuelPerks**
  - **Kroger 4x Fuel Points**

- **Kroger 2x Fuel Points**

All eight of these take up about the same amount of time. You have to go to Kroger/Giant Eagle, buy the gift cards. Then you have to deal with filling up gas cans if you choose to do that, and then emptying them into another vehicle or whatever. Or you could coordinate with a spouse and fill up both vehicles at once. This is technically against the rules, but I don't think they'll stop you.

- Chapter Ten: **Kroger 4x Fuel Points, with American Express BlueCash, Gas with the Kroger Visa, Swagbucks**
This will take the same amount of time as the strategies above, plus another trip (to Best Buy). That usually takes me about 10 minutes plus drive time.

- **Using Apps to earn money** (like Perk, etc.) These will take you a lot of time for very little return. 30 minutes per day gave me about $15-$50 per month. That's $3.33 an hour at best. But if you're not doing anything else (like I wasn't as I sat there nursing the baby for hours and hours on end), that's $15-$50 that you didn't have at the beginning of the month.

- **Swagbucks** is an exception to this. I spend very little time on it daily and usually pocket over

$50 a month.
https://www.smartmomsplandisney.com/swa
gbucks/

- Chapter Seven: **YES Program**. If you were able to join a group and not manage it, it would not be very time consuming. But managing your own group would be quite a lot of work.

- Chapter Thirty-Two: **Lowering your taxes**- This could be a gigantic job where you overhaul your entire life, or you could just do a few things.

Appendix C:
Strategies to Use if Your Trip is Soon

I get a lot of messages that start out, "Will your book help me if I'm going to Disney World in three months?" And the answer is a resounding "Yes!" But if you're going to Disney next month, things are a little harrier.

Below, I have given you a list of the strategies that you can employ, but before we get into that, I want to tell you one thing that has helped several of my last-minute readers. In fact, I found myself explaining this so many times that I knew I needed to put in in the second edition.

The "I've already paid for my trip, is it too late to save money" plan:

Ok, first, no, it's likely not too late for you to save a bunch of money if you've already paid Disney. The good news is that they will accept gift cards and refund your original form of payment. Now, I'm putting this here, knowing that they could change that policy at any time, so please ask in the private Facebook group (https://www.facebook.com/groups/1884149335165 319) before you do this, because if the policy has changed we'll likely know about it and can steer you correctly.

Here's what you do:

1. Buy discounted Disney gift cards from one of the options below.
2. Call Disney (or your travel agent) and ask them to accept these as payment and refund your original form of payment.
3. Go to Disney World for less than you otherwise would have!

You might have to rush around a little to get this done, but even if you just save 5% on $3000, that's $150.

Savings that can be had quickly:

- You can certainly sign up for the **Eight Websites** and use them to purchase some of the funds you need. You won't see your bonuses in time for your trip, but it's still money saved even if you get it after you return. It's not a problem since it's in cash. Chapter Two.

- **Sam's Club**- If you have the Discover or Chase Freedom Card, you can pop on into Sam's and pick up some gift cards today at 3-4% off with a bonus of 5% from Discover or Chase Freedom, assuming it's the bonus category for that quarter and you've activated the bonus. Take a look at Chapter Three.

- **Target is quick**. Even if you don't have a RedCard, you can likely go into the store and sign up and be approved on the spot. You won't have to wait for anything to come in the mail, you can just buy your gift cards at 5% off and be on your way. You may have even better luck getting the debit card quickly. Chapter Four.

- **Grocery store savings** can be quick. You may not be able to get 4x fuel points at Kroger, but 2x for sure and maybe you'll even get lucky and get 4x. Giant Eagle and the other stores don't have time sensitive situations on their fuel programs. Meijer is less likely to be timed right for you, but if they are, that's quick. Review Chapter Five.

- **Raise** can be your friend in this instance. You don't have time to sit around waiting for Kmart, Walgreens and Bed, Bath and Beyond gift cards to be discounted as low as they can go, but you can grab them at whatever you see them at.

Make sure they are ecards unless you have time to wait for the mail. And be sure to review Chapters Six and Seven.

- Most of the **Checking and Saving Account Bonuses** take less than 90 days to accomplish, but if your trip is sooner, you can start the process and cash in when you come back. Those bonuses are cash so you can apply it to everyday life. Chapter Nine.

- I would say you need at least five weeks to make the **Disney Visa** work for you. If you sign up, get the card and immediately spend the $500, you should have the $200 in two weeks. Chapter Ten.

- **Chase Sapphire** will take some time, but the bonus is in cash or Ultimate Rewards points, so if you can't make it in time for Disney, you can use it to replenish your savings upon your return. Chapter Eleven.

- Look over the **Resort Hacks** in Chapter Fourteen and check for any **Agency Exclusives** (Chapter Fifteen) also. You might also check for any **Confirmed Reservations** last minute (Chapters Sixteen and Seventeen.) These are all sort of long shots, but if it works out, you could save quite a lot, so it's worth taking a chance to look.

- **Military Discounts** should be available last minute, especially on tickets. Resorts might be a little tougher, but possible. Chapter Eighteen.

- You can upgrade to an **Annual Pass** at any time. If you are buying a package with tickets, it's very easy to upgrade those to Annual Passes at Guest Services. If you do it the first day, you can get the benefits for your whole trip. Look in Chapter Nineteen.

- **Authorized Resellers** don't take any extra time. Just make sure that they can email you the tickets. I've not come across any that won't. Chapter Twenty.

- **Convention Tickets** and **Tickets at Work** could conceivably work last minute. You may have a package booked that includes tickets, but you can call and change or cancel it if you found a convention rate. Tickets at Work only does tickets, so you could get tickets from them and change your package to a room-only reservation. See Chapter Twenty-One.

- You can add one of the **Dining Plans** right up until the night before you leave for your trip. It used to be 3 days before, but lately they've been saying they can add it up until the night before. Take a look at Part V and see if you should consider adding one of the plans.

- You can definitely save money on food, gas, and hotels last minute. Check out Part VI. The only things that might not work quickly are the Southwest cards and flights (because you might have those booked already.)

- Chapter Thirty-Three can help you with making your trip **Tax Deductible**. If you already own a business that you need to travel to Orlando for, you could certainly turn your vacation into a tax-deductible trip in no time.

Appendix D:
Strategies Without Credit Cards

I get it. You were young and dumb and your credit is a mess. I don't even blame you since a lot of people screw their credit up before they know any better. Our schools don't teach you how to manage credit or how to do anything about having bad credit either.

If you're in the bad credit boat, do something about it. Pull your credit report from the three bureaus and make sure it's accurate. If not, get the inaccuracies off. Talk to the people who are reporting negatives for you. Work out a payment plan. You can do this! Check out the workbook bonus pages for more guidance.

Or maybe your credit is just fine, but you LOVE Dave Ramsey. That's cool. I like him. I don't agree with him on a lot of things, but we do agree about debt. It's bad. Or maybe you just don't want credit cards for your own reasons, and I completely respect that. This appendix is a list of strategies from this book that you don't need a credit card to use. You'll find that you can use the vast majority of the book.

Here you go:

- Chapter Two: Eight Sites. You can use a debit card for all the maneuvers in this chapter. Save $150+

- Chapter Three, Six and Seven: Buying gift cards (Walmart, Sears, Kmart, Walgreens, Bed, Bath and Beyond) from Raise, Cardpool or Card Cash and using them to buy Disney gift cards. Walmart is your best option since you can use them at Sam's Club and get that additional 4% back. See if you can acquire a cash back debit card to stack. 7-10%

- Chapter Four: Target RedCard Debit Card- 5%

- Chapter Five: Kroger, Giant Eagle or Anderson's Fuel Programs, Meijer's Fuel programs. You will miss out on a little of the stacking if you don't get the BlueCash card, but that's only a small portion of the overall total. You can probably get around 15%-18% off without a credit card.

- Chapter Seven: ShopDisney (5% and stacks with a cash back debit card) and sharing rooms (50% and stacks with discounted gift cards) do not require a credit card.

- Chapter Eight: You don't need credit to take advantage of the opportunities here. .25%-2% APR

- Chapter Nine: You won't need to have good credit to open a checking account or savings account. Great opportunity. This could easily net you $1,000 per year.

None of the strategies in Part III, IV, V or VII require a credit card or good credit. The only strategy in Part VI that does require a credit card is the Southwest card maneuvers. The chapters in these parts that do not require credit cards are as follows:

- Chapter Twelve: Disney Resort Basics

- Chapter Thirteen: Disney Resort Discounts

- Chapter Fourteen: Disney Resort Hacks

- Chapter Fifteen: Agency Exclusives

- Chapter Sixteen: Deluxe for the Price of Moderate? Or Value?!?!

- Chapter Seventeen: Renting DVC Points Wisely

- Chapter Eighteen: Military Discounts

- Chapter Nineteen: Annual Passes for Everyone

- Chapter Twenty: Authorized Resellers

- Chapter Twenty-One: Lesser Known Ticket Savings Tricks

- Chapter Twenty-Two: Intro to the Dining Plans, Changes to the 2018 Plan

- Chapter Twenty-Three: "Should I Get the Dining Plan?"

- Chapter Twenty-Four: Dining Comparisons

- Chapter Twenty-Five: Hacking the Disney Dining Plan

- Chapter Twenty-Six: Stretching the Dining Plan

- Chapter Twenty-Seven: Hacking Disney Dining Without the Dining Plan

- Chapter Twenty-Eight: Flights

- Chapter Twenty-Nine: Rental Cars

- Chapter Thirty: Driving, Food, Hotels and Gas

- Chapter Thirty-One: Staying Offsite

- Chapter Thirty-Two: Lower Taxes, Please

- Chapter Thirty-Three: Tax Savings via Disney

- Chapter Thirty-Four: Saving on Life and Applying It to Disney

- Bonus Chapter Thirty-Five: Planning for All the Hidden Expenses
- Afterword: Learning to Find These Strategies Yourself

Appendix E:
Strategies to Use
Time and Time Again

Over the last year, several people have said to me, "Your book is awesome and I saved so much money. But now that I've done that, how do I get to Disney World again next year?" There are lots of things that are repeatable (ahem, over 55 trips later and I'm still saving), and I got tired of typing them out, over and over again so I decided we need another appendix.

Here are strategies that you can use many times in order of how we talked about them in the book:

- Chapter Two: Eight Websites. Not only can you continue to run your discounted gift cards through there, but you can even open fresh accounts and abandon or close the other accounts. That would enable you to earn the bonuses again. I would suggest waiting a while to do this and using a different email address for the new account. Some of the sites will be more conducive to this than others. You could get into the habit of opening a new email for each trip and using that to open as many of these as possible to cash in on the bonuses.

- Chapter Three: Sam's Club and BJ's are sustainable, but the Discover card doubling trick will only work that first year. You can close it, leave some time and then re-open it if you're really committed. You can open another Discover card too (spouse or another type).

- Chapter Four: Target's strategies are completely sustainable.

- Chapter Five: the grocery store strategies are all completely sustainable.

- Chapter Six: The big box strategies are all sustainable.

- Chapter Seven: Your Mileage May Vary? Yup, sustainable. If they worked for you, they'll likely keep working for you.

- Chapter Eight: All the strategies to get you through the pain of not having the DVA are sustainable.

- Chapter Nine: As long as you close them in time, you should be fine to open more accounts and get the bonuses again.

- Chapter Ten: Not sustainable unless you close your account and re-open it. You need to leave it closed for 2 years. What is sustainable is referring the card. You can earn $500 a year referring your friends who are heading to Disney.

- Chapter Eleven: Chase Sapphire Preferred same as above. You can close and re-open, but it takes two years. You can earn $500 a year in referrals though.

- Chapter Twelve: Disney Resort Basics-sustainable.

- Chapter Thirteen: Disney Resort Discounts (including Annual Pass resort savings info)-sustainable

- Chapter Fourteen: Disney Resort Hacks-sustainable. Over twenty trips with some of these hacks.

- Chapter Fifteen: Agency Exclusives-sustainable. I've been using them for four years.

- Chapter Sixteen: Deluxe for the Price of Moderate? Or Value?!?!- sustainable. I have been doing it for years.

- Chapter Seventeen: Renting DVC Points Wisely- sustainable

- Chapter Eighteen: Military Discounts- sustainable as long as you remain eligible.

- Chapter Nineteen: Annual Passes for everyone- sustainable

- Chapter Twenty: Authorized Resellers- sustainable

- Chapter Twenty-One: Lesser Known Ticket Savings Tricks- sustainable unless you quit your job and lose access to Tickets at Work.

- Chapter Twenty-Two: Intro to the Dining Plans, and Changes to the 2018 Plan- sustainable

- Chapter Twenty-Three: "Should I Get the Dining Plan?"- sustainable

- Chapter Twenty-Four: Dining Comparisons- sustainable

- Chapter Twenty-Five: Hacking the Dining Plan- sustainable

- Chapter Twenty-Six: Stretching the Dining Plan- sustainable

- Chapter Twenty-Seven: Hacking Disney Dining- sustainable

- Chapter Twenty-Eight: Flights- sustainable except for the Southwest cards/Companion Pass. The only way you can make that work continually is to cancel the cards and then re-open them. The timing is tricky, but I have read accounts of people online who manage to do it with only a small period of time where they don't have the Companion Pass.

  - Chapter Twenty-Nine: Rental Cars- sustainable

  - Chapter Thirty: Driving, Food, Hotels and Gas- sustainable

  - Chapter Thirty-One: Staying Offsite- sustainable

  - Chapter Thirty-Two: Lower Taxes, Please- very sustainable

  - Chapter Thirty-Three: Tax Savings via Disney- sustainable

- Chapter Thirty-Four: Saving on Life and Applying It to Disney- sustainable

- Chapter Thirty-Five: Planning for All the Hidden Expenses- sustainable